**Mystery
and Its Fictions**

MYSTERY
and Its Fictions:
From Oedipus to Agatha Christie

DAVID I. GROSSVOGEL

The Johns Hopkins University
Press / Baltimore and London

Copyright © 1979 by The Johns Hopkins University Press

All rights reserved. No part of this book may be reproduced or transmitted in any form or by any means, electronic or mechanical, including photocopying, recording, xerography, or any information storage and retrieval system, without permission in writing from the publisher. Manufactured in the United States of America

The Johns Hopkins University Press, Baltimore, Maryland 21218
The Johns Hopkins Press Ltd., London

Library of Congress Catalog Number 78–20516
ISBN 0–8018–2201–7
Library of Congress Cataloging in Publication data will be found on the last printed page of this book.

Illustrations: JEG Design

For Jill

Suave mari magno . . .

Contents

Acknowledgments

First, I would like to thank two friends, John W. Kronik and Josué V. Harari. Without the help of each, this book would still be a (less readable) manuscript.

To Professors Frederick M. Ahl, George Gibian, Roberto González Echevarría, Richard Klein, Pietro Pucci, Enrico M. Santi, and at least a couple of anonymous readers, deep appreciation for emendations, suggestions, discussions.

To Alain Seznec, whose efforts to free time for undertakings of this kind have benefited scholars (and even an occasional critic like myself), grateful acknowledgment.

To my editor, William P. Sisler, gratitude for his discernment, efficiency, and willingness to allow the author his lead in aspects of production that might have been contentious.

Lastly, to my fretful but always devoted and generous typist, Helen H. Calhoun, thanks for patience in ferreting out our combined errors and in doing over so many times so many different pages.

A Word to Start

The third of the Fates is called Atropos. She is the one who cuts the thread of life; she is the figure of Death. But she is also *not* a figure, since she is the one around whom one cannot turn, the one who cannot be turned around: we can assign her neither a place nor a shape. Atropos is herself only, and unknowable. She is not even a turn of phrase: to the extent that Atropos is a name, she is not to be grasped through even the spurious equivalency of language; Atropos is the one for whom there is no trope, no figure of speech, no metaphor, no equivalence. Atropos is absence and mystery; she is fascinating and fearsome. Neither her absolute danger nor her absolute absence ever discourage us from trying to penetrate whatever we believe to be concealing her.

**Mystery
and Its Fictions**

Introduction

A past beyond recall and the end of present
being remain shrouded within shadows
that are too deep for the glimmering of awareness to dispel: those concealed poles are a source
of attraction and of fear that neither attraction
nor fear, however strong, can affect. If one
thinks of awareness as a Heideggerian *Dasein*,
those shadows are simply the *tension* of awareness: the unknown is the pull of an onwardness,
a motion-towards, a pro-ject (*Entwurf*: "understanding—whatever may be the essential dimensions of that which can be disclosed in it—
always press[es] forward into possibilities"[1]).
The Heideggerian "understanding" is thus a

1. Martin Heidegger, *Being and Time*, trans. J. Macquarrie and E. Robinson (New York: Harper & Row,
1962), p. 184. This motion forward is the reverse

1

gerund, a concept informed with imminence, but no more; the most dazzling epiphany cannot reduce this darkness, which remains intact, however much it is forced to yield, and at an unvarying remove, however hard it is pressed. The permanency of its remoteness and intractability becomes the commensurate permanency of a need to overcome it. It may happen that the leap forward that cannot close the distance between the leaper and his object is turned into what Camus terms a leap of faith:[2] at such moments, "understanding" appears to accept its limitations and assume that final answers can be vouchsafed only to another form of awareness, one of transcendental power—for example, God.[3] This kind of gnoseological dodge simply locates the unknown within a name that does not have a specified dimension; one of the primary attributes of the deity is mystery.[4] And to assume that a god can dispel the shadows that conceal total understanding is still to assume, as does the pro-jected consciousness, that total understanding is somehow possible.

Even in God, the shadows remain; it is God who becomes shadowy. The incompleteness of human understanding makes a god incomplete; even the all-knowing God cannot demonstrate that He exists beyond mystery. Since man's intelligence cannot fathom the mystery that is God's alone to fathom, God becomes a form of the darkness

---

equivalent of an equally unknowable anteriority. If the Vénus de Laussel is the earliest record of a paleolithic culture's questioning of the unknown, the unknown it questions is that of origins: the figure represents a mother earth in whom are enshrouded the mysteries of birth and renewal: the beginning implies an ending, the end a beginning. (P. J. Ucko and A. Rosenfeld, *Paleolithic Cave Art* [New York: McGraw-Hill, 1967].)

2. Albert Camus, *The Myth of Sisyphus and Other Essays,* trans. J. O'Brien (New York: A. A. Knopf, 1955).

3. A part of this discussion weaves through notions of "God" and "god." Since we are arguing that man contrives figures to fill the unendurable void that is mystery, we use *God* to designate the Judeo-Christian concept (usually without an article) and *god* for other divinisations.

4. All mysteries remain mysteries within God: *in Deo abscondita.* The Book of Sirach details some of the mysteries: God's plan for men (see Daniel, ch. 2: only God in heaven can reveal mystery, that is, a vision of the future); astronomical and meteorological phenomena; the nature of human behavior. Monotheism would be, according to this speculation, the residual quandary after scientific investigation has dissipated a sufficient number of the former quandaries of which were born a multiplicity of divinities.

that He was meant to dissipate. God hides; God reveals in order to render manifest that He hides. Paul writes to the Corinthians that his own voice, even as it speaks for God, is but the "demonstration of the Spirit and the power" (1 Cor. 2:16). However much God reveals, the mystery remains, and man's intuition that there is forever something beyond his knowledge is confirmed (confirming at the same time the power and the mystery of God). Man is chastened by these confirmations; the Book of Sirach warns man not to look too closely at the mystery (3:21–22), and Matthew counsels against casting pearls before the swine (Matt. 7:6): to attempt penetration of a primal mystery is to be guilty of arrogantly exaggerating the power of reason once reason has accepted that it is bounded by a far greater reason. It is also dangerous to trespass: the shadows beyond knowledge are not necessarily death, but the extinction of awareness is equivalent to the extinction of life. Mystery may not mean death, but the odor of death is sensed in the absolute refractoriness of any mystery that states the limits of man.

Thus it may not be an inaccurate ellipsis to suggest that the life-force[5] cannot come to terms with the evidence of any mystery concerning it just as it cannot come to terms with the evidence of death. Failing to derive understanding from the mediation of an all-knowing god, man does not give up the possibility of mediation: a wholly silent god is no more conceivable than a wholly silent mystery. From the start, even a monotheistic god is envisaged as a dialectical force: *mystery* comes to mean *council* or *counsel*;[6] the secrets, which a notion of god hides, are debated within a divine assembly of beings who determine the fate of the world and among whom god is only a presiding presence. But such a splitting of the divine entity allows only a presumption of communication: the evidence of that communication does not become manifest. Man is confirmed once again in his conviction that mystery must be decipherable—has indeed been deciphered: there remains only to decipher the decipherer. It is at this juncture that the initiate is born, a human mediator on this side of

---

5. The French *élan vital* conveys more forcefully than its English equivalent the *tensing-towards* implicit in the process.

6. The Hebrew word for *mystery—sôd—*meant originally *council* or *assembly*. When, in the Book of Job, Satan speaks to the Lord, it is in the midst of an *assembly* of "the sons of God" (Job 1:6–12). Zeus, the giver of laws, holds *court* on Mount Olympus.

mystery, positioned between the ambiguous divinity and man. The initiate presumably knows, but he is instantly caught up in the paradox that preserves the indefectibility of a primal mystery: if he reveals what he claims to know, he destroys instantly one of the two terms (mystery/man) on whose coupling his raison d'être depends.[7] He can therefore only suggest that he knows: the mystery remains intact; this attempt at a bridging fails like all the others.

Mystery extends beyond god: god represents only man's most strenuous effort to overcome mystery. The frustration of that effort results in theological and moral consequences that do not concern us here. What does concern us is man's continued effort to overcome the threat and the temptation presented by the unknown even after the failure of divine mediation, when he realizes that he is irremediably confined to this side of mystery. Unable either to grasp or to abandon mystery, he resorts to a familiar fraud: he attempts to absorb mystery in speculation; he invents incarnations with which he can cope. Literature plays a part in this process, and most literature is tinctured to some extent with the effects of that concern. An intercessory image is created, similar in its position to that of the initiate, and corresponding to the *ritual* wherein the initiate demonstrates and secretes his knowledge. But whereas the initiate is eventually absorbed by the mystery he mediates, the image remains wholly within the grasp of man. (God is already part of such an image: though He is supposed to be immaterial, and against every Judaic injunction that His name not be spoken nor His shape conceived, Christianity contrives a rich iconography derived from the Trinitarian consciousness that follows the New Testament and the concept of the *persona*, a term designating the mask whereby the Greek actor rendered visible the character he represented.)

The enumerations of divine mysteries in the apocryphal Book of Sirach and Heidegger's pro-jected consciousness have in common the assumption of an unknown affecting man, creating a state of being that he cannot accept and towards which he is forever tensed.

---

7. The intercessor becomes so much a human repetition of the concealing/revealing god that he may well be divinized in turn: the mystery swallows up its human interpreter. The most popular divinity of ancient Egypt, Osiris, giver of agriculture and civilization, was a former intercessory king who had died and been raised to life again. The man Jesus becomes Christ, the "Son of God." (He preserves His humanity to the extent that He does not thereafter conceal/demonstrate God but commiserates with man about the divine absence.)

When, after seven centuries of Christianity, Western fiction begins to find emblems for this dilemma, it fashions them from a sense of the darkness and danger that lurk on the other side of understanding. In the earliest epics, the intercessory figure is that of the warrior-king functioning as the instrument of a god by whose divine right he exists, and for the benefit of the landlords who make up his retinue. The virtues of the king are an awareness of his intercessory role, martial skill and bravery, and generosity to his vassals. Although the king's victories result in economic benefits, the enemy against whom he contends is not an economic entity; although that enemy is destructible, it is not even a part of the known order: instead, it is a figure of singular evil whose predominance would destroy through alteration those to whose preservation the king is committed. The superior skill in battle of the intercessory king thus leads to a moral victory and the comfort that, mysterious and awesome though it may be, the evil has sufficient specificity to be apprehended.

In the first English epic, Beowulf contends against two principal foes, Grendel and the dragon, whose natures are indicative of the kind of forces that confront each other in the epic. Grendel is a threat far greater than any that might normally arise within the social structure where the danger, however intense, would be familiar in its form and circumstances. Grendel, to the contrary, is a shadowy figure, a monster banished from mankind, that dwells in darkness. In simple fact, Grendel is the embodiment of the dark province beyond men's understanding: he is a devil sent by fate who wears God's anger. The incarnation of the awesome force of the unknown has a single purpose: to present that unknown within a body that can be overcome. Through this literature, and Beowulf, the eighth-century landlord conjures the power of darkness.

The dragon is a similar figure with a more discernible pedigree. That figure of mystery is likewise a predator of the dark, holding sway within the gloom of night. However, the dragon has familiar lineaments: he is a "worm" who coils himself, a reminder of the serpent in Eden. This paternity recalls the purposeful evolution of the Edenic snake. When the serpent tempts Eve, it does so as an open and visible figure—one of seduction, not of fear. The snake as we know it—a creature easily concealed and generally held to be deadly—is the figure *after* its retributory punishment, once God has literally cast it down. It is after the Fall that the serpent, condemned with Eve, is reduced to crawl in the dust (Gen. 3:14). In that lowly position, it is both humiliated and in danger. But by virtue of that same abasement, it is concealed and endures as a lurking danger to mankind (Gen. 3:15).[8]

The unknown beyond is sensed as a danger. The threat that is hidden and informed with a power greater than man's contrives a sense of what Freud terms the "uncanny," the specific yet unspecified aspect of what excites dread. Freud's argument in "Das Unheimliche" is circular (more interesting in the psychoanalytic examples it discloses than in the logic of its progression), hinging mainly on the belief that the repressed past is a ghost whose reappearance unsettles us and the conviction that the unconscious cannot entertain the thought of its own mortality.[9]

Freud's investigation begins as a philological exercise (as so often in Freud, it ends as a literary exercise): he is concerned with showing how *heimlich* (*familiar*, literally *homelike*; on the same subject, see Heidegger's "Being-at-home") eventually coincides with its opposite, *unheimlich* (a little as in English a *familiar* may well be a supernatural spirit, one frequently embodied in an animal). In the first part of his development, Freud goes to dictionaries for a number of definitions, some of which are of particular interest to us. In D. Sanders's *Wörterbuch der deutschen Sprache* (1860), he finds for *unheimlich* "concealed, kept from sight, so that others do not know about it." And in Schelling he finds a parallel definition: "everything is uncanny that ought to have remained hidden." Freud thus finds in the public domain evidence for the fact that the uncanny is the frightening return of something that was once benign. Anticipating his conclusion that fiction has more ways than life to create the uncanny, Freud then proceeds to a detailed explication of "The Sandman" by a master of the uncanny, E. T. A. Hoffmann.

Briefly told, "The Sandman" is the story of Nathaniel, who, in the midst of an otherwise happy life, recalls obsessively the events sur-

---

8. The phallic snake, symbol of fertility in other lores, may well arise out of a similar sense of the unknown that can penetrate human existence with the power to affect it vitally. Once again, death and renewal are part of the same cycle: the mystery of penetration into life at the start, the mystery of an unknown otherness at the end. (See more on this in chapter 2.)

9. Sigmund Freud, "Das Unheimliche," in *Studies in Parapsychology* (New York: Collier Books, 1971).

rounding his father's death. In his childhood, his nurse had told him that the Sandman throws handfuls of sand into the eyes of children who won't go to bed so that their eyes pop out of their sockets for the Sandman to carry off to the moon where he feeds them to his children. Seeking to discover the identity of the Sandman, Nathaniel hides in his father's study one evening when his father is entertaining a lawyer named Coppelius. Nathaniel is discovered in the study and Coppelius is about to drop hot coals from the hearth into the child's eyes when his father intercedes. A year later, the father dies under mysterious circumstances in the same study and Coppelius disappears.

As a university student, Nathaniel believes that he recognizes Coppelius in an itinerant optician, Giuseppe Coppola, who terrifies him by offering to sell him "eyes." These turn out to be harmless eyepieces. Nathaniel buys a spyglass from Coppola and through it discovers in the house of Spalanzani, opposite his, the beautiful and still Olympia. Nathaniel is so enamored with this vision that he forgets Clara, his fiancée. But Olympia turns out to be a mechanical doll in whose making Spalanzani and Coppola have collaborated; at the end of a quarrel between the two men, Coppola leaves with the eyeless doll. Spalanzani picks up the bleeding eyeballs and throws them at Nathaniel, from whom Spalanzani believes Coppola has stolen them. This precipitates an attack of madness in Nathaniel, who relives the experience of his father's death and attempts to strangle Spalanzani.

When he recovers from the sickness that ensues, Nathaniel is about to marry Clara. But on a day that the couple has climbed to the top of a tower, Nathaniel, still using the fateful telescope, catches sight of something strange—presumably Coppelius—in the street below. In a sudden fit of madness, Nathaniel attempts to push Clara over the railing. She is saved, but the raving Nathaniel tumbles to his own death, confirming the prediction of Coppelius to the crowd that the madman would soon come down from the tower by himself.

For Freud, this story about sight and the fear of losing one's eyes is a reminder that such fears occur in childhood as substitute castration fears (we will return to this question in our examination of Oedipus the King). Since these fears derive from the presence of the father, the Sandman becomes a figure representing the child's ambivalent feelings: the father both threatens to blind (castrate) the child and intercedes to save his sight. It is the "good" father who dies in the office; the evil father-imago (Coppelius) survives, causing the son's madness and eventual death. (This dual representation is maintained in the Spalanzani-Coppola pairing.) Freud finds confirmation for this theory in Grisebach's account of Hoffmann's own relationship to his father.

The doll Olympia allows Freud to introduce the notion of the "double" and the related concepts of animism and primary narcissism. In the games of children, a doll is likely to be treated as a live person: the "double" is originally a spare, an insurance against destruction of the ego (the need endures in the belief that grants mortals a body and a soul). But as repression transforms emotional affect into morbid anxiety, the unwonted reappearance of the doll, long after the existence with which we informed it has been overlaid, represents another form of the obsessive and unsettling Freudian ghost. Primary narcissism (a "primitive" notion as well as an aspect of childhood), which overestimates mental processes in order to withstand the otherwise "inexorable laws of reality," encourages an animistic view of the world that peoples it with the spirits of human beings. Traces of such a former belief can be reactivated—the uncanny corresponds to the stirring of those vestiges within us:[10] if we animate an inanimate object with the repressed memory, it will be fearful and strange for showing so plainly what, in Schelling's formulation, "ought to have remained hidden."

The inanimate doll that returns as the trace of a former life is the more logically midwifed by this former animism because of a "primitive" fear of the dead that still abides in us: the deceased is a menace to the survivor whom he threatens to carry off with him. Freud's argument intertwines the concept of the repressed past and the fear of death as it is more generally and more immediately understood: the unconscious cannot entertain the idea of its own extinction. Even though he begins by criticizing the central thesis of Jentsch (whose paper "Zur Psychologie des Unheimlichen" he uses as a springboard for his own)—an analysis of the uncanny as a sense of "intellectual uncertainty"—Freud concludes his argument by allowing that the sense of intellectual uncertainty is important in determining what it sees as the threat of death. The circularity of Freud's argument, at

10. Sigmund Freud, *Totem and Taboo* (New York: W. W. Norton, 1962), pt. 3.

this point, is due to the fact that he is talking about two kinds of death, or more precisely, about two locations of the sense of death. The fear most generally held sees death as a looming in the future (the "aheadness" of Heidegger); Freud's argument accepts this sense at times but also establishes the fear in the individual's repressed past. Freud the clinician is more interested in the latter location since exposure of the ghost is curative. But, significantly, the psychoanalytical interpretation requires for its understanding the sense of death in its more familiar form.

The fear of losing one's eyes, which Freud believes to be a substitute fear for that of castration, evolves through a similar circularity. Among the explanations attempted for this complex theory is the association of such fears with primal losses—those of the mother's breast, the feces, the detachable penis. This sense of loss represents the first sense of *separability* in a world that was previously whole, the first sense of *limitation* in a world that was previously unbounded. The sense of those boundaries contains the sense of death as we have used it in this speculation: an awareness that our being is circumscribed in a way that is ineradicable and utterly unacceptable, which we henceforth fear and tend towards/against.

We lose little more than Freud's psychoanalytic speculation if we assume that "The Sandman" tells about a threat to human sight (and about the ultimate failure of sight) in order to convey a sense of the fascination and danger inherent in mystery when mystery is felt to contain that which might abrogate our pro-ject. Nathaniel's eyes are threatened by the beyond into which he attempts to cast them. We never really know what it is that Nathaniel sees, or attempts to see. Indeed, we do not even know whether the threats he senses derive from a region beyond the scope of sight or are merely inventions of his buffeted mind. We know only that his eyes are cast at mysteries that are not to be fathomed (and are therefore *cast back* at him). What is "uncanny" about Hoffmann's story is the mood it creates: we may not know towards what beyond Nathaniel is tensed, but his sense of that beyond is our own. In considering the kind of fictional verisimilitude that is most favorable for the development of that sense, Freud suggests a fundamental definition (to which we will have occasion to return in subsequent chapters): uncanniness can attach to fiction only to the extent that the fiction is located within a mundane and familiar world. The fairy tale, Homer's mythological creatures,

Dante's spirits, Shakespeare's ghosts (or Beowulf's world, once we have identified his monsters as symbols) may be variously gloomy or impressive, but no aura of the uncanny surrounds them. Their being contrives an acceptance of the supernatural world and that acceptance coerces ours: they are posited as existing on the other side of a boundary that they, in fact, cancel. In order to be the equivalent of what we may sense beyond the reach of our *own* possibilities, the fictional uncanny requires the absolute contrast of a realistic story depicting an everyday world. Modern realism (whether that of Kafka, Borges, or Robbe-Grillet), which favors this mode, rejects the symbolic as does Freud's prerequisite for the establishment of the uncanny mood. The uncanny can become such only within a world believed to be real (a condition never likely to be wholly achieved in the reading of fiction, and one that is difficult for the critic to allude to since, by definition, he is never in such a position of belief when he functions as a critic). This consideration is important because it determines the nature of the fictional hero beset by the uncanny: that hero must accept as *real* all intimations of the uncanny so as to act as a mediator of the reader's acceptance—the reader's acceptance of that hero being possible only inasmuch as he is otherwise a mundane part of his mundane context. Nevertheless, Todorov suggests a useful limitation of the hero's powers of acceptance: he must never accept the evidence of his fantastic world either without a struggle or totally ("total faith or total incredulity would lead us beyond the fantastic").[11] Todorov is interested in preserving this residual doubt because he requires it for a distinction between the fantastic (defined in terms of that doubt) and the uncanny, which he understands (as we do) to be "an experience of limits."[12] Since the reader never quite surrenders his disbelief, it is likely that his skepticism preserves even within the uncanny that doubt through which Todorov wishes to define only the fantastic: in Blanchot's words, and for all readers of fiction, "art is as if"—but seldom more.[13]

11. Tzvetan Todorov, *The Uncanny*, trans. R. Howard (Ithaca, N.Y.: Cornell University Press, 1975), p. 31.

12. Todorov, *Uncanny*, p. 48. Todorov sees this experience of limits as a reminder of ancient taboos and a primal experience of transgression. This would be in fact a second step following upon what we have defined as a first sense of fragmentation and limitation within the infantile world.

13. Maurice Blanchot, *La Part du feu* (Paris: NRF, 1949), p. 26.

Freud remarks that folklore, without striving for uncanny effects, readily adopts an animistic point of view: fiction, if it so chooses, has many more ways of creating the uncanny than has real life. Though folklore is not quite literature (or is literature only to the extent that it is the *dress* of a collective unconscious), literature frames and privileges: its special economy allows it to synthesize a moment or a sense that might otherwise be dissolved in an existential flow. Inasmuch as Freud is interested in investigating such a sense and uses Hoffmann's fiction as his exploratory ground, it should be noted that Freud and Hoffmann are engaged in utterly dissimilar pursuits. In rendering the effect of the uncanny, Hoffmann (contrary to Freud) cannot explore Nathaniel's inner world. Even though the story's uncanny events are told so that the reader may wish to infer that they are but a part of Nathaniel's madness, the "uncanniness" of their effect is possible only when they are thought to be part of a world that is *external* to the hero. The clinician who places himself within the deranged mind of his subject establishes a stable dwelling for himself—somewhat like the fiction that, in assuming a supernatural context open to the reader, cannot generate a sense of the supernatural. But Hoffmann is interested in unsettling the quietude of his reader by unsettling the quietude of Nathaniel.

In a literary sense, it might be said that Hoffmann is more "modern" than Freud because, paradoxically, his tale is closer to the epic that motivated this digression, locating for the reader a world that calls for the reader's response or speculation rather than his rehearsal of that world within the mind of the fictional character. Beowulf, like Nathaniel, accepts his world as real. His monsters may be alien to the social order upon which they intrude, but there can be no doubt that they *are*; in the familiar world of Beowulf's lieges, those monsters represent "an event that cannot be explained by the laws of this same familiar world"; [14] but the fact that they cannot be explained does not dematerialize them. Whatever self-searching they might awaken in Beowulf is subordinate to his inherent definition— that of the figure who must eventually destroy them. As conveyors of an otherworldly mood, they can determine self-searching only in those who are susceptible to their threat—the listeners of *Beowulf*, the ones who, through self-comparison, will be able to measure the

14. Todorov, *Uncanny*, p. 25.

extent of Beowulf's epic stature. Because Beowulf exists for other reasons, the threatening mood around him is real but external: he lacks an inner mood that might be affected by the external one; he cannot be "explained" except as part of a tautological definition. It is only when the (less-than-epic) character has an inner world, and is therefore susceptible to the external threat, that his "explanation" is possible—an explanation in which Western literature has long been interested and that, for an equally long time, gave its protagonists a tincture of anxiety (determining the eventual reaction of writers like Sartre and Robbe-Grillet against the "tragic" propensity of that literature). However, when the reality of the fear is *intended* (as in the case of Nathaniel), its analysis *explains it away* to the reader whom that fear was supposed to contaminate.

With reference to his reader, Hoffmann's purpose is the opposite of Freud's, creates an "outer" rather than an "inner" world and corresponds to another moment and another mode of response to the human predicament (suggesting that Freud, in addition to providing a key to modern consciousness, is also, as Harold Bloom suggests, the inheritor of an older literary tradition).[15] At some time between *Beowulf* and that modern consciousness,[16] and during an extended period of time, Western fiction is less interested in describing a world beset by the mystery of ultimate realities than in describing the effect of that mystery upon an individual consciousness—engaging in a metaphysical rehearsal that is not unlike the psychological exploration of Freud. During that period of Western literature, even the most compellingly external presence cannot prevent such speculative and internalizing returns. The failure to apprehend the unapprehendable turns into a speculative brooding about the limits of the self. In the following *dizain* by Maurice Scève, written in 1544, the very love object becomes an instance of personal and metaphysical failure:

> Le jour passé de ta douce présence
> Fut un serein en hiver ténébreux,

15. For example, in *Poetry and Repression: Revisionism from Blake to Stevens* (New Haven, Conn.: Yale University Press, 1976).

16. Or "post-modern," as our current exacerbation sometimes terms the present transiency. Since human consciousness does not conform exactly to a critical chronology, the scheme suggested here, while generally accurate, shows considerable overlapping at both ends and is not infrequently confirmed by significant exceptions.

Qui fait prouver la nuit de ton absence
A l'oeil de l'âme être un temps plus ombreux,
Que n'est au corps ce mien vivre encombreux,
Qui maintenant me fait de soi refus.
Car dès le point que partie tu fus,
Comme le lièvre accroupi en son gîte,
Je tends l'oreil, oyant un bruit confus,
Tout éperdu aux ténèbres d'Egypte.[17]

(Which translates roughly as "The day spent in your sweet presence/ Was lovely and calm within the winter gloom,/And shows the night of your absence to be/A time of greater darkness to my soul/Than is for my body this burdensome life/Which now refuses itself to me./ For since the moment you left me,/I, like the rabbit crouched in his lodge,/Tense my hearing towards a nameless sound,/All in dread of Egypt's night.") The Petrarchian antitheses, whose function it is to describe a perfect and perfectly effective mistress (she turns the darkest winter day into its vernal opposite, and gloom into light), serve to represent a menacing darkness as the poet, swinging back into himself, is overwhelmed by ill-identified but somber forebodings. Egypt, a biblical symbol of oppression for the Jews (*Mizrahim*), becomes an *audible* sign of impending jeopardy. What began as a compliment to a lover ends as the statement of an inner dread that reduces the lover to ineffectualness: the internalized concern sees only its own danger in an awareness of limits that are sufficiently threatening to negate the effective radiance of the love object. The imagining of an absolute (Petrarchian) mistress compels thoughts of the absolute, and these, as one might expect, state themselves in terms of the fearful boundary that frustrates every absolute possession: the winter desolation that returns because of the mistress' withdrawal introduces the metaphysical desolation of a consciousness that cannot possess the world sundered by an absolute absence.

Unable to cross over or dismiss the fateful boundary that hems it in, the frustrated awareness establishes surrogates for the beyond on this side of the divide: a false boundary is posited, but one that is permeable, inviting a mock penetration of the unknown through an

17. Maurice Scève, *Oeuvres complètes* (Paris: Mercure de France, 1974).

active participation (that of the initiate and the initiatory ritual) or a speculative one (through the "rehearsive" nature of art or myth). In literature, the refractory mystery may be rehearsed as the *sense* through which it discloses itself in actuality ("The Sandman") or as a meditation on the mystery's effect (depth psychology, metaphysical speculation). In either case, literature is thought to be, if not quite reality itself, then at least informed with our own brooding on that upon which the fiction, or its characters, brood: the literary event is as "true" as the existential event in proportion as it is able to effect an identical brooding in the reader. It is here that the distinction between "high" and "low" literary genres is born, from the more-than-theoretical belief that such a transference of self to the mediatory mana of a certain kind of fiction is possible ("high") and not to another ("low").[18] Within a given culture, the constituents of such a literature and the culture itself are likely to be mutually defining, establishing a circularity whose closure is best demonstrated by the efforts that are made to break out of it. An anthology like *Man and His Fictions* was compiled in the belief that "what distinguishes Literature from that kind of writing that is not Literature is not entirely clear" (the uncertainty being "indeed one of the questions that this book asks you to consider"); it wonders what gives us the confidence to assert that "*King Lear* is in, *Tarzan* is out."[19] It is a confidence implicit in the compiling of such an anthology that, by the very fact of its existence, constitutes a canon, with the sacramental implications of the term—implications that a reading of the table of contents confirms. The book is composed, much as one might expect any college anthology to be, of pieces that can be recognized as "high" literature

18. This fact makes notions of "high" and "low" idiosyncratic and transitory: the "genuineness" of the genre is largely determined by the credence the individual respondent invests in it; the determination of the genre's "value" is his —what appears as "high" art within a particular culture may be no more than kitsch or exoticism in another.

19. A. B. Kernan, P. Brooks, and M. J. Holquist, eds., *Man and His Fictions: An Introduction to Fiction-Making, Its Forms and Uses* (New York: Harcourt, Brace, Jovanovich, 1973), p. 1. Tarzan is the emblem of the "low" genre even though Edgar Rice Burroughs (not represented in the anthology) might have meant to create in the character, who is part Lord, part lord of the apes, a figure of Lear-like solitude within two cultures whose shortcomings are implicitly criticized: the primitive bestiality of the jungle and the less honest complexities of the civilized code into which the hero was born. See Richard A. Lupoff, *Edgar Rice Burroughs: Master of Adventure* (New York: Carnaveral Press, 1965).

or that have a sufficient cultural patina (a prior acceptance by other interpreters of a level of culture corresponding to that of the authors) to qualify.

With the exception of a few pages of the comic strip "Superman," the most decisive descent of *Man and His Fictions* from the empyrean of a "high" genre is provided by the section entitled "Bedrock of Fiction: The Detective Story" (a descent somewhat mitigated by the fact that its only representatives are Sir Arthur Conan Doyle and Sophocles).[20] To explain why the detective story might be the occasion of such a descent requires a preliminary analysis of the genre.

If we accept that a certain literature is an attempt to come to terms with the mystery of what lies beyond the reach of consciousness, then the mode of the detective story is to create a mystery for the sole purpose of effecting its effortless dissipation. As Todorov points out, it is a curiously articulated fiction, in which what happened is kept from the reader while what he is told is less than relevant to what has happened.[21] Other paradoxes: the genre features a hero, the detective, whose existence is a mere function of the mystery he is solving, while that mystery is, in fact, a patent knowledge over which a veil has been drawn at the first page that cannot extend beyond the last.[22] Finally, it has at its start a corpse to which is attached no sense of death. As a genre, the detective story is optimistic and self-destructing. Its coy mystery, served by its mechanistic detective and its antiseptic corpse, is free of the odor of death that is usually associated with the beyond. The intensity of the consciousness projected towards that beyond is replaced in the detective story by an expectation: the duration of the story (its reading) is the time we must wait for the pieces to fall into place; the intensity of the "mystery" is voided by our awareness of that mystery's transitoriness.

20. A view (Sophocles as a detective story-writer) rejected at about the same time by one of the coauthors (M. Holquist, "Whodunit and Other Questions: Metaphysical Detective Stories in Post-War Fiction," *NLH* 3 [1971–72]).

21. Tzvetan Todorov, "The Typology of Detective Fiction," in *The Poetics of Prose*, trans. R. Howard (Ithaca, N.Y.: Cornell University Press, 1977).

22. It is of this kind of striptease ("unveiling") that Barthes speaks in *The Pleasure of the Text* (trans. R. Miller [New York: Hill and Wang, 1975]), contrasting the expectation of an ultimate exposure with the more subtle pleasures of "penetration." I will leave out of account, in this discussion, the sexual implications of the pro-ject, especially as I do not believe that "penetration" is ultimately possible. However, the sexual thrust of the question cannot be denied.

This transitoriness exaggerates to the point of parody the shrinking of the mystery contained within fiction: a concern formerly *like* the one induced by the reader's existential reality is reduced, in the detective story, to the dimensions of a small game; the metaphysical mode is replaced by a mode of play. In this respect, the detective story resembles other genres—the adventure story, the spy novel, the thriller—whose interest is in the fashioning of a trajectory largely for its own sake, the sustaining "mystery" corresponding to that part of the trajectory that is not yet completed by the reader. The temptation of these genres is that of characterless plot—events are more important than the people engaged in them. By contrast, other small genres, like the love story, or the horror story, claim greater interest for the protagonist than for the event that engages him.

The temptation of the detective story to become pure abstraction— what Dorothy Sayers calls a tale of detection in which the means of logic that lead to the apprehension of the criminal are of far greater interest than the criminal—represents its desire to engage the participation of the reader. Since the metaphysical mode (identification with someone essentially like the reader in his concerns) has been abandoned (along with the concomitant tension/interest of those concerns) in exchange for the reader's interest in an *unfolding* ("how will it come out?"), the detective story ("detective" being adjectival, since there is no actual *detective* to invite identification) invites the reader instead to participate in that unfolding, to play the game actively rather than through the passivity of a demonstration. Since the hero of the detective fiction is a void created by his functional dependency on the "mystery," the reader is offered that same dependency so as to become, through his own ratiocination, the character that fictional ratiocination is unable to create.

The temptation of the detective to become wholly abstract can never be more than a temptation. The ideal represented by that temptation is the problem or puzzle that uses functional symbols and can dispense with the articulation of a story. But the game of detective fiction derives from the telling of a story and so creates at least functional characters. It is therefore also subject to the reverse temptation to use its mode as a pretext for other inclusions: the detective story is always in danger of becoming something else. With the advent of the "hard-boiled" genre (Dashiell Hammett, Ross Macdonald, or Raymond Chandler), the detective story becomes a saga of the American industrial city as the locale of a man facing the corruption of individuals and of government. Although Philip Marlowe's drinking, drabness, and dames do not succeed in making him much less of an abstraction than his more exclusively ratiocinating forebears, the moral and political implications of the events into which he is thrown suggest the lineaments of a character.[23] At an extreme, a writer like Simenon is unabashedly interested in the inner life of his detective: his stories are largely a waiting by the hero and the reader for an anticlimactic "solution," a waiting spent *within* Maigret, whose vision ultimately contrives what Simenon's fiction is really about—the sketch of particular social types and milieus. In Simenon, the genre quite loses sight of itself.

In spite of these temptations to become something else, and in the face of repeated predictions by historians and critics of the genre's imminent demise, its requisite stylization has remained largely unchanged for well over a century, at the very hub of the large number of mutant genres it has spawned. This, together with the critical evolution of the reader, has resulted in a new incarnation of the traditional detective story that has become defining for a substantial part of modern fiction.

I have attempted to show elsewhere[24] how a reader who is less and less credulous (literally, a reader who is less and less a *believer*) distances himself from the fiction-maker's word (primitively associated with the Creator's Word—art as a form of logos) and requires of the fiction-maker increasingly elaborate strategies of reader entrapment. From an external depiction of the world that was eventually robbed of its mimetic magic, there evolved what we still think of as the traditional novel, whose probing of its character was compatible with the concerns of an equally self-questioning reader. Whether such a novel had a social purpose (to effect an improvement in its reader's circumstances), whether, on the contrary, it was seen to be determined by the social (and psychological) circumstances of that reader, or whether it was thought of as the rehearsal of a fundamental

23. Lineaments that are sufficient for a recent critic to read into them elaborate sexual ambivalences, the threat of aristocratic transcendency to a benevolent bourgeoisie, etc. See John G. Cawelti, *Adventure, Mystery and Romance* (Chicago: University of Chicago Press, 1976).

24. David I. Grossvogel, *Limits of the Novel* (Ithaca, N.Y.: Cornell University Press, 1968).

experience through symbols and myths (the kind of literary activity with whose analysis we have been primarily concerned so far), the statement of that fiction assumed a human grounding: however anxious or tragic, it was optimistic to the extent that it resulted from an anthropocentric conviction that was evident, at the very least, in the control of the authorial voice.

Every new form of fiction derives from the loss of a neutral ground —the loss of a way of saying, or of a belief in what was being said, that was previously thought to be possible. The acceptance that a poet once articulated something like the breath of god made the mimetic moment of fiction possible: a first death of god turned the reader inward and encouraged the rehearsive propensity of the novel that probed its object through ever greater descents that came to be known in time as depth psychology. But this internalization still assumed the equivalent of a god, a center or fixity, the neutral ground that allowed a *point of view*: whatever human mysteries the probing might fathom, it had to presuppose a probing author who transcended them. Paradoxically, the greater the depth of the probing, the more the distance between the prober and his object subverted the prober's credibility, the magnitude of the quest dwarfing the quester. With the loss of this anthropocentric grounding, new strategies started to alter traditional fiction: the resolutely antimetaphysical mode of the detective story opened the way for a new fictional metaphysics.

The epic nature of Beowulf rests on two necessary assumptions: that the reader (to use an anachronistic term) of *Beowulf* believe in the monster with which Beowulf contends, but that there be no *inwardness* in Beowulf that allows *him to believe*. The monster must be an (ir)reducible otherness for both Beowulf and the reader that confirms the hollowness of the first and the belief of the second. If Beowulf should believe in the monster as does the reader, then he is subject to the same fears as the reader and his integrity—his absolute definition (he-who-kills-the-monster)—is altered. If the reader does not believe in the monster, he cannot believe in the epic stature of Beowulf: belief in that stature results from the confrontation by the reader of Beowulf's emptiness of fear and the fear induced by the reader's own belief. (The same mechanism is at work in "The Sandman" even though Nathaniel believes in, and fears, his otherness:

the reader can credit Nathaniel only if he can credit Nathaniel's fears; the difference between Nathaniel and Beowulf derives from the fact that "The Sandman" is not really about Nathaniel: it can easily dispense with him.)

The modern consciousness may *know* that Beowulf is an epic figure but it does not *believe* it: it no longer believes in his monsters. This distinction between knowledge and belief forces the writer of the psychological or metaphysical novel to internalize within the consciousness of the character those monsters that formerly compelled belief in that character through their externality. A more modern Beowulf is defined not as he-who-kills-Grendel but as he-who-broods-over-Grendel (or the consequences of the symbol Grendel). As opposed to the "emptiness" of the original Beowulf, such a character is *full*: a metaphysical universality flows through him, composing his inner world as it does the reader's. Within this universality, the character's circumstantial definitions can be no more than secondary.

This loss of a necessary specificity served to further dissipate the *sense* of mystery in the writer whose fiction fastened upon an unknown that it described as being increasingly resistive to any kind of appropriation. A sense of the mystery, like that of the uncanny, required a specificity, a *familiarity* that could be subverted, but there was nothing to subvert in the psychological novel: it had become twice bland—recognizable in its concerns but without a need for compelling features, familiar in the hero's depth but lacking a surface. A favorite with intellectuals since the nineteenth century, the detective story offered, by contrast, the necessary specificity of its circumstances against which the "mystery" (however fraudulent) was played. It was the possible subversion of its world by something *external* (a subversion that the familiar world of the detective story made possible) that eventually attracted the novelist who felt that his traditional form had become too abstract and equable for the exigency of its concern.

Alain Robbe-Grillet, one of the first to speak of this kind of subversion (and one of its practitioners), found in the courtroom a metaphor to contrast both genres. Assuming that a court of law is convened to discover truth, Robbe-Grillet referred to the ineluctable quality of the "exhibit"—the document formally introduced as evidence in the proceedings.[25] He contrasted this *evidence* with the words and the *seeming* imposed on the document in an effort to make it conform to constructs (the prosecutor's, the defendant's, etc.) that are given as real but are no more than verbal. This corresponds to the evidence of a nonsignifying world that a kind of literature attempts to endow with significance, even though that significance can pertain only to the endower. The intent of this appropriation through words (through literature) is to overcome what we mistakenly term *our* world—an attempt to cope with what Robbe-Grillet senses as a refractory *otherness* that we are determined to subdue ("en venir à bout"). The process describes the attempt of the metaphysical novel to assimilate a world that *is simply there*, while losing in the process the sense of that world's unassimilableness. But it also describes the process of detective fiction in which a familiar object, the repository of a final truth, is disguised by words (the misleading story) that attempt to give that object a spurious *meaning*.

Other than such familiar, humble, and ultimately irreducible objects, the detective story offered its reader only a vacancy: the reader was invited to become the (nonexistent) detective by separating (and discarding) literature from those objects. The reader remained external to that literature and, to that extent, the game proposed by the detective story engaged the reader on the level of a parafictional reality. But a mystery so constructed could not convey a *sense* of mystery: the detachment of its reader prevented the story's everyday circumstances from being counterpoised to a credible *otherness* within it. The ultimate vacancy of the genre was recapitulative and total: at the end of the book, the mystery was turned into transparency extending from cover to cover. The writing of a metaphysical mystery (a fiction that would convey a sense of the mystery rather than its analysis) required only that the seal closing the traditional detective story be broken so as to transform it from containment to open-endedness. Once this was done, the reader faced a vacancy without remission, a fictional world whose final page had been removed so as to open that world to the nonascribable meaninglessness of his own. The sense of an existential alienation was returned to a genre from which the resolvable mystery had been removed.

25. Alain Robbe-Grillet, "A Future for the Novel," in *For a New Novel*, trans. R. Howard (New York: Grove Press, 1965).

Through the same process of habituation that had made of the psychological novel something too familiar for the *sense* of a mystery to which its argument referred, the metaphysical detective story eventually lost the quality of strangeness that had constituted its original appeal. It endures nevertheless because the reader's detachment, which replaced his earlier participation (his *sense* of strangeness), corresponds to the detachment required by the game-playing of the genre in its original form. But the elements of the game afforded by the open-ended genre are multiple and bend the mystery back, within the play of interreflecting mirrors contrived by the text and its words, into the reader's existence. Subsequent chapters examine some elements of this new literature, which has become for the modern reader a part of his tentative and problematic reading of an increasingly alien world. The text that first proposed itself as a description of the mysterious, and later as a reflection upon it, now proposes a more visceral participation: it offers itself as a deciphering, as another form of the obdurate otherness at whose shifting limits the probing continues.[26] In suggesting this more visceral rehearsal of the reader's experience at the point where experience fails, this new realism aspires to the status of parafiction.

26. Even here, the more "primitive" text shows affinities with the modern text. The "description" it proposed was largely a function of the reader's readiness to believe that description. But the runic quality of poetry reminds us of its religious and incantational origins: the versification in Dante's didactic epic is an invitation to discover still other meanings in it.

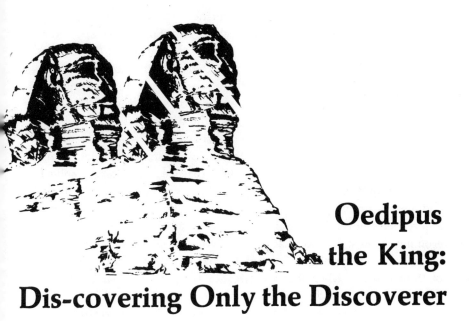

Oedipus
the King:
Dis-covering Only the Discoverer

On a first reading, *Oedipus the King* might sound, indeed, like a work of detective fiction: there is a killing, a quest for the murderer, a resolution when, at last, all questions are answered. But then, it is difficult to talk of a first reading of *Oedipus* (while it is difficult to talk of anything but a first reading of a detective story). And then there is a peculiar stench that tells us even more strongly that this is not a detective novel: it is the odor of the corpse that, literally, smells to high heaven. Strong enough to offend the gods, that smell provides a number of clues: it suggests that this corpse is not simply a cipher in an abstract puzzle. As the Sphinx implies, the riddle concerns *man*, real people—us. That the gods are involved indicates that it may concern even more than us—or concern us in a fundamental way. The game proposed here, though it begins with riddles, cannot be contained or controlled by the mind. A further departure from detective fiction (and a radical one): the reader, like Sophocles' spectator, knows the answers beforehand;[1] he knows that when Laius and Jocasta had their son, the oracle predicted that the son would kill his father; that the baby was therefore exposed to die on Mt. Cithaeron but brought by a shepherd to Polybus, king of Corinth; that as an adult, Oedipus learned from the oracle that he would kill his father and wed his mother, and, believing his foster parents to be his real parents, fled Corinth; that at a crossroads he met, quarreled with, and killed Laius; that he proceeded to Thebes, solved the riddle of the Sphinx, gaining the kingship and Jocasta's hand, and thereby bringing to fruition the full prediction of the oracle. What the reader knows beforehand is a story, albeit one whose ironic economy is so satisfying that it may have helped Aristotle formulate his belief in the primacy of the plot—that encapsulation of a scheme of things which, when it is right, contains a relation that is so true that the poet's main duty is to discover it.[2] But knowing the plot, the reader cannot be interested in only the plot: its repetition must be for him the occasion of a more important rehearsal.

To return to the corpse: Laius was a king thought to be childless, several times guilty before the gods, and, in fact, a father—the implications of his death are as complicated as those of his life. As might befall mortals, he is cursed from the start, caught up in the web of more ancient maledictions: it has been decreed that his lineage must end with him; even before the oracle spelled out the consequence of having Oedipus, Laius had been warned. In *Seven against Thebes*, Aeschylus recalls an earlier part of the myth:

> I speak of an old breach
> of law, long since begotten,
> but bitterly swift to bring

1. The modern reader also knows all that has been said *about* the play, from Aristotle to Freud. Yet every reading, *any* reading, is an attempt to discover: if the play is *readable* after twenty-three centuries, it warrants the critic's return to it. He is, after all, still another reader.

2. See Gerald F. Else, *Aristotle's Poetics* (Cambridge, Mass.: Harvard University Press, 1957), especially p. 320.

retributive disaster;
and yet lingered on
to the third generation.
Three times the Lord Apollo
in the midmost Pythian navel,
the prophetic center, spoke:
if Laios were to live
childless, without issue,
then the city would be safe.
But madly overcome
by lust, the body's folly,
despite the speaking god
Laios begat his doom.[3]

If one considers the myth without the complex, the curse upon Laius is that of barrenness. For a family to be without issue is a curse; for a king, it is a national calamity as well. It is here that the fundamental prohibition against incest (according to Lévi-Strauss, a "pre-social" awareness in its universality and elemental nature) is enunciated as a social law.[4] In Laius the social and divine injunctions are intermixed and cause him to sin at least twice: once in resisting the divine prohibition not to have children, once in thinking that he might be able to resist a prohibition that is divine. The many involutions of the Oedipal tragedy result from an *after*-thought.

In killing Laius, Oedipus is only the executor of the gods. But passing sentence on Laius does not undo all that Laius has done: there is still the condemnation of Cadmus that endures in Oedipus; and he has his own oracle. To kill one's king is bad enough; to kill one's

3. Aeschylus, *Seven against Thebes*, trans. Anthony Hecht and Helen H. Bacon (New York: Oxford University Press, 1973), verses 740–55.

4. Lévi-Strauss notes that in Madagascar the prohibition against incest among the lowborn applies to the mother, sister, and cousins, whereas to the king or lord, only the mother is *fady* (prohibited): the head of the clan is given more progenitorial chances; but by an interesting reversal of cause and effect, sterility in a couple is assumed to be due to incest, whether known or unknown, and a cleansing ritual is routinely offered. ("Nature and Culture," in *The Elementary Structures of Kinship* [Boston: Beacon Press, 1969].) Since procreation implies, in a patrilineal scheme, that it is a procreator who must be procreated, the Greeks specified that conduct of the all-important funerary rites devolve first to the son. (On this and other forms of patrimonial preservation showing the importance of family and children, see J.-P. Vernant, *Mythe et pensée chez les Grecs* [Paris: Maspéro, 1966]).

own father is terrible. Parricide was, for the Greeks, the unthinkable crime; Solon's civil code specifies no penalty for it: to countenance the penalty would have meant to countenance the possibility of the crime. Like his father, Oedipus belongs to the gods, and they impart a dreadful echo to deeds that would otherwise be within the province of men to heal.

But here, even men condemn. In a sense, Oedipus is innocent (of at least his most heinous crimes): his parricide, like his incest, is committed in a state of ignorance. However, that ignorance was not as mitigating for the Athenian mind as it might be for ours: there is the awful evidence of the hand. Time and again (lines 106, 107, 231, 236, 1332, etc.), Oedipus insists that his deeds were done *by his hand*. Thomas Gould reminds us that the Greeks distinguished between two kinds of guilt: their most awesome court, the Areopagus, tried the culprit who had done the deed by his own hand; a lesser court, the Palladion, tried those who plotted but did not actually carry out the deed. How guilty Oedipus remained for the spectator of Sophocles can be inferred from the fact that whereas even voluntary homicide, if it was not actually perpetrated by the culprit, was tried by the Palladion, even *involuntary* homicide was tried before the Areopagus.[5] Even among men, the magnitude of Oedipus's crime overshadows the circumstances of its resolution. His crime calls into question the very nature of criminality.

But there remain the gods. In every human encounter with human limits, the beyond, the godhead, is what defines those limits. Against the ignorance of men, the gods are knowledge. But in the story of Oedipus, the deeds are too monstrous for all who are caught up in them not to know—even when what they think they know differs from the truth. In Sophocles' play, Jocasta voices a fundamental awareness. She says, "How many times have men in dreams, too, slept/with their own mothers" (lines 981–82). She speaks, as if it were a truth generally known, of a truth that is generally unspoken: she refers to the desire of incest as if it were common, when the injunctions of gods and men designate it as a centrally polluting calamity. Is she right? If the desire is so common, why do the gods and men conspire to keep it so consistently hushed? If the desire

5. *Oedipus the King*, trans. Thomas Gould (Englewood Cliffs, N.J., Prentice-Hall, 1970), p. 29. All subsequent quotations refer to this edition.

is uncommon, why then, again, this huge conspiracy of silence? Why *our own* silence, if it corresponds to our innermost desires? Why our own silence if it does not?[6] The play by Sophocles (very likely the myth itself) breaks that silence: the consequences of that rupture are parallel to those of the action the play rehearses, and this parallelism contributes to make of it something more than a play. In some very intimate way, Oedipus's crime contaminates us.

Why the breaking of that silence should still awe us today is the question that attracted Freud to the Sophoclean drama. In its psychological mechanism, he saw the working out of infantile impulses that he believed to be psychologically defining. As we have noted in his analysis of "The Sandman," Freud is apt to seek in literature confirmation for evidences that have already been established in the clinic, resulting in readings that might be open to question. Since such reservations do not impinge on the clinical evidence, that clinical instrument might be useful indeed to break through (over and above certain symbolic hermeticisms of the play) that which prevents *us* from being affected by the play as once we might have been. For Freud's sense of our present awe notwithstanding, it is likely that we are not moved by *Oedipus* as strongly as was the Athenian audience.[7]

To assume that Jocasta is not talking about the universality of incestuous desire (in a desperate attempt to make it seem less terrible) would be to achieve what she herself cannot achieve: to take away from the gods and Oedipus the full burden of the curse. To assume that the gods and Jocasta are not concerned with a central human mystery reduces the play to little more than archeological evidence. Even though the modern mind (which has little left to be shocked

---

6. Questions not answered by ethnologists who want Jocasta's words to mean simply that one cannot have faith in oracles, and for whom *mother* is a symbolic transposition of *mother earth* (as in the dream of Hippias, related by Herodotus, 6:107). See, for example, J.-P. Vernant, "Oedipe sans complexe," *Raison présente* 4 (1967): 3–20. On the relation of mother to mother earth, there remains more to be said.

7. One thinks, for example, of the disproportionately long scene (and coliloquies) given Oedipus after his blinding, and, especially, his own weeping (lines 1467ff.), with the evident invitation to the audience to weep as well—an invitation that, according to Gould (*Oedipus the King*, p. 163), was all too readily taken up (see Plato, *The Republic*, trans. H. D. P. Lee [Harmondsworth, Middlesex: Penguin Books, 1955], 10. 603ff.).

by) inhibits visceral response, there is little doubt that it confronts *Oedipus the King* with a familiarity whose uneasiness denies the control of expertise and commentary. The nature of this uneasy familiarity must influence the main questions addressed to a second reading of the play; its full power lies beyond the metacritical buffers of modern readings that talk about the reasons for the play's power in order to avoid direct exposure to that power.

It is perhaps an indication of these defenses that the modern sensitivity tends to *read* the play, when we should be speaking (assuming that we should be "speaking" at all) of a *performance* rather than a text, ritual rather than art: in every meaning of the expression, the play was intended originally to allow the spectator to *observe the ritual,* that is, to confirm to the ritual, to participate in it. The performance, as opposed to the assimilation of reading, is an *otherness* that the spectator is invited to *enter*—his *becoming a part of* being implied in his *separation from* (while a private—"mental"—reading invites him to continue being only himself, even as he is changed by his reading).

Ritual is born of luck and repetition. The circumstances under which the miraculous event first took place are scrupulously repeated in order to achieve repetition of the miracle; ritual as repetition is an attempt to control the caprice of miracles, an attempt to make them portable. Marie Delcourt outlines the further steps through which this mimetic process, attempted at first for the satisfaction of a specific wish, may become, once the original wish has been lost sight of, a scrupulously self-repetitive function for the benefit of a god: religion replaces a forgotten desire.[8] One is not supposed to offend the touchy gods, but the reason is buried within the distant unconscious.

Aristotle took note of this repetitive propensity and ascribed it tautologically to an inborn pleasure in imitation: the adult repeats the triumphs of the child during its time of learning. Imitation would thus hark back to a moment when mystery seemed, with greater justification, to be more assimilable. In order to explain why the repetition of an inherently painful experience—tragedy—should be equally desirable, Aristotle introduced the notion of catharsis: in the concepts of pity and fear, he located the extremes of attachment and

8. Marie Delcourt, *Oedipe ou La Légende du conquérant* (Paris: Droz, 1944).

repulsion of which the spectator might cleanse himself through a surrogate object. The Aristotelian shift from pleasure principle to cathartic function was amended by Freud: instead of Aristotle's pleasurable reminder of childhood patterns, Freud considered the trauma involved in the loss of a pleasurable infancy—the infant's separation from the mother and his subsequent rivalry with his father. In Freud's historical determinism, that rivalry harks back to an original murder of the father, a murder indefinitely replayed within the human psyche that grants the dead father vengeful powers stemming from his inhibitionary power in life. Thereafter, tragedy allows the spectator to relive this intimate and primordial drama by either associating with the hero as a father figure (oppressed by the gods) or with the hero as a son figure (oppressed by the father). In either case, the "pleasure" of tragedy is masochistic; an ineradicable trauma is rehearsed with a compulsiveness that displaces (and confirms) the pleasure principle.[9]

For Freud (as for Aristotle), *Oedipus the King* was the tragedy par excellence: it questioned directly the event whose occurrence left an identifying mark on mankind and explained the functioning of subsequent tragic mechanisms. Oedipus's oracular fate is certified, for Freud, by his human nature—the son's desire to kill the father in order to possess the mother. Whether or not one accepts the Freudian hypothesis, the play remains a question addressed to the irreconcilable enigma that sets limits to human understanding; *Oedipus the King* is an emblematic fable about a desire to know that ends in blindness. Freud (as already noted in chapter 1) particularizes the unknown within a circularity: the unknown is merely the repression of a truth previously known. Indeed, for even the non-Freudian, *Oedipus the King* unfolds as a pattern of such circularity and burying. Oedipus is a man who has *already* acted: he must now read his acts in order to know who he is. Similarly, the gods have already spoken: in answer to the repeated questions of mortals (Laius twice; Oedipus in Corinth, and in Thebes through Creon), the gods can only repeat themselves. When, through his stepbrother, Oedipus questions them a last time, they can only tell him about his past.

That circularity extends to Oedipus's knowledge: like the others, he knows even as he does not know. When Creon tells him the version of Laius's death that is current in Thebes, a version that has Laius struck down by several bandits, Oedipus reverts in his response to an automatic singular.[10] Repeatedly, Sophocles allows innocent words of Oedipus to become prophetic, as when the latter speculates about the (ever singular) murderer of Laius: "Whoever murdered him may also wish/to punish me—and with the selfsame hand" (lines 139–40); or when he speaks about his present circumstances: "it's I who have the power that he had once,/and have his bed, and a wife who shares our seed" (lines 259–60); or again, when he vows vengeance for the death of Laius, "as if for my own father,/I'll fight for him" (lines 264–65)—words whose irony has seemed especially significant to modern adapters of the play (see Gide's *Oedipus*).[11]

The key Oedipus is looking for is in the past, submerged. Oedipus, the stumbler, trips over its present evidence—in vain. But as in Proust's cobblestones, the truth is *underfoot*. (The oracle, to that extent at least, plays fair with Oedipus: he of the swollen foot [*Oidipous*, which in addition to the usual meaning, "swell foot," suggests the root *oida*, "I know," or *eidon*, "I see"] is asked a riddle about feet: "What is it that is four-footed, three-footed and two-footed?"[12] Confronted with yet another surfacing of the truth in the words of Tiresias, the irritation of Oedipus finds the prophet to be obstructive, but his own prophetic voice finds Tiresias to be "underfoot" (line 445).

In *Oedipus*, knowledge, like the mystery to which it is counterpoised, is *hidden*: it is *below*; the boundaries of the unknown may be displaced but they are familiar. As elsewhere, the unknown reveals itself only through such hints as preserve it. Human knowledge is impure. Of the unknown, we know only that it is absolute—*that absolute* is its purity. Oedipus, aware of the distinction between gods whose purity locates them within the unknown and the mortal who only professes purity (lines 830–33), seeks intercessors. I have already

---

10. Verses 122–24. And again, to the chorus that tells him, "He is said to have been killed by travelers," Oedipus answers, "I have heard, but the one who did it no one sees." Even accepting that the Greek text says "but the one who saw it no one sees," Oedipus's obsessive conviction that there is but one murderer makes no doubt: in his very next speech he says, "He won't fear words: he had no fear when he did it" (line 296).

11. André Gide, *Oedipus*, trans. J. Russell (London: Secker & Warburg, 1950).

12. See M. L. Earle, *The Oedipus Tyrannus* (New York: American Book, 1901), p. 40.

sketched out the short cycle that turns the intercessor into a form of the unknown: every intercessor evidences this duality (the part that claims to know and is impure, the part that cannot tell and is godlike), including those gods who are not content to remain figures of pure mystery. Apollo, whose oracle is the most famous in Greece and who therefore is invoked by all the principals in *Oedipus*, is such an ambiguous figure, an emblem and instance of opposing forces— the desire to know and the impenetrability of mystery. At first Apollo is a figure of absolute truth, associated with the sun (Phoebus Apollo) —pure radiance unmixed with revelation. He slays Python (the figure of darkness and the underworld) with his arrows (rays). But once the god is associated with mystery, he is contaminated by the forces of darkness and becomes the more dangerous Apollo Loxias, the oblique, who, like any mediator of the beyond, embodies within himself the radiance/darkness (disclosure/concealment, promise/ danger) that states the unknown.

Apollo's oracle at Delphi, the Pythia, received her knowledge as emanations from below. These, entering her, put her in the mystic trance that spoke the prophecy. Her name derives, of course, from Python: the sexual source of truth is related to a sense of origins (see chapter 1, note 7): the cave in which dwelled Python (sometimes thought itself to be oracular, or the guardian of Gaea's oracle) is a *stomion* ("small mouth"), a Greek word for vagina. The shrine had among its most holy objects the *omphalos*, a sacred stone that marked the exact center of the world and was Apollo's seat. Like the *stomion* itself, the *omphalos* is sacred, prophetic and a *voice* (though it means "navel," *omphalos* is homonymically related to the root of the Greek word for the divine voice, *omphé*): darkness, depth, midpoint, mystery, danger, and truth are articulated in the prophetic voice that speaks from Delphi.[13]

The Sphinx, which has similar origins, is not a fortuitous agency. She is (in Sophocles' Greece, at least) a female monster, not unlikely the result of an incestuous coupling (begotten by Echidna and her son

---

13. See Marie Delcourt, *L'Oracle de Delphes* (Paris: Payot, 1955), pp. 34–35. Modern research has found no chasm in Delphi for the sacred emanations and doubts therefore that there ever was a Pythia who went into trances while sitting on the sacred tripod. Possibly. Still, what we are dealing with here is not archeology but the projections of imagination. The question is not whether these events occurred, but why they were *imagined in this form*.

Orthus, though some say by the more legitimate Typhon), and, through her mother, part snake.[14] The Sphinx was a common ornament of Apollo's temples (not only at Delphi, but also at such shrines as Didyma and Amyclae), and Sophocles stresses the mythic characteristics that associate her with Apollo and the prophetic nether regions. Instead of being sent to Thebes by an underground divinity and ravaging the city for many years, as in other accounts, the Sphinx of Sophocles appears in Thebes between the departure of Laius for Delphi and the arrival of Oedipus, seemingly as a specific instrument of Apollo, whose prediction she helps fulfill.

The ancestry and definition of the Sphinx combine that which, for the Greek mind, was horrible, dangerous, and prophetic: she represents the temptation to know and the danger of indulging that temptation; her name may be derived from the Greek word "to strangle": as in the Book of Sirach, elucidation of ultimate mysteries is perilous. The sexual origin and danger of truth are once again manifest in her. According to legend, the Sphinx either strangled, ate, or killed her victims (all of them young males) sexually. Generically, her name could denote a prostitute (a "Megarian Sphinx"). Oedipus refers to her in a traditional way as a "dog" (line 391), an appellation that may derive from her shape, but that may also have connoted the sexual equivalent of *bitch*.[15] Gould notes further that "stories of men caught

14. According to Hesiod, she too dwelled in a cave from which she sallied forth to snatch and devour passersby.

15. It does not weaken this argument to invert it by saying that the name was simply applied to dangerous and/or sexual women; one would still have to ask why. The sexual conception of the Sphinx's evil is apparent when she is contrasted with the other female agent of Apollo, the Pythia: both are female in utterly different ways. The Pythia is pure: only a god can enter her (a not uncommon religious belief). The Sphinx's sexuality derives from her fertility, her potential parenthood (emphasized by the monstrosity of her lineage). Like the very mother earth, the actual mother carries in her knowledge of a *beyond* (see chapter 1, note 1): a woman who is to be the receptacle of the god must therefore be "pure" (desexed), as is the Pythia or Vestal. If she is not, she must be cut off from initiatory rites, since the initiate must have his knowledge *imparted* to him (Jewish women, though not kept out of the Synagogue, are relegated to its outer fringes). The Sphinx is never connected with the sacred rites: she is only the destructive instrument that serves them, as an apotropaic force (she wards off the evil eye) or as an executing agency. The son of the mother must always become, in a certain sense, the initiate who learns, outside the mother, about the mystery she carries in her. He does so after he outgrows her, at puberty, when his sexuality enables him, in his turn, to create another mother. The explicitness of *Oedipus the King* demonstrates just such an initiatory rite.

in a vice-like grip during intercourse have frightened boys since time out of mind, but the most common confirmation of this phenomenon, surely, is among dogs. Cf. Lucretius, 4. 1201 ff.":[16] something of the *stomion* in which the prophetic snake first dwells endures in the monster issued from it.

The private truth of Oedipus (which is, in fact, part of a far more extensive and public truth) is down below, as well: the partially concealed or subconscious awareness of the son who has killed his father who now dwells underground, threatening to escape with a vengeance. (That Freud should have seen in this fear the emblematic nightmare of the human race for the killing of a primitive father is not overly surprising.[17]) Pausanias (9.26, 2–4) refers to a variation of the myth that suggests an even closer connection between the threatening father and the Sphinx: according to his version, the monster was in fact an illegitimate daughter of Laius.

The unknown against which Oedipus is tensed since birth is given the traditional faces that suggest the absence of a face: it is dark, it is dangerous, it is elusive. Its manifestation as revelation/concealment alternates images of light and dark. The Pythia ("Golden Pytho," line 151) prophecies (an ultimate truth) within a sanctuary that is, literally, golden with the treasure of those who seek an answer. This is the oracle thought of as revelation. But the Delphic god is unable to explain or hide; "he gives a sign" according to Heraclitus: the plague, semiotic evidence of pollution in Thebes, is the destructive fire of Ares (lines 190–92), associated with that of Hades, the "sunset" god (line 179); both contrast the radiant fire of "golden" Artemis, which shields and enlightens (lines 206–10). In assigning blind Tiresias to the forces of darkness ("You are the child of endless night," line 374), Oedipus mistakenly identifies himself with the forces of light: he mistakes his desire to know for evidence of knowledge. In fact, Oedipus must be swallowed up at last by the darkness he tried too aggressively to penetrate. The scream he utters as he confronts his truth is "dreadful"—*deinon*, the adjective whose repetition is associated with *daimōn* and turns the meaning of the latter

---

16. Gould, *Oedipus the King*, p. 73.

17. The Sphinx appears to be a conventional figure of nightmares in Greece. (See Delcourt, *L'Oracle de Delphes*, in particular pp. 119ff.)

from neutrality, or even benevolence (that of a superhuman being), to an evil representing the supernatural or the uncanny (lines 1258ff.).

It is the full horror of the womb as truth, and truth as tragedy, that Sophocles sets forth, a bloody and awesome initiatory rite rather than the stately game within which the modern awareness contains it. The Theban curse that begins with the assault by Cadmus on the sacred snake of Ares preserves the form and the attributes of the snake, ending the Sophoclean tragedy (the earlier of his two Oedipal dramas) with a fateful return to a womblike darkness—that of truth as it is contained within the somber *stomion*, the vital center ("earth's navel, the untouchable," line 898).[18] Oedipus blinds himself in a final act that is not unlike a symbolic prelude to intercourse with Jocasta, now dead and lying on the ground (line 1267):

> he snatched the pins of worked gold from her dress,
> with which her clothes were fastened: these he raised
> and struck into the ball-joints of his eyes. (lines 1268–70)

The curious word *ball-joints* (*arthra*) is the one previously used to designate the "ball-joints" of Oedipus's feet where he was yoked (line 718) and that have always identified him ("The ball-joints of your feet might testify," line 1032):[19] the oracle has been as open in its signs as in its words.

This *visibility* of the oracle is well served by the visibility of the stage. Like the ritual itself, the stage invites the spectator's comprehension and participation (two dissimilar stances): the spectator observes the stage action as once he might have "observed" the ritual. And what he observes is, in fact, a kind of ritual.

Ritual, which begins as a surrogate satisfaction of desire and ends as pure sacrament once its solemn appeal is reduced to mere solemnity, is renewed in the extremism of the Sophoclean tragedy

18. For the euphemistic "navel" that designates the oracular crevice in mother earth, see Gould, *Oedipus the King*, pp. 23–24.

19. Herodotus and Aristotle use *arthra* as the word for "vaginas." There was no lack of evidence for Otto Rank to speculate that, in blindness, Oedipus returns to the womb. (See Otto Rank, *The Trauma of Birth* [New York: Harcourt, Brace, 1929].) The signs Oedipus carries on his ankles are revealing indeed.

that once again describes and invites an exacerbation of comprehension through a myth about human understanding. Aristotle's extremes of pity and fear, resulting from a dramatic action that commits and distances its spectator to the utmost, are in *Oedipus the King* the forbidden absolutes of sexual desire and murderous violence. That these forbidden absolutes are absolutes indeed is evident in the punitive vigilance within which a society like ours, which thinks of itself as rational and founded on the justness of law, still contains them. The play of Sophocles, like ritual, is concerned with uncovering what our social and psychological overlays usually cover up (and for that reason, if no other, to read *Oedipus* as if it were part of that overlay, an assertion of moral verities or social codes, is, once more, to evade its dangerous core). But like the ritual, which is not the miracle itself, tragedy proposes only a partial participation, a participation that is never achieved at the expense of a more distancing understanding, and catches the spectator in a double pull. A part of him otherwise submerged by reason(s) recognizes itself on stage, but because that stage is also separate, such recognition is never altogether uncritical: to use the expression of André Green, the theater is the place of misunderstanding.[20] The explicit authorial voice that mediates the novel is absent: instead, within the dimensionalizing reality of the stage (starting with its live actors), its *words* become for the spectator an evidence of *being* (binding him through his understanding) and of *being there* (distancing the spectator through his spectatorship). This double pull of the spectator in the theater corresponds to a double pull within us (awareness/repression). In *Oedipus the King*, where play and myth (like ritual) are concerned specifically with the analysis and demonstration of that double pull, the normally rehearsive nature of the theater is translated as an even more intimate rehearsal within the spectator.

Again like ritual, this stage is in part wish fulfillment, but of a special kind. Phantasies (Freudians would think of primal phantasies) that an innermost self buries and recognizes are enacted for our culpable enjoyment; punishment follows, but that retribution (thanks to the distancing stage) falls on another: we are relieved, even as we weep for the guilty victim within us. And as long as we recognize that the mystery is really not broached by our broaching,

20. André Green, *Un Oeil en trop* (Paris: Minuit, 1969), p. 12.

we are once more enticed to the outer limits of our understanding and repeat, in our exacerbated attempt upon those limits, the sacred ritual through the wish-fulfilling myth that, in *Oedipus*, is given as stage play.

To the spectator in us, the insignificance of the characters' posturing that responds so inadequately to a tragic dilemma is patent; our ritual rehearsal also allows us to know what the actors in the drama do not know, and in their groping ineffectuality we measure the absolute nature of that dilemma, we learn about the impossibility of learning (our *head* learns). Twice (lines 70 and 603–4), the Pythian name is punned on (*Pythika: pythoit;* "so that he might learn"): paralleling the advice given Oedipus to look inside himself rather than to an oracle he refuses to understand, the pun returns the spectator from the dramatic ritual to himself, to the only truth that can inform an otherwise empty performance (a strategy rather to be expected of Apollo, or his play—reminiscent of the inscription over his Delphic temple, "Know thyself"). When the chorus introduces Jocasta (the repository of a ghastly truth that she herself does not know, though we do) to the messenger from Corinth, it says, "This is the wife and mother of his children" (line 928). Our privileged understanding interrupts this social platitude after the fateful word *mother* and gives it its full resonance of horror, which then spills over the break provided by our awareness into the rest of the verse. The second sight in Tiresias, the second sight in Oedipus that he cannot recognize until he does away with eyes that mislead him (the second sight of the psychoanalyst?), is thus granted the spectator. Its purpose is to teach him what it teaches the characters about the uselessness of second sight, but that truth is sufficiently well hidden within us to require more than ordinary perception; its uncovering requires the understanding of the mind as well as other kinds of understanding.

The blend of awe and understanding that the Athenian playwright could expect of his audience is replaced in today's audience by either an inadequate acceptance of the myth or too specialized a comprehension of it. The latter reads the oracle no longer as an omen but as a *text*. To paraphrase a formulation of Lévi-Strauss, the modern reader moves from the visible foot to the head: he reads with Oedipus's intelligence and insistence the oracle's *words*.[21]

21. Claude Lévi-Strauss, *Structural Anthropology*, 2 vols. (New York: Basic Books, 1963–76).

The obliquity of oracles is axiomatic. In the Oedipal tragedy, the oracle is no less oblique: it is the manner of its concealing that is different: like D-- in Poe's *Purloined Letter*, it conceals through openness; in order to confuse, this oracle speaks plainly (perhaps because it speaks before us, and we also know). It is the plain truth of the oracle that is difficult to understand: this oracle not only is frank but also says a great deal.

When the various people of the tragedy encounter their oracle, they believe its words and show their belief by trying to evade them. Laius has a child, then attempts to do away with it; Oedipus leaves Corinth with too much precipitation; later, he looks *around him* for culprits, full of zeal, but with instructions only imperfectly understood. These errors are due to an urgency that precludes a thorough or full reading: the readers are being told more than they give themselves time to decipher. This is true even of Oedipus, who is dogged in his determination but whose mind is too quick: he can solve only a certain kind of riddle. The moment the main threat is discerned through such a reading, the reader hastens off to counter what he has read, believing that his thin text offers him alternative possibilities, not knowing the many ways in which it states a full and unremitting condemnation.

The first invitation to dwell a little longer on the text is implicit in the game played by the Sphinx. Oedipus gives her a general answer, and the Sphinx, eager to play out her part in the charade, jumps off to her death. Oedipus's instant intelligence produces the generic answer "man" without pondering sufficiently a question about "feet" (even though his second sight reads the text with more acuity). Upon reflection, Oedipus might have thought of a more specific answer— not "man," but "a man," himself. After all, Tiresias knows who it is that walks on three legs towards twilight: he tells Oedipus that the latter will "go and point before him with a stick" (line 456). And there are other clues: early on the priest urges Oedipus: "Do not stumble! Put our land on firm feet!" (line 51). While Creon recalls that the Sphinx has "asked us to turn/from the obscure to what lay at our feet" (line 130–31). But the fact is that Oedipus, hobbled at birth (and for life), is fated to be a stumbler—the priest's advice notwithstanding, he must "stumble" on a truth he cannot clearly make out.

Beyond the words of the text, there is another, more pervasive, truth. The swollen ankles are more than a summary of Oedipus's life ("A fearful rebuke these token left for me," line 1035): they are a palimpsest within which can be read the more significant piercing of the eyes (and within which the Freudian analyst can read still other histories); similarly, the modern reader looks within his text for a writing by the automatic hand that is the instrument of a second sight.[22] That reader encounters at the fateful crossroads a "secret ravine" (line 1398), a "narrow place" (line 1399), which are reminiscent of the great womb, the oracular mouth of truth, and which put Oedipus in mind (line 1403) of the tragic repetition that characterizes the process of his doom (the double roads that converge at the place of his crime; his reentry into Thebes and his mother; the seed twice sewn in Jocasta).[23] These forms of a doubling, and of a doubling back, are emblems of a truth located in the past and of its *act*—the double assault that Oedipus has perpetrated on his parents and that, in a final and fateful *return*, he perpetrates on himself in a double self-immolation.

That doubling back is also the emblem of the reader's relation to his text. The reading of a text concerned with reading requires a particularly accurate appraisal of the fictional trajectory determined by those misreadings. But it is only the possibility of such a *return* in any instance that can define what we call a text—something that differs from the translucence of other kinds of communication through an opacity that requires not only a *reading* but a *reading into*. The characters in *Oedipus the King* and the rest of us read the same signs: the mystery that lies beyond them concerns us all equally. But the modern reader tends to seek his truth elsewhere, transferring the mystery to the signs themselves, questioning them rather than himself.

22. See a similar notion in the title and argument of Green, *Un Oeil en trop*.

23. To which Gould adds the double horror of the double feet and double eyes, the double goad that Laius brings down on his son, the double doors leading to Jocasta's bedroom, the double curse that will drive Oedipus into exile, etc. (*Oedipus the King*, p. 47).

Agatha
Christie:
Containment of the Unknown

Oedipus the King is a sample, not a solution, of the perdurable mystery. The spectator knows what will happen before the fictional event unfolds, but that knowledge and the confirming resolutions do not allay the spectator's sense of mystery. After Oedipus has been led away at last, there remains within each spectator an intimate sphinx who continues to ask him fateful and unanswerable questions. The experience of Oedipus was meant only to reinforce his awareness that no man can compose with the gods: the spectator could not be in ignorance before the start of the tragedy. If there are benefits to be derived from this type of rehearsal over and above the Freudian pleasure in repetition and the masochistic reexperiencing of primal frustrations, it is in the kind of grandeur that the awareness of an original condemnation confers on the victim who confronts his knowledge: Oedipus's quandary is the spectator's as well, and the latter shares in his dignity; far beyond the fiction, the part of *Oedipus* that its spectator lives out in his own experience is *real*.

The "reality" of Oedipus is in its metaphysical discretion: it assumes as an inalienable given that there are dark regions that can be alluded to only, not broached. The awesomeness of the Oedipal myth is that of a remarkable mechanism intended to instance and comment upon the assertion of those limits. For Oedipus as well as the spectator, there is no possible transgression: when the truth so doggedly sought is finally understood in the fullness of its perfect circularity, there remain just as many oracles to decipher as before. Oedipus learns to displace limits in order to learn about the permanency of limits.

The detective story does not propose to be "real": it proposes only, and as a game, that the mystery is located on *this side* of the unknown. It replaces the awesomeness of limits by a false beard— a mask that is only superficially menacing and can be removed in due time. It redefines mystery by counterstating it; by assuming that mystery can be overcome, it allows the reader to play at being a god with no resonance, a little as a child might be given a plastic stethoscope to play doctor. Judging by the large number of its participants, this kind of elevation game is sufficient for the greatest part of the fiction-reading public.

Agatha Christie wrote her first detective story, *The Mysterious Affair at Styles*, in 1920. Thereafter, and for over half a century, she was the most popular purveyor of the genre.[1] During that time she wrote works that would not fit quite as well within the narrowest definition of the genre. But detective fiction is a form that loses definition in proportion as it extends beyond its intentional narrow-

---

1. At least in the aggregate. Even if one excludes the handful of Agatha Christie's works that were not detective stories, a total sales of well over 400 million by 1975, translated into 103 languages, is undeniable proof of her huge readership. Her play *The Mousetrap* (an adaptation of her short story "Three Blind Mice" that first appeared in 1950) opened in London in 1952 and set a record for the longest uninterrupted run in theater history. (See Nancy Blue Wynne: *An Agatha Christie Chronology* [New York: Ace Books, 1976].)

ness—a truism confirmed by the lasting appeal of even as rudimentary a work as *The Mysterious Affair at Styles:* after the book had gone through many printings by Lane, in England, by Dodd, Mead and Company, by Grosset and Dunlap, Bantam Books was able to issue ten printings of the novel between 1961 and 1969. In 1970 there followed another edition by Bantam, which has reached so far eleven printings. The publicity on the cover of the eleventh capitalizes on other Christie successes—the well-known and final *Curtain*[2] and the extended run of the film *Murder on the Orient Express* (from her 1934 *Murder on the Calais Coach*). The detective story requires characters only in sufficient numbers, and sufficiently fleshed out, to give its puzzle an anthropomorphic semblance and to preserve the reader from boredom for as long as the veil of its "mystery" is drawn. When it restricts itself to this kind of functional stylization, it exposes little to the dangers of age: how many novels written at the end of the First World War could find such a ready, face-value acceptance today?

To say that the detective story proposes a puzzle is not quite accurate either: one must assume that only an infinitesimally small number of Agatha Christie's half billion readers ever undertook or expected to solve her stories in advance of Jane Marple or Hercule Poirot. What the detective story proposes instead is the *expectation* of a solution. The detective story offers confirmation and continuity at the price of a minor and spurious disruption. The continuity that it insures includes, ultimately, that of the genre itself: nearly every part of the world within which *The Mysterious Affair at Styles* is set must surely be dead and gone by now (if it ever actually existed), and yet thousands of readers who have never known that world still accept it as real, with little or no suggestion of "camp."

That world was the one possibly enjoyed for yet awhile by the English upper class after 1918.[3] Styles is a manor scarcely ever de-

2. Agatha Christie, *Curtain* (New York: Dodd, Mead, 1975). *Curtain* was meant to be published posthumously, but was written in the early part of the 1940s.

3. Agatha Christie was among those who perceived most shrewdly the disappearance of that world. In one of the best of her later stories, *At Bertram's Hotel* (London: Collins, 1965), the mystery became clear to Miss Marple when she realized that an antebellum place like Bertram's simply could not exist in postwar England. And in *Curtain*, when Poirot and Hastings return for the last time to Styles, it is no longer a private estate but a hotel.

scribed—"a fine old house,"[4] and little more: like nearly every other part of this world, it is a functional cliché. It has many rooms (whose communicating doors can be mysteriously bolted, and, even more mysteriously, unbolted) available to house a large, landowning family, several summer guests, and a full complement of servants (all these people are, of course, equally valid suspects). Among so many people, love has adequate means to bloom, or hit a rocky course, for the sake of a secondary plot that keeps the action from slowing down. The mood out of which Styles Court is built cannot fail to include "a broad staircase" (p. 9) down which you descend after you have "dressed" ("Supper is at half-past seven"—"We have given up late dinners for some time," pp. 8–9); an "open French window near at hand," with, just beyond it, "the shade of a large sycamore tree" (p. 5) where tea is punctually spread out in July; and a tennis court for after tea. Styles Court exists only in our expectation of what it might be if it were a part of our imaginings. It comes into being through a process of diluted logic that assumes, since mystery is given as an unfortunate condition that can, and should be, eliminated, that life without such unpleasantness must perforce be agreeable and desirable. In a place like Styles, the plumbing is never erratic (unless for the limited purpose of serving the plot), personal sorrow is as evanescent and inconsequential as a summer shower, age and decay cannot inform the exemplary and unyielding mien of its people: the young know that they will be young forever, the professionals are admirably suited to their faces ("Mr. Wells was a pleasant man of middle-age, with keen eyes, and the typical lawyer's mouth," p. 54), and the good-natured fool (the one character who is only seldom a suspect) will neither mature nor learn, however many of life's grimmer vicissitudes he is exposed to. In such a garden of delightfully fulfilled expectations, there rarely occurs anything worse than murder.

Where the corpse of Laius was a scandal that affronted even the gods, the poisoning of Emily Inglethorp at Styles is an event that is just barely sufficient to disrupt the tea and tennis routine. "The mater" (as John Cavendish calls her, not being any more than the

4. Agatha Christie, *The Mysterious Affair at Styles* (1920; New York: Bantam Books, 1970), p. 4. This, the seventh printing of this edition, announces, with pride and all caps, that "NOT ONE WORD HAS BEEN OMITTED." All subsequent quotations refer to this edition.

others one to derogate from his own cliché—even though she is not quite his mater, but rather his stepmater) cannot be, after all, "a day less than seventy" (p. 1), has already been left by her first husband "the larger part of his income; an arrangement that was distinctly unfair to his two sons" (p. 2), and, as if that didn't clinch it, she has recently married again, a younger man this time, who "wears very peculiar clothes" (p. 72)—a certain Alfred Inglethorp, described by John Cavendish as a "rotten little bounder" (p. 2). If one adds to the list of the dispossessed spunky and cute little Cynthia Murdoch with "something in her manner [reminding one] that her position was a dependent one, and that Mrs. Inglethorp, kind as she might be in the main, did not allow her to forget it" (p. 8; though presumably forgetting herself that sweet Cynthia does volunteer work in a dispensary that is a veritable arsenal of violent poisons); Evelyn Howard, the blunt and sensible friend with whom Mrs. Inglethorp has quarreled; John's wife, "that enigmatical woman, Mary Cavendish" (p. 9), who keeps disappearing with the mysterious Dr. Bauerstein, by no coincidence "one of the greatest living experts on poisons" (p. 11), it begins to look as if not doing away with Mrs. Inglethorp would be the height of irresponsibility, so clearly must her disappearance signify, instead of murder, the righting of an order she has grievously upset.

It is not the act of murder that casts a pall over this idyllic landscape. The pity of murder is that, as slugs ruin lettuce beds (something that would be unheard of at Styles, of course), murder spoils what was otherwise good. Styles St. Mary (or Jane Marple's identical St. Mary Mead) is not the world of high romance: it is the bucolic dream of England, with its decent pub for food, half-timbered lodging and ruddy fellowship, its fine old homes belonging to the landed gentry and the moderately well-to-do (that is to say, nearly everyone), and the quaint (but immaculate) homes of the less than well-to-do. Those who dwell in this land by right are good, or at the very worst, lovably eccentric: the immorality of murder is patent in the way it injects them with a tincture of suspicion and, for awhile (for no longer than will tax the tolerance of the reader, who is never to be completely cast adrift but must remain in sight of the sound land soon to be recovered), darkens the vision of a pristine Devonshire belonging to two English girls who recalled their "childhood and young girlhood as a pleasant time of infinite leisure with ample time for thinking, imagining and reading."[5]

The people in that landscape are as tautological as the landscape itself: an adjective or two are sufficient to call their identity to mind. There is "Miss Howard. She is an excellent specimen of well-balanced English beef and brawn. She is sanity itself" (p. 103). The reader's store of familiar images conjures her out of seven words when he first encounters her: "A lady in a stout tweed skirt" (p. 4), the moral qualities of stoutness combining with the British virtue of tweed to convey the instant vision of a hearty, hardy, and honest soul. Thereafter, Evelyn Howard turns into the manifest emblem of her inner nature: "She was a pleasant-looking woman of about forty, with a deep voice, almost manly in its stentorian tones, and had a large sensible square body, with feet to match—these encased in good thick boots" (p. 4). Agelessness, together with an utter lack of gender or esthetic qualities, confer on her the quintessential merit visually attributed to John Bull.

In another part of this predictable landscape, there is a "parlour maid" with no apparent duties but to confirm our expectation of finding her there. She is simply and suitably named Dorcas, with neither a family nor a face. Like lawyer Wells and Evelyn Howard, she is a pleonasm: "Dorcas was standing in the boudoir, her hands folded in front of her, and her grey hair rose in stiff waves under her white cap. She was the very model and picture of a good old-fashioned servant" (p. 39).

But once murder has been committed, the tautological evidence can no longer be trusted: even Evelyn Howard or Dorcas may actually have done it. And so might Cynthia Murdoch, though she is "a fresh-looking young creature, full of life and vigour" (p. 8): however clearly she may stand for innocence and the simplicity of first love, once there has been the nastiness of Mrs. Inglethorp's poisoning, even her very selflessness in the wartime dispensary must become as suspect as Lucrezia Borgia's efforts to entertain. Or again, the finger might point at the stepsons: under more normal conditions, they would be, as

---

5. Wynne, *Agatha Christie Chronology*, p. 262. It is said that Agatha Christie wrote *The Mysterious Affair at Styles*, when still quite young, on a bet with her sister that she could do a detective story.

befits their station, the respectable and tenanted failures of the manor (John, the barrister without a practice; Lawrence, the doctor who never made it). But now, even John's justifiable indignation at an interloper is subject to scrutiny (" 'Rotten little bounder too!' he said savagely. 'I can tell you, Hastings, it's making life jolly difficult for us,' " p. 2). And as for Lawrence, he must suffer something like character in what might otherwise be an acceptably innocuous face: "He looked about forty, very dark with a melancholy clean-shaven face. Some violent emotion seemed to be mastering him" (p. 9).

At least Lawrence is clean-shaven: even under stressful conditions he preserves certain unmistakably British characteristics. But there are also those with beards; and when beards are out of style, they give the impression of disguising something that is unsavory (or, in the paradox of the mystery story, of proclaiming an unsavoriness that might not necessarily be there).[6] At Styles St. Mary, there are three outlandish beards; the real ones (belonging to Dr. Bauerstein and Alfred Inglethorp) and the false one thanks to which the criminal's accomplice is able to disguise an otherwise noticeable identity. When Hastings first catches sight of Inglethorp's beard, he confides, "He certainly struck a rather alien note. I did not wonder at John objecting to his beard. It was one of the longest and blackest I have ever seen" (p. 6)—even though John Cavendish, however outraged he might have been, has limited his tonsorial comments to the following words: "He's got a great black beard" (p. 3). Hastings is speaking about an objection that does not need to be voiced in order to be evident: there is something unnatural about Alfred's beard, even though it is quite real; in Styles St. Mary, it proclaims itself as being alien. It is unfamiliar, repugnant, adverse, and may well signal danger. The antifashion becomes a form of the anti*physis*. "It struck me," muses Hastings, "that he might look natural on a stage, but was strangely out of place in real life" (p. 6): it is this being out of place, this strangeness that contradicts "real life," that is the most evident consequence of the crime that has been committed.

---

6. The trend had been towards the clean-shaven since the Anglo-Saxon 1880s. In cities beards were still worn, but mainly by older and professional men. The eleventh edition of the *Encyclopaedia Britannica* (1909) suggests that by the decade in which *The Mysterious Affair at Styles* is set, the upper classes showed an inclination to shave clean.

If one can equate in a beard degrees of evil with the depth of its roots, Dr. Bauerstein's is even more threatening. Since Bauerstein is required merely to trigger a sense of revulsion that awaits his coming, there is little for Agatha Christie to do once she has named him. Her only portrait of the bad doctor proclaims him "a tall bearded man" (p. 11). But this is sufficient to plunge the good (and deeply intuitive) Hastings into an agony of metaphysical forebodings: "The sinister face of Dr. Bauerstein recurred to me unpleasantly. A vague suspicion of every one and everything filled my mind. Just for a moment I had a premonition of approaching evil" (p. 12). This is because Dr. Bauerstein comes by his beard even more naturally than Alfred Inglethorp: in the words of John Cavendish, "He's a Polish Jew, anyway" (p. 118). As far as Hastings and Cavendish are concerned, Bauerstein would wear a black beard even if he were clean-shaven: his beard, like his name, is a stigma that classifies him in the reader's mind regardless of the role that he might be called on to play in the story.

Alongside these aliens whose difference shows in their person like a plain and unmistakable curse, there are the ones in whom strangeness is better concealed. Like that of the others, its source is in the reader's prejudices, but it is allowed to show as only a flickering of danger. The sphinxlike Mary Cavendish turns out to be Russian on her mother's side (" 'Ah,' " says Hastings, " 'now I understand.' 'Understand what?' " asks Mary Cavendish. " 'A hint of something foreign—different—that there has always been about you' " p. 133). Or there is farmer Raikes' wife, believed to be dallying with a number of the men, who is understandably a "young woman of gypsy type" (p. 12). Besides such naturally endowed women, transparent little Cynthia Murdoch has only her poison dispensary, and Evelyn Howard her gruffness, to justify the suspicion the death of Mrs. Inglethorp has cast upon them all.

These characters lay no claim to being people: they are dyspeptic evidence of a déjà vu. Out of such reminders of minor unpleasantness within the world, the detective story creates the temporary annoyance to which it reduces an otherwise all-enclosing mystery. The suggestion of the foreigner, the gypsy, the Jew, echoes such fleeting moments of dyspepsia. Alfred Inglethorp and Dr. Bauerstein do not exist any more than does Dorcas—they are only shadows upon which have been hung the ostentatious beards that activate our minor qualms.[7] They are our prescience of evil, as they are Hastings's—and with as little warrant: if we cease to believe in beards, the trigger mechanism fails to operate and with it the sense of mild discomfort induced by the detective story in order to create the gap, within which it is situated, between two contrastive moments of imagined control. Even though today's sales figures would seem to show that the small phobias depicted in *The Mysterious Affair at Styles* are still much a part of our lives, it should be pointed out that they are not exclusive; there are others: their only requirement is that they be relatively mild but recognized by a large number of readers. Over the years this kind of precise dosing has become increasingly difficult to maintain. Since 1920 the world has continued to shrink, and the idea of the "alien" as represented by someone who is not quite like us has had to be modified. Lately, Ian Fleming was still recruiting his cast of villains rather exclusively from among the ranks of those whom his English hero would recognize as distinctly non-British (primarily central Europeans and Asiatics), but the minor annoyance that once was their nearly reflex consequence now required their sinister part to be bolstered. One was more likely to rub elbows with them, and the world had become increasingly tense (perhaps, in part, because of such elbow-rubbing?): in a universe that had lost, along with its green areas, its bucolic problems, the minor annoyance of such "alien" presences, already tempered through familiarity, would be the more likely to pass unnoticed. James Bond was thus required to confront, instead of village poisoners or even large-scale embezzlers, foreigners intent on nothing less than taking over the whole planet. With Ian Fleming, the detective story, as it often does, becomes something else.

But in 1920 Agatha Christie could still rely on her world and the responses of her people. The canniest person in *The Mysterious Affair at Styles* is neither the criminal (doomed to defeat within the

---

7. And by them hang some of the illogicalities that crowd upon one when he attempts to see the shadows for more than what they are. Dr. Bauerstein turns out to be a red herring, in this case a German spy—that is to say, someone who presumably works under cover. Yet his function in the novel is to draw attention to himself *through* his cover (his beard). As for Alfred Inglethorp, the simple-minded but eminently British Hastings sees through him from the start ("A wave of revulsion swept over me. What a consummate hypocrite the man was," p. 29); but the intelligent Poirot, who sees Inglethorp as a mechanism rather than as an emblem, unfailingly finds him (and his schemes) to be "clever" and "astute" (pp. 172ff.).

expectations of the genre) nor, obviously, the singularly inept narrator, Hastings. But it is not Hercule Poirot either: it is Agatha Christie herself. She moves in a world she knows so well she can pretend not to be a part of it, counting on the reader's prejudice that associates him with her characters, while she herself avoids contamination. Her mode allows her to show the guilty and the innocent in what appears to be the same light by dissociating herself ostensibly from the convention on which she relies, while in reality she knows that she is casting suspicion on those who should not be suspect. Farmer Raikes' wife is a gypsy, but pretty enough to turn the appreciative (if empty) head of Hastings: the narrator seems quite ready to become a part of the immorality that appears to radiate from her, but the author has done no more than provide us with factual evidence about her origins and her encounters. That Hastings (and the reader) should fall sway, with the rest, to a belief suggested by the word "gypsy" is a consequence that Agatha Christie will not reject but that she has done nothing to encourage.

Again with Hastings, we sense that the mysterious and dangerous part of Mary Cavendish is Russian. However, danger and mystery (when kept within bounds) are also part of the attractiveness of someone who is more than just a pretty face. If we allow our Slavophobia to suggest that Mary might be one of the suspects, the author has no objections, but that Russian ancestry is certainly not given as a valid clue to assist us in solving the riddle. As for Dr. Bauerstein, with whom Mary increases the chances of her possible guilt through association, he is rewarded with the backhanded compliment that Jews are in the habit of receiving from anti-Semites: he is (like that other beard, Alfred Inglethorp) "A very clever man—a Jew, of course" (p. 129). Poirot's words echo those of Mary Cavendish, whose semialienism is spurred by a fit of pique at husband John: " 'A tinge of Jewish blood is not a bad thing. It leavens the'—she looked at him—'stolid stupidity of the ordinary Englishman' " (p. 118). And on this note of worldly dismissal, the author (her seeds sewn as she intended them to be) turns her back on such pretty squabbling among foolish mortals.

In the detective story world of a mystery made portable, the initiate is the detective who benefits, unlike the initiate in the real world, from the reduction of the mystery. He enters his realm with the full intention of becoming, in due time, an unequivocal discloser of something that, for once, can be disclosed. The assurance of the detective's infallibility results in structural difficulties that are further evidence of the skillful dosing required by the genre. Too manifest an expectation of the detective's success will weaken fatally the delicate tension that must be maintained during the time of subtle unpleasantness that extends between the crime and its resolution. However infallible the detective (and, in the traditional genre, all are equally infallible), he cannot be so percipient as to reveal instantly the sham for what it is. In proportion as Poirot's foes were relatively easy to dispose of at the time of his first introduction to the world, Poirot himself was proportionally the more flawed. Other than the remarkable activity of "the little grey cells" of his brain (for the publicity of whose performance he is the main impresario), Poirot has little to recommend him to us or to denizens of Styles Court. From the first he is marred by the same imperfection as the other aliens—his conspicuous foreignness: nowhere is it more evident than in the fact that he is *short*. Even before he appears, he has been patronizingly dismissed by most of the Britishers in the cast. To Hastings, he is "a marvelous little fellow" (p. 7); to Cynthia, "a dear little man" (p. 17). Dorcas is immediately on her guard: "in her attitude towards Poirot, she was inclined to be suspicious" (p. 39). Even Manning, the gardener, casts "sharp and intelligent" eyes at Poirot that are filled "with faint contempt" (p. 58). Of course, this is meant to be a joke on Manning, Dorcas, and all the rest, but it is a double-edged joke nevertheless; though it confirms Poirot in the end, it helps to blend him a little better with the "alien" quality of murder until the final and brief moment of his triumph.

Starting with his insufferable shortness, everything about Poirot confirms the others' opinions of him:

Poirot was an extraordinary looking little man. He was hardly more than five feet, four inches, but carried himself with great dignity. His head was exactly the shape of an egg, and he always perched it a little on one side. His moustache was very stiff and military. The neatness of his attire was almost incredible. I believe a speck of dust would have caused him more pain than a bullet wound. Yet this quaint dandyfied little man who, I was sorry to see, now limped badly, had been in his time one of the most celebrated members of the Belgian police. (Pp. 16–17)

The author was aware of the faintly ridiculous figure cut by Poirot when she baptized him. She named him after a vegetable—the leek (*poireau*, which also means a wart, in French)—to which she apposed the (barely) Christian name Hercule, in such a way that each name would cast ridicule on the other. Virtues that might have been British in someone of normal stature were undercut by Poirot's height—five feet four inches. His moustache, characteristic enough of the military class at a time when the razor was making its presence felt among most other classes of British society, lacked an adequate body for virile support. The elegance one would have expected of an Englishman could only "dandify" a body that was not up to standard requirements. And the last resort of dignity was reserved, traditionally, for men of tolerable size.

Such indignities were visited on Poirot by virtue of his birth; but in the parts of his personality over which he might have been expected to exercise some self-control, he showed a deplorable tendency to indulge his foreignness. His English was unaccountably Gallicized ("The mind is confused? Is it not so?" p. 30; "Ah! Triple pig!" p. 64; "Mesdames and messieurs! I speak! Listen!" p. 97; "enchanted, Madame," p. 140), with altogether too many exclamation marks, too much boastfulness (frequently voiced by the redundant "I, Hercule Poirot," after which, to compound everyone's embarrassment, "he tapped himself proudly on the breast," p. 137), and an excess of continental posturing ("He made an extravagant gesture with his hand. 'It is significant! It is tremendous!'" p. 30—a trait that distressed even the plain folk at Styles St. Mary: "A little chap? As waves his hands when he talks? One of them Belgies from the village?" p. 74). Even Poirot's single greatest asset—his brain—is ostentatiously displayed in a head exactly like an egg.[8] But perhaps the most serious injury inflicted by Poirot's shameless exuberance is the extent of the overstatement into which he forces those who must describe him, starting with the hapless Hastings.

However, these imperfections notwithstanding, Poirot is not entirely dismissible, either. Part of the artificial surprise of the detective

8. In a manner reminiscent of our own mildly contemptuous "egghead," which demonstrated what Colin Watson terms the public's inclination "to be in awe of knowledge but to distrust intelligence" (*Snobbery with Violence* [London: Eyre and Spottiswoode, 1971], p. 168).

story is contained within the detective who triumphs, as he brings the action to a close, over even his own shortcomings. (A layer of the genre's optimism derives from the individualism it champions: threats to law, order, and ethnic purity, with which the amorphous aggregate of the police cannot cope, are within the power of a single individual to master.) Agatha Christie is faithful to her method in distancing herself from the aspersions cast at her detective. Not only is his intelligence the brighter for having to shine through his mannerisms, but he has been endowed by his maker with a saving grace of no mean consequence: Gallicized as he might be, Poirot is still not quite French. Rather, he is as Nordic as can possibly be someone using the French language—he is Belgian. And he is Belgian at a time (World War I) when "gallant little Belgium" (the smallness of the country perhaps atoning in part for Poirot's own diminutiveness) is overrun by Germany.[9] The good Dorcas sums it all up with the perspicacity of rural Devonshire: "I don't hold with foreigners as a rule, but from what the newspapers say I make out as how these brave Belges isn't the ordinary run of foreigners, and certainly he's a most polite spoken gentleman" (p. 107).

Lastly, Poirot is conferred a kind of honorary citizenship in being awarded a sacrificial, native goat—Hastings—used for purposes of contrast and to ask Poirot questions, the withholding of whose answers is necessary for suspense within the story (very properly, the predetermined time during which disclosure of what was known all along is *suspended*, held up). Hastings is wholly functional: until the arrival of Poirot, that is to say, before the story can devolve from a dialectical process, Hastings is the sole reliance of the reader. He is considerably more urbane than John Cavendish (and far less cliché-ridden); he appraises Lawrence shrewdly; he is suavely avuncular with Cynthia. But once Poirot enters the scene, Hastings becomes no more than a bumbling foil: he sounds for all the world like John Cavendish, he becomes the ludicrous suitor at whom Cynthia Murdoch simply laughs, and he spends most of his time with Poirot being insulted. Just as the unsatisfactory Watson is positioned between

9. Part of whose evil lies in the fact that an Anglo-Saxon can never be quite sure of exactly what races have gone into its making. Colin Watson notes the privileged status of Belgium at the time, in that by 1918, "the British [had] unaccountably neglected to coin a derogatory epithet for the inhabitants of Belgium" (*Snobbery*, p. 166).

the reader and Sherlock Holmes, Hastings acts as the reader's inter-cessor to the intercessor—though he is manifestly the most obtuse of the characters. Presumed to be the spyglass through which the reader is able to "follow" Poirot, he in fact prevents the reader from seeing much; Poirot is clear on that score, if on few others: "As you know, it is not my habit to explain until the end is reached" (p. 32), or: "Do as I ask you. Afterwards you shall question as much as you please" (p. 57). The reader, tainted by the identity of his own ig-norance with that of dumb Hastings, is subsequently disposed to accept the kind of praise that straight men have bestowed on their betters since the Anytus of the Socratic dialogues ("'Dear me, Poirot,' I said with a sigh, 'I think you have explained everything,'" p. 180): according to his temperament, he will be prepared to admire either Poirot or the author.

And so, the trivial unpleasantness that was contrived for the pleasure of ending it is brought to a close. A spoilsport old lady has been eliminated, foreigners (or those who act like them) have either been justly punished or made to disappear. Those who were only half-foreigners, but actually good, emerge as their better halves. The lovers are reunited, the upper-middle-class ritual is once again resumed. Law, order, and property are secure, and, in a universe that is forever threatening to escape from our rational grasp, a single little man with a maniacal penchant for neatness leaves us the gift of a tidy world, a closed book in which all questions have been answered.

The detective story treats the reader's expectations and prejudices with gentle solicitude. Alongside its disposable annoyances, the planetary triumphs of James Bond are unsettling: the evil he over-comes is of such magnitude that, even when undone, it leaves a menacing trace. We are left wondering whether the secret agent with license to kill is not, in his apotheosis, a reincarnation of what he has eliminated. In a novel by Ian Fleming, an anxiety caused by the aware-ness that such a tale could be told seeps through the closed covers within which that anxiety was meant to be contained. The anxiety we feel is, of course, more than its fiction intended, and its seepage is an accident. But that seepage makes the world that writes Bond into being much like ours: both are one. Agatha Christie's world, on the other hand, was never more than nostalgia and illusion. Her con-tinued success suggests only that the illusion has not yet receded completely beyond our ken.

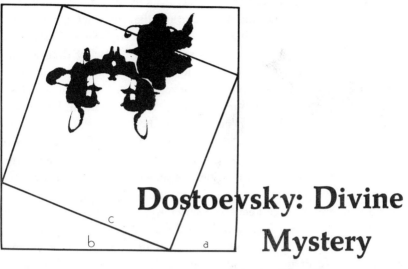

Dostoevsky: Divine Mystery and Literary Salvation

The detective story proposes a trajectory: the questions it asks are important only to that trajectory, not to the reader. If the spectator does not share Oedipus's fearful puzzlement more deeply and more intimately than mere *learning* would allow him to, the play is reduced to little more than moral allegory. That the puzzlement of Oedipus may transmit its fearfulness to the reader is what makes it different from Poirot's: the detective's perplexities derive from circumstances that have little to do with the reader; the latter only *lends* his attention to them.

In proportion as the characters of the detective story compel more interest in themselves and less in their trajectory, the mystery withheld by the contrivance of a plot—the disclosable mystery—is absorbed by the characters and resists ultimate disclosures. Were it not so, *The Brothers Karamazov* would be a detective story. It has a likely victim,[1] a number of equally likely suspects, and a resolution that tells us exactly who committed the crime as well as how and for what reasons.[2] Like Mrs. Inglethorp, the victim is shown as someone who richly deserves his fate. Fyodor Pavlovich is "a trashy and depraved type and, in addition, senseless."[3] He is a "buffon" with, nevertheless, a shrewd and less-than-honest sense of how to make money. Having made it, he remains avaricious, "depraved," and "sensual." He is a terrible father; Dmitri Fyodorovich, his oldest son and the prime suspect, will wonder "Why is such a man alive?" (p. 65)—a question pondered in different ways (the difference in reflection being the essential difference between characters) by all three sons and also by the bastard son Smerdyakov, whom Fyodor Pavlovich keeps as a servant.

Since all three sons have pondered the question, all three may well be guilty.[4] Dmitri is passionate and violent, a creature of intense moods and feelings. Ivan, like Raskolnikov, is the intellectual in whom flights of theory can veer away from common humanity. Even the youngest, Alyosha, the saint, is afflicted with the Karamazov curse; in a moment when Rakitin is not simply the butt of Dostoevsky's contempt for Europeanized unbelievers and "socialists," Rakitin judges Alyosha: "You're a Karamazov too, you know! In your family, sensuality is carried to a disease" (p. 70)—a judgment confirmed by Dmitri: "All we Karamazovs are insects [of sensual lust], and, angel as you are, the insect lives in you, too, and will stir up a tempest in your blood" (p. 96).

1. As soon as we extend the narrow concerns of the detective story's trajectory, even the victim claims our attention. Here, as in *Oedipus*, the corpse smells and there are consequences attendant on the murder that have more to do with us than with the police.

2. But since this is not a detective story, the resolution resolves precious little: the disposition of the mechanics in this case is effected so as to show how unimportant those mechanics are.

3. Fyodor Dostoevsky, *The Brothers Karamazov*, ed. Ralph E. Matlaw (New York: W. W. Norton, 1976), p. 1. All subsequent quotations refer to this edition.

4. The fact that this is not a detective story allows the author to tell us that all three indeed *are* guilty, though none committed the crime.

Additionally, the list of suspects contains the usual servants, among whom, of course, is Smerdyakov. But Dostoevsky remains even closer to the surface of the *faits divers* by adding the transparent motivation of money. The dissolute and spendthrift Dmitri has become his father's rival for the attention of Grushenka. Dmitri learns from Smerdyakov that Fyodor Pavlovich has put aside three thousand roubles as an inducement for Grushenka to visit him. Dmitri, who has reason to feel that he has been done out of his mother's inheritance by Fyodor Pavlovich, makes threats that are widely heard: when the bloody corpse of Dmitri's father is found, all signs point to Dmitri.

In the detective story, this kind of "motivation" vouches mainly for the occurrence of events and their logical succession. But in Dostoevsky, event is less important that motivation. The *faits divers* is not even the contrivance that merely allows the development of an idea: it is, to start with, the illustration and *evidence* of an idea. Assuming the detective story could contemplate a crime as "loaded" as parricide,[5] that crime would still remain largely an abstraction, since a genre concerned mainly with the outline of a trajectory cannot afford the presence of either a real father or a real son (or for that matter, as we have seen, a real murder). Dostoevsky's novel reaches an abstract level of a different kind and for utterly dissimilar reasons: it cannot show parricide without pondering its nature and its significance as more than a police problem. Dostoevsky's reader is held by concerns that the novel reawakens but *does not* create; those concerns are, to begin with, private ones of Dostoevsky: for neither author nor reader is the novel to be simply an esthetic hiatus or an escape from existential awareness. *The Brothers Karamazov* is of interest to us to the extent that it is an existential part of Dostoevsky's own struggle with refractory and illusive instances of a mystery that is also ours.

In a letter to A. N. Maykov (25 March 1870), Dostoevsky writes that his projected *Brothers Karamazov* (which he thought of, at that time, as *The Life of a Great Sinner*) will be about "the existence of God," that question being "the very one I have struggled with con-

---

5. Agatha Christie removes the possibility of matricide in *The Mysterious Affair at Styles* by specifying that the heirs of Mrs. Inglethorp are *not* her children: they are the children of her deceased husband—legal wards, not blood relations.

sciously and unconsciously all my life." Dostoevsky's choice of the verb indicates that *The Brothers Karamazov* will be neither a theological nor a moral treatise—the answers, if there are any, are simply not that clear; the "struggle" is not stayed by the presence of God. René Girard notes as a general truth the two choices that confrontation with the unknown allows—dependency on God or the assertion of human pride.[6] That dependency requires, however, quiescence within God once He is accepted along with the limitations against which pride otherwise contends. But in Dostoevsky, neither alternative is ever possible. Dostoevsky knows, and accepts, many of the absolutes for which God stands, but he remains, nevertheless, "struggling"—unwilling to acknowledge that pride must necessarily cede those absolutes to God. There is a fundamental rift and tension at the heart of Dostoevsky's world that affects his vision and his characters. As Temira Pachmuss has shown, it is impossible to envisage Dostoevsky's order of things bereft of incompatible dualities.[7]

As suggested previously, a world located within the embrace of an all-knowing God assumes that questions about ultimate mysteries can be suspended in the assurance that their answer is immanent within an intelligence greater than man's. This assurance *humanizes* the intractable mystery without making it any less intractable: the mystery *appears* to be resolvable without being resolved. Anything less than the quiescence of an absolute reliance on God leads to a sense of dualism—the knowledge of a self-evident *here* and the intuition of a more problematic and fascinating *beyond*. One may assume that there is a flaw in the human mind that allows it to be aware of a death it cannot transcend (limits, the unknown, irreducible dualities) but that forces it to contend against that awareness: the mind uses the power that its intuition achieves in order to resist that intuition. This conflict accounts for two divergent though not necessarily discrete temptations that were intensified at the time when Dostoevsky was thinking about *The Brothers Karamazov* (or that went into the thinking of *The Brothers Karamazov*). Assuming the flaw to be in the human mind, there are those who sense that it can be overcome

6. René Girard, "Au fond de toutes choses, il y a toujours l'orgueil humain ou Dieu," in *Dostoïevski: Du double à l'unité* (Paris: Plon, 1963), p. 166.

7. Temira Pachmuss, *F. M. Dostoevsky: Dualism and Synthesis of the Human Soul* (Carbondale: Southern Illinois University Press, 1963).

through a rush at the absolute (God, Reason, Beauty, Perfection). And there are those who believe that the transcendental effort must be attempted within man seen as a creature of society. In Russia, during the second half of the nineteenth century, those who believed in the possibility of a realizable Eden were confirmed by the action of powerful social forces. Industrialization was accelerating the pace of change within the Tzarist empire (the emancipation of 22 million serfs—one third of the entire population—in 1861, with the start of more widespread land holdings, the slow rise of a working class; the shrinking of distances thanks to the steam engine, electricity, the telegraph, with a resulting infiltration of "Westernizing" ideas; etc.). But that change still contended with the traditions of a country that had remained largely feudal and agricultural: change was slowed, but as it occurred, it appeared to be the more dramatic.

Dostoevsky was caught up in this ferment, at once tempted and repelled by its manifestations, and not always able to reconcile them, and his own impulses, in a harmonious system. The contradictions and the passions that often turn his theory into an intellectual shambles (as evidenced, for example, by some of the essays in *The Diary of a Writer*) also went into the substance and the circumstances of his characters and contributed to their hugeness—the genius of the novelist rejecting the impossible simplicity of an either/or. Like their author, his people are tensed and torn between a necessary here and an unspannable beyond, the ones who are less wracked becoming morally suspicious: the simple utopian and the simple criminal are equally delinquent because of their simplicity (which has nothing to do with the far more difficult "simplicity" of the Christian). If Dostoevsky's criminals appear to fare better than his utopians, it is because the deed of the former works against a more complex aggregate of human vectors than do the theories of the latter.[8]

It is this awareness of human complexity that makes the simple characters "comical." Sometimes that simplicity is in the oversimple eye of the beholder. Myshkin, the reincarnation of Don Quixote in *The Idiot* (1869), suffers conflicting forces not apparent to those who

---

8. Freud drew an even closer connection between the complexity of the Dostoevskian criminal and the sympathy of the author, associating Dostoevsky's epilepsy with guilt over his father's death and tying his "admiration" for his fictional murderers to their ability to kill, as it were, in his stead.

can only measure his failure to achieve a kind of social behavior that is generally expected. But Fyodor Pavlovich is a "buffoon" because of a congenital defect—an inadequate human resonance to the difficulty of being in the world. Though he experiences that difficulty, and has the intelligence (and even some of the book learning) to comprehend it, he tries to reduce it to insignificant words.

It is not the death of a "buffoon" like old Karamazov that interests Dostoevsky—Fyodor Pavlovich is hardly more important than Mrs. Inglethorp: like her, he is a presence sufficiently hollow not to impinge on the events that will be articulated about him and his murder. Only the appropriate magistrates will try to know the physical circumstances of his death: the others will ask questions about themselves and *around* him—why such a man should have been imposed on them, who is responsible once he has been killed and the culprit discovered. That is the *mystery*—the police are concerned with only a "riddle" or a "secret."[9]

The concerns of the police are too simple to be of any consequence: the law is a yardstick applicable only to surfaces, and Dostoevsky mistrusts the integuments of people, or people too much concerned with integuments. "The Bernards," mutters the author through the mouth of a smiling and scornful Dmitri during the trial (p. 687). The reference is to a previous conversation between Dmitri and Alyosha (we will have occasion to return to it) and to Claude Bernard, the father of experimental medicine who so influenced Zola and who, at the time, was explaining hitherto unexplained parts of man by considering the functioning of the human organism as that of a chemical process. Dmitri makes the remark when "Rakitin's opinion of [Grushenka]" is mentioned. Rakitin's remarks are noteworthy: it is not the first time that he has been involved as a witness for the prosecution, "a young observer who has observed the Karamazov family at close quarters, and profoundly—Mr. Rakitin: 'The sense of their own degradation is as essential to these reckless, unbridled natures as the sense of their lofty generosity'" (p. 665). It is not that Rakitin is wrong—his character capsules are accurate enough; what elicits the scornful smile of Dostoevsky and Dmitri is that Rakitin's judgments, however correct, account for only a surface—as does Claude

9. See Ya. E. Golosovker, "The Words 'Secret' and 'Mystery,'" in Matlaw, *Brothers Karamazov*, pp. 857–61.

Bernard when he reduces the human mystery to a vasomotor or glandular function.[10] The scornful smile is aware of the thinness of that surface, compared to what it conceals, and judges those whose knowledge is limited to that surface.

Bernard and his followers were not the only ones who believed they were causing the darkness in man to recede through a process of despiritualization. In 1859 Darwin's *Origin of Species* removed man from the kingdom of god and replaced him within the animal kingdom. Philosophy and political theory were evolving likewise. Kirilov, in *The Possessed* (1872), represented an attack by Dostoevsky on Bakunin, who believed that men could achieve complete freedom through anarchism, collectivism, and atheism. In the same novel, the character Pisarev mocked Chernyshevsky who, independent of Marxist influence, advocated economic materialism as a way to socialism. The Tzarist 1860s acknowledged these forces in the liberal policies of Alexander II, whose reign (1855–1881) brought about, in addition to the emancipation of the serfs, local self-government, a reform in the law courts that introduced the jury system (something Dostoevsky was to remember in Dmitri's trial), extension of public education, relaxation of censorship, and tax reform. As was frequently to be the case thereafter, such liberalization afforded the clearer expression of more radical demands: in *Fathers and Sons* (1861), Turgenev gave currency to the term *nihilism* for the theory of those who wanted the economic and social order destroyed so as to prepare the way for a better one. Terrorism was the weapon of those who believed that the immediate objective—destruction—took precedence over any other: Alexander II was assassinated on the day he was issuing a limited constitution. His son swung the pendulum back to repressive reaction, exacerbating social upheaval that eventually culminated in the Bolshevik revolution. After a century that experienced repeatedly the buffeting consequences of these events, it is likely impossible to realize with what impact they affected those who lived through them. But it is as difficult to imagine Dostoevsky's prophetic

10. It was while working in Claude Bernard's Paris laboratory (November 1862) that the Russian physiologist Ivan Sechenov reported on the repressive efforts of thalamic nerve centers on spinal reflexes. It was Sechenov who outlined a first reflex study of behavior to which Pavlov later acknowledged his debt; he can thus be considered the father of objective (later known as behavioral) psychology.

and eschatological vision without reference to the apocalyptic 1860s in Russia.

For Dostoevsky, who had gone through a period of early radicalism prior to his exile, these forces of materialistic secularism were destructive (*Notes from Underground*, in 1864, had already castigated the technological opiate as a Crystal Palace of man's illusions and enslavement); Dostoevsky returned from exile to the turmoil of the sixties and, like the government some time later, gradually hardened into reactionary enmity. But the effect of that reaction on the writing of *The Brothers Karamazov* is subtle; in the novel, it stated the impossibility for a man to transcend through only the power of his reason the limits and the mystery that bound him. But Dostoevsky showed as well the desperate efforts of an individual will to achieve that transcendency nevertheless; within these huge confrontations of human desire and human limits, another kind of morality obtained —the architectonic imperative—and Dostoevsky was unable to remain bound by the constraint of the ideas he had intended to defend. In a novel that was to have been in its entirety, according to Dostoevsky's *Notebooks,* an answer to the negation of God, the Devil always got his due.[11]

Nathan Rosen has noted how, in his comments on the Book of Job, Zosima leaves out of account Job's assertions of self—his insistence on his own innocence and his request for an encounter with God in order to put forth his case.[12] Instead, Zosima dwells on the mystery of healing and acceptance. Zosima is a saint because of this acceptance; even though he occupies the initiate's position between two worlds, he feels no need to go against the warnings of Sirach— his "knowledge" is not a striving to know: "Much on earth is hidden from us, but to make up for that we have been given a precious mystic sense of our living bond with the other world, with the higher heavenly world, and the roots of our thoughts and feelings are not here but in other worlds. That is why the philosophers say that we cannot apprehend the reality of things on earth" (p. 299). This ac-

11. It was in this sense that André Gide thought Dostoevsky's creation to be "demonic." (See his *Dostoevsky* [London: Secker & Warburg, 1949], especially the fifth and sixth of his conferences at the Vieux-Colombier.)

12. Nathan Rosen, "Style and Structure in *The Brothers Karamazov,*" *Russian Triquarterly* 1, no. 1 (1971): 352–65.

ceptance is achieved not through religious passivity but through an active emotion—love: "Love a man even in his sin, for that is the semblance of Divine Love and is the highest love on earth. Love all God's creation, the whole and every grain of sand in it. Love every leaf, every ray of God's light. Love the animals, love the plants, love everything. If you love everything, you will perceive the divine mystery in things" (p. 298). But Zosima does not mean that the insight of even love will break the seal on the beyond—only that the beholder will become aware of that forbidding seal and, therefore, richer: "God took seeds from different worlds and sowed them on this earth, and His garden grew up and everything came up that could come up, but what grows lives and is alive only through the feeling of its contact with other mysterious worlds. If that feeling grows weak or is destroyed in you, the heavenly growth will die away in you. Then you will be indifferent to life and even grow to hate it" (pp. 299–300). It is this sense in Zosima that makes the assertive part of Job's mind and energy seem like the start of the frustrating quest to establish an equation with God.[13]

It is against the human fullness of Zosima that the arrogant shallowness of "the Bernards" is ultimately measured—an arrogance and a shallowness derived from the conviction that the mystery within and about man can be (and should indeed be) reduced, that his misery and greatness can be reasoned away. For the Bernards and the Rakitins, the understanding of the human condition is too simple; in the ironic words of Dmitri: "It's chemistry, brother, chemistry! There's no help for it, your reverence, you must make way for chemistry. And Rakitin does dislike God. Ough! doesn't he dislike Him!" (p. 557); "Life's easy for Rakitin. 'You'd better think about the extension of civic rights, or even of keeping down the price of meat. You will show your love for humanity more simply and directly by that, than by philosophy' " (p. 561). Zosima and Bernard represent the clash of two fundamentally different assumptions: the belief that the mystery is defining and immanent, and therefore divine in origin and good, and a sense of the unknown as a transiency that it is in the nature of man to overcome. Dostoevsky the man had no trouble knowing with whom he sided; but the writer placed *both* temptations within the

13. As I note in my conclusion, there are other ways of interpreting Job's "assertiveness."

hugeness of his characters in order to make visible Dmitri's agonized observation that "God and the devil are fighting . . . and the battle-field is the heart of man" (p. 97).

Ivan's devil is more than figurative—he emerges as a full-fledged character from Ivan's nightmares. That devil is, above all else, urbane —a fact that contributes not a little, in Dostoevsky's view, to his villainy: his repartee is prompt, his turn of phrase worldly and lib-erally sprinkled with French. It is not that the devil's French is par-ticularly offensive (that is a secondary, though still considerable, sin)—his primary sin is his fluency, his ability to speak so well and with so little effort.[14] His contempt for mankind shows most strik-ingly in the ease with which he turns the poignancy and depth of its mystery into salon conversation: he is a sophisticated version of Fyodor Pavlovich. This sophistication evidences, of course, another part of his depravity: he is Europeanized. His French is the affectation of those whose leisure for games of the mind has theorized them out of a sense of communion with the suffering of the underprivileged whom they reduce to the words of their games.[15] This represents for Dostoevsky both intellectual and moral shabbiness: the mind, which claims to understand, understands little indeed. Ivan's devil is hardly the adversary of God, to whom Dmitri refers: he is at the most a gibe at the rationalists, a reminder that Descartes' effort to prove rationally the existence of God resulted in a Western European drift towards atheism.

In the view of the Slavophile Dostoevsky, this intellectualizing reductiveness begins in the West. The Russians are God's chosen people, not unlike the Israelites of old, and for them to ape the modish

14. One might contrast the glibness of the devil's urbane speech with the more personal and complex sources that went into the writing of Zosima's speech, made up "of Biblical texts, recollections of [Dostoevsky's] visit to the saintly elder Amvrosy at the Optina Pustin monastery, various lives of the saints, etc.": see Nathan Rosen, "Style and Structure," which refers to the stylistic studies of Pletnev and Komarovich.

15. A constant of Dostoevsky's thought. Note, for example, his essay on "The Jewish Question" in *The Diary of a Writer*, 2 vols. (New York: Charles Scribner's Sons, 1949). In response to a letter accusing him of insensitivity to the plight of Russian Jews in spite of his professions of solidarity with, and compassion for, the oppressed, Dostoevsky answers that the fault lies with the Jews who, because they are victims, should have preserved a sense of kinship with the oppressed instead of remaining isolated from them.

theories of (Western) aliens is to risk alienation from the immediacy of an instinct that knows more than the ostentatious mind. This immediacy of knowing with more than the power of reason is something that the lavish ritual of Roman Catholicism or the adventurous mentalism of a Claude Bernard can only lose contact with. Though Dostoevsky occasionally acknowledges Russia's spiritual kinship with Europe,[16] he is not swayed in his "conception of a Russian destiny. 'Everything characteristically Russian,' he wrote, 'everything that is ours, pre-eminently national—and therefore everything genuinely artistic—is unintelligible to Europe.' For Dostoevsky, Russia was inseparable from the Orthodox Church, the unsullied vessel in which alone was preserved 'the Divine image of Christ.' "[17] Berdiaev has called attention to this Messianism of the Russians: they must be the ones to right the social order, but they must do so in the knowledge that this righting is only a necessity, not an end.[18]

The complexity of this Russian "soul" informs Dostoevsky's major characters, allowing them to enact the author's dislikes even as they give voice to his beliefs. In the conversation with Alyosha that prepares his trial reference to "the Bernards," Dmitri articulates for a time Dostoevsky's convictions:

"Damn ethics. I am done for, Alexey, I am, you man of God! I love you more than anyone. It rends my heart . . . to look at you, that's what. Who was Karl Bernard?"

"Karl Bernard?" Alyosha was surprised again.

"No, not Karl. Wait, I made a mistake. Claude Bernard. What is that? Chemistry or what?"

"He must be a scientist," answered Alyosha; "but I must say I can't tell you much about him, either. I've heard of him as a scientist, but what sort I don't know."

"Well, damn him, then! I don't know either," swore Mitia. "A scoundrel of some sort, most likely. They are all scoundrels. And Rakitin will make his way. Rakitin will get on anywhere; he is another Bernard. Ugh, these Bernards! They are all over the place." (Pp. 556–57)

16. For example, in his article on "The Death of George Sand," in *The Diary:* "We, Russians, have two motherlands—Russia and Europe—even in cases where we call ourselves Slavophiles" (1:342).

17. Irving Howe, *Politics and the Novel* (New York: Horizon Press, 1957, p. 54).

18. Nicolai A. Berdiaev, *Dostoevsky* (New York: Meridan Books, 1957).

Bernard is also Karl (Marx?), the interchangeable Western European —French or German—in any event a maker of systems intending to explain what God willed to be mysterious. Less dismissible is the Russian ("Rakitin") contaminated by Western ideas. But should the Russian not be contaminated and yet act in such an alien way, and without the counterpull of his native force, he is deemed to be congenitally deficient, like Fyodor Pavlovich, a "buffoon," the character whose inadequate definition turns him into a comic figure, the unidimensional fiction evidencing the loss of a moral dimension. If the fictional figure is redeemed as fiction, its complexity, like the linguistic complexity of a Zosima that distinguishes him from a minor devil-advocate, derives from (and demonstrates the catastrophic throes within) the character that bring on his suffering and, at last, his (moral) redemption.

When Rakitin opposes to "philosophy" civic rights or the price of meat as ways to improve the lot of mankind, two sorts of character are shown in the two kinds of morality: civic rights and the price of meat are inadequate responses to the mysterious ways of God. Not that civic rights and the price of meat are not dreadfully important: it is simply a question of not confusing refractory mystery and the possibility of solutions. Such matters as civic rights and the price of meat belong to the realm of men, and those who concern themselves with them should not therefore presume upon the divine mystery. But even that presumption is not necessarily as simple as Rakitin suggests: because the questions that belong to man are indeed dreadfully important, they represent a dreadfully important pull. Ivan has experienced that pull, and, because his is a better mind than Rakitin's, he has experienced it with even greater intensity.

"Ivan has no God. He has an idea. It's beyond me. But he is silent. I believe he is a freemason. I asked him, but he is silent. I wanted to drink from the springs of his soul—he was silent. But once he did drop a word."

"What did he say?" Alyosha took it up quickly.

"I said to him, 'Then everything is lawful, if it is so?' He frowned. 'Fyodor Pavlovich, our papa,' he said, 'was a pig, but his ideas were right enough.' That was what he dropped. That was all he said. That was going one better than Rakitin."

"Yes," Alyosha assented bitterly. (P. 561)

The shudder that goes through Alyosha and Dmitri (and is not pro-
voked by Rakitin) is not attributable solely to the fact that Ivan is
their brother; it begins with an awareness of the power of Ivan's mind
that projects him so far beyond the comfortable huddles of men,[19]
and shows also an intuition that his suffering will be commensurate.

The simplicity of a Rakitin, demonstrated by the complexity of a
like-minded Ivan, is possible to the extent that the character exists
primarily as a foil, as a reaction within the more important characters;
Rakitin has scarcely any other claim to existence. It is, however, in
the saintly characters that simplicity becomes a fictional problem, for
if it is true that the meek are blessed and shall inherit the earth, it is
less sure whether they are similarly blessed by novelists or can lay
equal claim to the fictional realm. And within Dostoevsky's complex
equation of fictional and moral fullness, the saint is in danger of losing either his fictional or his moral definition.[20] Perhaps mindful of
the relative failure of The Idiot's Myshkin, Dostoevsky chose to
leaven his latter saints with some of the earthy forces that contend
in his sinners. Zosima is sundered from his sinful (criminal?) past in
the world by the monastic cell: the seraphic elder is drawn against
the contrast of a former Zosima. This diachronic wisdom in Zosima
has no use for an Alyosha whose purity would be preserved within
monastic confines; Alyosha will have to go out into the world for
his virtue to contend against the frailty of his own nature:

19. The isolation and splintering that result from reliance on the analytic
faculties of the mind is frequently stressed by Dostoevsky. Howe notes that
Slavophiles "believed that Russia could and should avoid the path of the West;
and from their vantage-point in the social rear they were able to see the terrifying
consequences of the atomistic individualism that had sprung up in the West"
(Politics, p. 53). See also what Dostoevsky had to say about the "isolation" of
Europeans in The Diary (1:250).

20. A fact noted by many critics. Murray Krieger concluded that "Dostoevsky
did not totally succeed in his attempt 'to portray a truly beautiful soul'" (The
Tragic Vision [Baltimore, Md.: The Johns Hopkins University Press, 1973],
p. 211). Gide analyzed at some length the demonic influence at work in Dostoevsky
(see note 11 to this chapter), reminding us that Blake observed poetic freedom in
Milton only when he wrote about Satan and hell, not when he dwelled with God
and the angels. Dostoevsky himself makes mention of the problem on more than
one occasion; Konstantin Mochulsky notes that "Working on The Idiot, the
author confessed: 'depicting the positively beautiful is an immeasurable task'"
(quoted by Matlaw, Brothers Karamazov, pp. 789–90).

"When it is God's will to call me, leave the monastery. Go away for good."
   Alyosha started.

   "What is it? This is not your place for the time. I bless you for great
service in the world. Yours will be a long pilgrimage. And you will have to
take a wife, too, you will have to. You will have to bear all before you
come back. There will be much to do. But I don't doubt of you, and so I
send you forth. Christ is with you. Do not abandon Him and He will not
abandon you. You will see great sorrow, and in that sorrow you will be
happy." (P. 67)

The "great sorrow" to which the elder refers is the result of human
corruption as Alyosha will encounter it outside the monastery, starting with the legacy of the Karamazov blood in him—that power to
magnify the blandishments of love and reason into the agonies of
the flesh and mind that tempt the degenerate (he who has moved
beyond his race) to become god unto himself and others. Dostoevsky
never wrote the novel he had originally intended, the one that would
have described Alyosha's "long pilgrimage," but even so the earth
alloys the saint on several occasions. Like Christ himself by Satan
(see Matt. 4:1–11, which Dostoevsky frequently quotes), Alyosha
will be tempted by Ivan to entrap God within the snares of human
logic. After the sudden rotting of Zosima's corpse—an image of the
sudden disappearance of spiritual counsel and its replacement by the
evidence of human corruption—Alyosha remembers Ivan's words:
"He loved his God and believed in Him steadfastly, though he was
suddenly murmuring against Him. Yet a vague but tormenting and
evil impression left by his conversation with his brother Ivan the day
before, suddenly revived again in his soul and seemed forcing its way
to the surface" (p. 318). When Rakitin shows up in order to lead
Alyosha into further temptations, the tempter will be surprised by
the change in Alyosha, though he is unable to understand the torment
of the boy through whom the voice of Ivan occasionally speaks:
"Alyosha gazed a long while with his eyes half closed at Rakitin, and
there was a sudden gleam in his eyes . . . but not of anger with Rakitin. 'I am not rebelling against my God; I simply "don't accept His
world." ' Alyosha suddenly smiled a forced smile" (p. 319). Alyosha
will overcome his "rebellion"; later, when Rakitin leads him to
Grushenka, he will be saved from the other Karamazov temptation by
the prostitute herself. But in these and other encounters, Dostoevsky

establishes the dialectical tear that he requires for the definition of a human being, as opposed to the singleness of any idea—including that of Christian salvation.[21] And only out of this composite of experience and transcendency will the relatively *pale* figure[22] of Alyosha express his saintliness—embodied in the symbolic "well-grown, red-cheeked, clear-eyed lad of nineteen, radiant with health [who] was very handsome, too, graceful, moderately tall, with hair of a dark brown, with a regular, rather long, oval-shaped face, and a wide-set dark gray, shining eyes" (p. 19), but of an epileptic and "possessed" mother, and of a father who, though "shrewd and intelligent enough," was also "peculiar, repulsive, sensual" (p. 17), as well as "wicked and sentimental" (p. 19).

Less saintly characters are easier to portray, and of greater fictional stature, the forces that contend in them being allowed freer play in proportion as their resolution is not as clearly predetermined by the character's symbolism. (Each critic finds his own hero in *The Brothers Karamazov*, but only seldom is that hero the one Dostoevsky intended—Alyosha.) In Dmitri, the sensualist predominates; love has become degradation and hurt: "I loved vice, I loved the ignominy of vice. I loved cruelty; am I not a bug, am I not a noxious insect? In fact a Karamazov!" (p. 97). But Dmitri is no more a blissful sinner than Alyosha is a blissful saint: he remains tortured by his awareness: "God sets us nothing but riddles. Here the boundaries meet and all contradictions exist side by side. I am not a cultivated man, brother, but I've thought a lot about this. It's terrible what mysteries there are! Too many riddles weigh men down on earth" (p. 97). The cutting edge of his awareness will redeem his "sinful" love for Katerina Ivanovna, once he has endured her "virtuous" love born of *nadryv*.[23]

21. Akin to Dostoevsky's own tempering in the "furnace of doubt"—a recurrent awareness of his. For example, in his *Notebooks for the Brothers Karamazov*: "It is clear that I do not believe in Christ and preach Him like a child, but my *hosannah* has passed through a great *furnace of doubt*, as my devil says in the same book" (Matlaw, *Brothers Karamazov*, p. 770).

22. The word is Konstantin Mochulsky's, quoted in Matlaw, *Brothers Karamazov*, p. 789.

23. Usually rendered as "self-laceration": "The word comes from the verb *nadryvat'*, which means—apart from its literal meaning of tearing things apart, like paper—'to strain or hurt oneself by lifting something beyond one's strength'" (quoted by Edward Wasiolek, in Matlaw, *Brothers Karamazov*, p. 820; see also the article by Robert L. Belknap, in Matlaw, *Brothers Karamazov*, pp. 807–12).

From the start, Katerina Ivanovna and Dmitri mask their mutual attraction through like expressions of scorn:

She was the belle of the balls and picnics, and they got up charades in aid of distressed governesses. I took no notice, I went on as wildly as before, and one of my exploits at the time set all the town talking. I saw her eyes taking my measure one evening at the battery commander's, but I didn't go up to her, as though I disdained her acquaintance. I did go up and speak to her at an evening party not long after. She scarcely looked at me, and compressed her lips scornfully. Wait a bit. I'll have my revenge, thought I. (P. 100)

When Katya's father embezzles government money, she humiliates herself to Dmitri by asking him for the sum that would redeem her father's honor. Dmitri's impulse is to exacerbate her humiliation: "I looked at that one for three seconds, or five perhaps, with fearful hatred—that hate which is only a hairsbreadth from love, from the maddest love" (p. 103). It is this tangle of love and hate that dictates his response:

I went to the window, put my forehead against the frozen pane, and I remember the ice burned my forehead like fire. I did not keep her long, don't be afraid. I turned round, went up to the table, opened the drawer and took out a banknote for five thousand rubles (it was lying in a French dictionary). Then I showed it to her in silence, folded it, handed it to her, opened the door into the passage, and, stepping back, made her a deep bow, a most respectful, a most impressive bow, believe me! (P. 103)

In that low bow are expressed all the tempestuous contradictions in Dmitri—his first impulse (a "Karamazov one") as well as his love. He will be marked by that love, as he will be by the accuracy with which Katya reads the "noxious insect" in him ("She shuddered all over, gazed at me for a second, turned horribly pale—white as a sheet, in fact," p. 103). Katya recovers quickly, and for good: "all at once, not impetuously but softly, gently [she] bowed down to my feet—not a boarding-school curtsey, but a Russian bow, with her forehead to the floor."[24] Katya, the figure unredeemed, will keep the upper hand. She

24. Dmitri is caught up in a number of significant bows that, like a stage play in reverse, indicate the events that will follow in his life. At the monastery, he bows to his father; although "taken unaware," Fyodor Pavlovich is "equal to the occasion" and makes "his son a bow as low in return" (p. 59). But this mock anticipation of Dimitri's and Katya's bows is followed by that of Zosima, who has been a witness to the scene: he falls down on his knees before Dmitri and bows to the floor. His is the only selfless bow: it pays homage to the victim.

compounds her revenge by returning the money as soon as her
fortune changes and insisting on marriage: " 'I love you madly,' she
says, 'even if you don't love me, never mind. Be my husband. Don't
be afraid. I won't hamper you in any way. I will be your chattel. I
will be the carpet under your feet. I want to love you forever. I want
to save you from yourself' " (p. 105). Dmitri knows: "She loves her
own virtue, not me." However much Dmitri attempts to escape from
her pride, her self-love, and her forgiveness through unfaithfulness
and depravity, Katya remains steadfast in her vengeful self-
abasement. At the trial, she reduces Dmitri to a mere figment of her
exultant humility—how could the man who saved her father have
killed his own (which elicits from Dmitri the agonized "Katya, why
have you ruined me?" when the guilt he wants to assume publicly is
masked by the *nadryv* of her love)? It is only when Ivan proclaims his
own guilt that Katya finally breaks and confesses the hatred of her
love:

"I was lying against my honor and my conscience, but I wanted to save
him, for he has hated and despised me so." Katya shouted like a mad-
woman. "Oh, he has despised me horribly, he has always despised me, and
do you know, he has despised me from the very moment that I bowed
down to him for that money. I saw that. . . . I felt it at once at the time,
but for a long time I wouldn't believe it. How often I have read it in his
eyes 'you came of your own will, though.' Oh, he didn't understand, he had
no idea why I ran to him, he can suspect nothing but baseness, he judged
me by himself, he thought everyone was like himself!" Katya hissed
furiously, in a perfect frenzy. (P. 655)

The final summation of Dmitri's awareness—"We've hated each
other for many things, Katya, but I swear, I swear I loved you even
while I hated you, and you didn't love me" (p. 655)—explains the
redemptive process through which the "noxious insect" in Dmitri
is extirpated at last, so as to leave in him only the love out of which
it was engendered and to provide the human resonance necessary for
his acceptance of responsibility: "It's for the babe I'm going. Because
we are all responsible for all. For all the 'babes,' for there are big
children as well as little children. All are 'babes.' I go for all, because
someone must go for all. I didn't kill father, but I've got to go. I
accept it" (p. 560).

The final healing of Dmitri is possible because, in a sense, his is
a lesser passion. In the character of Ivan, who represents the mind

unbridled, destructive passion is shown with greatest intensity—
perhaps because the appetite of the mind can never be quite as simple
a self-indulgence as the appetites of the flesh; perhaps too because
the energy of the mind develops through a dialectical process that
adumbrates postures of conflict and self-laceration. In straining to
break free of human limits, Ivan comes up against the interposed
presence of God. He resents the three-dimensional limits that God
has imposed on men: "If God exists and if He really did create the
world, then, as we all know, He created it according to the geometry
of Euclid and the human mind with the conception of only three
dimensions in space" (p. 216). Ivan is the man who cannot brook
emprisonment within those three dimensions: "There have been and
still are geometricians and philosophers, and even some of the most
distinguished, who doubt whether the whole universe, or to speak
more widely the whole of being, was only created in Euclid's geometry; they even dare to dream that two parallel lines, which according
to Euclid can never meet on earth, may meet somewhere in infinity."

The mind of Ivan is able to think better worlds than God's—or at
least to show irreconcilable contradictions, foremost among which is
the suffering of the innocent (those for whom Dmitri will atone in
exile). The tear in Ivan results from his sense of the mystery and his
inability to dispel it: "It's not that I don't accept God, you must
understand, it's the world created by Him I don't and cannot accept"
(p. 216). That tear, and the other Karamazov lust ("I have a longing
for life, and I go on living in spite of logic. Though I may not believe
in the order of the universe, yet I love the sticky little leaves as they
open in spring," p. 211), will eventually save even Ivan—the wrench-
ing and contradictions that make him different from a shallow and
comfortable atheist like Rakitin. Ivan's is a passionate intelligence:
the inability of the Karamazovs to touch any part of the world lightly
gives depth to what might otherwise be romantic blasphemy or arrogant self-indulgence. When he asserts "that for every individual . . .
who does not believe in God or immortality, the moral law of nature
must immediately be changed into the exact contrary of the former
religious law, and that egoism, even unto crime, must become not
only lawful but even recognized as the inevitable" (p. 60), he voices
the awful freedom of man alone, without the sustenance of authoritative answers. Camus, who continued Dostoevsky's thought, described
how the existential awareness that slips out of the tenuous idea of

order (God) is suddenly overwhelmed by the evidence and the totality of chaos (the absurd). Zosima notes the clearsightedness and the dodges of despair in Ivan: "The question is still fretting your heart, and not answered. But the martyr likes sometimes to divert himself with his despair, as it were driven to it by despair itself. . . . But thank the Creator who had given you a lofty heart capable of such suffering; of thinking and seeking higher things, for our dwelling is in the heavens" (p. 61).

Ultimately, Ivan must be vanquished by the Euclidian limitations imposed on him: God remains He-who-will-not-answer. There is left only the devil, master of illusions, to act as the fraudulent intercessor, to sustain the mind's hope long enough for it to break. The stature of Ivan is extended into his devils. There is first the fourth Karamazov, the bastard Smerdyakov, half-brother, half-character, half-man: he lacks the soul born of inner torture, the double possibility, the dual vision. He lacks humor (as opposed to Fyodor Pavlovich, who tries to have him read Gogol, whom Smerdyakov finds merely "untrue") and intelligence (he is unable to "get through ten pages of Smaragdov['s *Universal History*]," p. 113), but he is the disciple of Ivan and the part of him that acts. He reduces the torment of Ivan that concedes the *logic* of murder to the simple, inhuman and incomplete *act* of murder. Smerdyakov murders Fyodor Pavlovich in cold blood, accepts a trivial reason (the money, for which he has no use), and kills himself, having accomplished in its entirety an act devoid of human resonance or purpose. In him, the act is a demonstration of the emptiness of action. In the breakdown of Ivan, however, it echoes as the irreducible force of the mystery that "Euclidian" man must endure.

Besides Smerdyakov, who shows the limits of thought in action, there is Ivan's devil, who mocks that thought by becoming Ivan to Ivan and confining him within the futility of the mind's logic. And yet Ivan's thought is powerful. In the parable of the Great Inquisitor, it individuates a new Trinity—the trinity of need in mankind, which analyzes the nature of mystery. Mystery is seen as the provision of an authoritative answer ("authority"), the mystery revealed ("miracle"), and refractory mystery. The Grand Inquisitor displaces Christ only as much as he needs to: of the former religion that failed men as they are, he retains mystery, though not as the absolute compatible with absolute freedom that Christ had allowed. He allays that absolute through miracles and answers—a subtlety that underscores the Inquisitor's "better" understanding of mankind and his "greater" love for it. The accuracy and the power of Ivan's thought went beyond the novel, where it had shaken Alyosha, to shake the prosecutor for the Holy Synod, K. P. Pobedonostsev, who worried that the position of the Grand Inquisitor might not be refutable and to whom Dostoevsky had to write a letter of reassurance from Ems (24 August 1879).

There was, in fact, no reason for Pobedonostsev to worry: had he been a more insightful reader, he would have realized, as Dostoevsky assured him, that the entire novel was the refutation that he required: from the start, Dostoevsky's literary salvation was bound up with the complexity of his heroes that insured their salvation as well. Though the book is a thing of sounds and words that may awaken within the reader a momentary resonance beyond intellective meaning, it is also a thing of sentences and thoughts—an object of the mind; and when it describes and comments upon a human lust to possess the unknowable, that lust will be more convincingly experienced within the mind that perceives it as a passion of the mind: therefore, Ivan's greatness and his power of conviction. The limits of man are also the limits of language: ultimately Ivan breaks, his words and his mind unavailing; but the author need only take note, and Pobedonostsev's lesson becomes an evidence.

Within the cross-reflecting pieces of the broken mirror, the entirety of the Karamazov nature is realized and magnified. An unimportant crime, committed by an unimportant character, is intensified and prolonged in every part of the sundered hero. The mystery of circumstances becomes the mystery of the human condition, the killing of the earthly father an image for the killing of the Spiritual Father— an effort to recover a lost innocence in a cataclysmic act that would transcend the bounds of mystery. At the trial, a not-quite-demented Ivan says, " 'I should think that I am in my right mind . . . in the same nasty mind as you . . . and as all these . . . ugly faces.' He turned suddenly to the audience. 'My father has been murdered and they pretend they are horrified,' he snarled, with furious contempt. They keep up the sham with one another. Liars! They all desire the death of their fathers' " (p. 651). Ivan, the protagonist of reason, speaks at last, and for all men, the irrational truth that defies systems and moral codes, Zosima's as well as Ivan's. If Zosima is wiser, it is only because his own break occurred earlier and he now realizes that man *is* that break, not the whole and wholesome creation of a logical mind.

The Grand Inquisitor is ultimately a fool (and of such proportions that the silent kiss of Jesus appears to be ironic): though he reads men correctly enough, they are no more happy within his logical scheme, however cynically the scheme accounts for their debilities. The only happy man is Zosima: he enters the scene only long enough to demonstrate contentment through the serenity of his death. That serenity is his alone (little more than an awful stench for those who have not progressed as far), for he alone has learned to accept the mystery as an active *experience* rather than trying to come to terms with its *nature*, rejecting the passivity of the saint and the systems of the Inquisitor alike. Within the delicate balance of his dialectical awareness, Zosima is the sum of Dostoevsky's sundered people who, in the coil and recoil of their passion, in groping and in pain, must learn to give up the temptation of the either/or that tears them apart.

In the end, "the peasants stand firm." The jury convicts the wrong man, who is the right man, understanding what they have done, not understanding. Their judgment is Dostoevsky's last comment on another of the new ideas that came into being during the sixties, intended to help God do His job better. It is also a measure of how difficult it is to fathom a human being, and the final word on the indwelling mystery.

Camus:
A Sense of Life,
the Unknowable Death

There is little need to document the influence of Dostoevsky on Camus and, more particularly, that of *The Brothers Karamazov*, the Copeau adaptation of which Camus helped stage and in which he acted the role of Ivan while yet in his twenties in Algeria. It is not so much the specifics of influence that concern us here as the persistence in different times of a need to confront the unknowable and the limits of human understanding.

The heroic size of Dostoevsky's characters derives from the magnitude of their buffeting from absolute to absolute: no lesser a barrier than God can be thrown up against these madmen. The three brothers Karamazov confront God at the point where the passion of even their magnificent effort fails, whether that passion derives from the need of an absolute knowledge that would transcend the contradictions that tear their souls, or from the absolute physical possession that would also be a possession of the world. Ivan cannot possess the world through the great power of his mind any more than Dmitri is able to through the hungering of his flesh. For awhile the hugeness of the Karamazov desire contends with sainthood even in Alyosha. The failure of Alyosha, and that of his brothers, is underscored by the wisdom of Zosima, who has filtered out of human desire the need for mastery and so allowed a sense of God, a sense of mystery, to replace the contest with God.

Camus's *The Rebel* (1951) turned to questions raised by Dostoevsky through what Camus termed the "indignation" of Ivan; the irresoluble contradictions that lead others to a God in whom all contradictions are resolved led Ivan to confront a God of contradictions. Camus's analysis creates a Dostoevskian character bereft of many conflicting temptations and much torment, while in his own fiction, Camus comes closer to Dostoevsky through characters who are ultimately aware of the absurd limits that constrain them.[1] Camus's analysis emphasizes the sense of an injustice that enters into Ivan's or Dmitri's sense of God—the faith of neither being adequate, for example, to accept the misery of children.[2] But in a novel like *The Stranger*, Camus knows that the mystery for which God occasionally stands cannot be reduced to emblematic tokens or events: like Dostoevsky, Camus ends with a character who can neither accept the event nor do anything about it.

Of Ivan, Camus says, "If he had faith, he could, in fact, be saved."[3] The same reprieve is offered Meursault, after his crime, by the exam-

1. It is this sense of "scandal" before a world whose irrationality will not yield to human reason that motivated the central part of Sartre's philosophical criticism of *The Stranger*. I will strive to show that Camus is less concerned with the mind than Sartre was. And it should also be recalled that Dostoevsky found the power of reason to be singularly unavailing; the real fools are the Bernards for believing that they can reason away man's mystery: the Slavic instinct knows more than such arrogant Western minds.

2. In making of Ivan a more single-minded character, Camus equates him with Dostoevsky. He forgets that Ivan goes mad while Dostoevsky only became angry.

3. Pp. 56–57. Quotations from *The Rebel* are from the translation by Anthony Bower (rev. ed. [New York: A. A. Knopf, 1971]).

ining magistrate and the prison chaplain. "While I was talking, [the examining magistrate] thrust the crucifix again just under my nose and shouted: 'I, anyhow, am a Christian. And I pray Him to forgive you for your sins. My poor young man, how can you not believe that He suffered for your sake?' "[4] And, more in character, the chaplain balances the uncertainty of temporal salvation with the assertion of spiritual salvation: "He said he felt convinced my appeal would succeed, but I was saddled with a load of guilt, of which I must get rid. In his view man's justice was a vain thing; only God's justice mattered" (p. 148). But Meursault is not Ivan. God exists for Ivan within his very denial: Meursault simply does not believe in God. Or rather, Meursault refuses to allow an idea of God to become the hope against which the knowledge of his limitation contends. Meursault either asks no questions (part 1) or understands the absolute nature of his limits so clearly that even his steadfast refusal of those limits cannot sunder them into the two parts of a dialectical principle. Meursault's refusal is wholly within him: there is no God against a part of whom he might be tempted to argue.

The key to the Meursault of part 2 is in that of part 1: he is "like everybody else" (p. 81) except for one, signal difference—he is unable to accept any perceptions but his own. He is polite, compliant, cooperative, but something deep within him remains irredeemably singular. He is a *stranger*—a strange mixture of utter honesty and utter selfishness. Given a chance, a hint, a lead, society will be quick to analyze that singularity. Upon his mother's death, he is unable to sham the expected display of grief that he does not feel; nor can he feel because of her death an attachment that he did not feel while she was alive. He cannot accept the value of newness or ambition as his boss expects him to when he offers Meursault the prospect of moving to Paris and traveling. He is unable to leave the evidence of sensual gratification in order to follow Marie's speculations about love and marriage. It is his inability to understand or accept the usual classifications that accounts for his loyalty to Raymond Sintès, a brutal and cowardly criminal: Raymond's criminality does not concern Meursault because he has not experienced it and general categories are too abstract to mean anything to Meursault.

4. P. 86. Quotations from *The Stranger* are from the translation by Stuart Gilbert (New York: A. A. Knopf, 1946).

Double negatives replace in him the affirmation that he is as yet unable to make: he has no reason not to oblige Raymond.

The Meursault of part 1 is an unquestioning creature of his own sensations: he has a nervous system but no imagination. Instead of living within the comfort of an emblematic and remote god who still questions, Meursault lives within the embrace of a glaring sun, his only truth, which affirms the evidence of animal life and the power of immediacy. On the day of his mother's funeral, Meursault is more aware of the sun than of the funeral's significance. It is the sun and the sea of Algiers that make Paris and the prospect of other worlds pale. And his desire for Marie has the taste of the salt and the heat on their tanned bodies.

The characters of Dostoevsky belong to several collectivities: the Russian nation is as much a reality to them as is God. Their outbursts of hatred and love for their fellow men deny a fundamental loneliness. Meursault appears after the death of God and the end of nations: he is alone, and at the time of his greatest contentment (part 1), he knows only the truths of his singleness: he experiences moments that are separate from each other and suggest neither past nor consequence, and whose value dies with them. He speaks in the past indefinite—the French tense for actions that have been completed—and in a first person through which can be heard the voice of the author. At this moment, like the author, he is suspicious of words, uses them sparingly without allowing them to become metaphor or hyperbole. He neither judges nor compares;[5] he merely describes phenomena of equal value:[6] the spare rhythms of his speech and its discontinuous

5. The judges are usually the only ones guilty in Camus's moral system. As René Girard's clever *boutade* has it, clues in *The Stranger* lead not to the murderer but to the judges ("Camus's *Stranger* Retried," *PMLA* 79, no. 5 [December 1964]: 523). But this is not because of the judges' position in a social structure; it is because of their function, which presumes that there can be guilt and a definable process in the actions of men.

6. At this point, Meursault and Camus evidence the lesson of Léon Brunschvicg and other French philosophers who questioned the power of human reason: the human mind comes up against what it cannot explain and must fall back on representation and classification. (See John Cruickshank: *Albert Camus and the Literature of Revolt* [New York: Oxford University Press, 1960], p. 50.) When Husserl allows that, beyond the ability of human thought only to describe, further significance is imparted by extratemporal essences, he introduces for Camus the notion of a leap of faith. (See "The Myth of Sisyphus" in *The Myth of Sisyphus and Other Essays*, trans. J. O'Brien [New York: A. A. Knopf, 1955], pp. 44ff. Quotations from *The Myth of Sisyphus* are from this edition.)

matter-of-factness sound like its signified: they contrive a kind of philosophical onomatopoeia. Meursault is, in part 1, the denizen of an existential Eden before a necessary and humanizing fall: he has an exemplary emptiness adequate to make of him an existential anti-hero, but he has not yet begun to ask questions. Until Meursault's encounter with the Arab on the beach, he has not been touched by any sense of mystery; he may have found the propositions of men to be on occasion unintelligible or remote from an immediately veri-fiable evidence, but he has not yet encountered the absurd.

In *The Stranger*, as in *The Brothers Karamazov*, there is the stench of the corpse—the moral consequences for a killer of a killing that society might absolve if it were given a chance to. The Arab killed by Meursault, like old man Karamazov, represents a part of society that society would as leave amputate. In both cases this negative presence must become full, the victim must be reborn with sufficient life, with sufficient human presence to inform the victim's killer: in death, old man Karamazov must become a man, a father, within the consciousness of his sons. The Arab must become, within the consciousness of his murderer, the human evidence that will make manifest the human evidences in all others. The Arab will never attain that kind of life for the examining magistrate: "However, as he continued talking, I did my best to understand, and I gathered that there was only one point in my confession that badly needed clearing up—the fact that I'd waited before firing a second time. All the rest was, so to speak, quite in order; but that completely baffled him" (p. 85). But as to Meursault, it is at that precise point, between the first and second shots, that his awareness wakens. The second shot (and the others) prevent the killing from being a mere inadvertence, an accident that society, in its dismissal of the Arab, is ready to dismiss.

For the primitive Meursault of part 1, the sun worshipper, the killing is a coincidence: the sun borrows Raymond's gun in Meursault's hand. The sun literally drives Meursault on: "It struck me that all I had to do was to turn, walk away, and think no more about it. But the whole beach, pulsing with heat, was pressing on my back" (pp. 74–75). The "same sort of heat as at [his] mother's funeral" (p. 75) takes charge of both participants:

I couldn't stand it any longer, and took another step forward. I knew it was a fool thing to do; I wouldn't get out of the sun by moving on a yard or so.

But I took that step, just one step, forward. And then the Arab drew his knife and held it up towards me, athwart of the sunlight.

A shaft of light shot upward from the steel, and I felt as if a long, thin blade transfixed my forehead. (P. 75)

The sun borrows the Arab's blade in the same way as it borrows the gun in the hand of Meursault. It then blinds Meursault:

At the same moment, all the sweat that had accumulated in my eyebrows splashed down on my eyelids, covering them with a warm film of moisture. Beneath a veil of brine and tears my eyes were blinded; I was conscious only of the cymbals of the sun clashing on my skull, and, less distinctly, of the keen blade of light flashing up from the knife, scarring my eyelashes, and gouging into my eyeballs. (P. 75)

There only remains for the sun to depress the trigger in order for the drama to be played out: "Then everything began to reel before my eyes, a fiery gust came from the sea, while the sky cracked in two, from end to end, and a great sheet of flame poured down through the rift. Every nerve in my body was a steel spring, and my grip closed on the revolver. The trigger gave" (p. 76).

Meursault has been an absence at the most fateful event in his existence: it is that absence that he must now enter. He must shake off the sun and become responsible for the death of a man:

And so, with that crisp, whipcrack sound, it all began. I shook off my sweat and the clinging veil of light. I knew I'd shattered the balance of the day, the spacious calm of this beach on which I had been happy. But I fired four shots more into the inert body, on which they left no visible trace. And each successive shot was another loud, fateful rap on the door of my undoing.[7] (P. 76)

In firing four more shots deliberately, Meursault moves out, cancels the sun, becomes responsible for (and aware of) the death of a brother.

---

7. There are a number of unsatisfactorinesses with Stuart Gilbert's translation of this passage. The conjunction "but" ("But I fired . . .") establishes a false link across what is the most portentous gap in the entire narrative. The French adverb *alors* of the original only locates a separate moment in time. The translation "on the door of my undoing" for "*sur la porte du malheur*" strays further from the author's intent. "Undoing" is an unfelicitous word when the four last shots have been, in fact, an act of conscious *doing*, and when, through them, Meursault is not bringing on his own destruction, but rather, in a real sense, his rehabilitation. The French *malheur* confirms this awareness of a human destiny. Compare Camus's Caligula, who notes that men die alone and *are not happy*.

He is now ready to give a meaning to the exemplary vacancy that he had heretofore demonstrated with no purpose.

For Meursault, prison represents the reality of human constraint, the necessary limitation of a human gesture that he had not been aware of previously. Meursault's previous world had the dimensions of the sun—it was as natural and as unlimited. He now learns that the true human dimension is that of the prison and of the prisoner condemned to death, and that life is still possible, is in fact only possible, under such conditions. For the first time in his existence, Meursault has something to strain against.

This *tension towards*—which may sometimes be of such force as to create, in the defeat of the effort, a god at the point where the effort breaks—that tension *against* may also become an affront by the undefeated *against god* once that god has been created by others. The prison priest invites Meursault's resignation, attempting quite literally to *turn aside* the forces of Meursault's desire, suggesting that God is *inward*:

These stone walls, I know it only too well, are steeped in human suffering. I've never been able to look at them without a shudder. And yet—believe me, I am speaking from the depths of my heart—I *know* that even the wretchedest amongst you have sometimes seen, taking form against the grayness, a divine face. It's that face you are asked to see. (Pp. 148–49)

But Meursault refuses the kind of redemption Dmitri finds in prison; Meursault knows that the irrecusable *otherness*, God or man, is *outside* of him, outside the cell *that he is*:

This roused me a little. I informed him that I'd been staring at those walls for months; there was nobody, nothing in the world, I knew better than I knew them. And once upon a time, perhaps, I used to try to see a face. But it was a sun-gold face, lit up with desire—Marie's face. I had no luck; I'd never seen anything "taking form," as he called it, against those gray walls. (P. 149)

It is the fact of those walls that has become of paramount importance in the awareness of Meursault: they are now the motor force of his desire, its human information and the source of its strength. Bereft of the solar principle that informed him in the days of a presumed freedom, Meursault is starting to grasp that he exists instead by virtue of the coiled spring within him tensed against a barrier that has come down forever between him and an absolute *beyond*.

Meursault has evolved from a form of passive heliotropism to the dynamics of a pro-ject, and in this dynamic state he no longer represents a clear statement. At the moment when a judge names him criminal and brings his life to a term upon that definition, Meursault has become, in fact, a *process*. It is not by inadvertence that his spare, clear, discontinuous descriptions of part 1 have yielded to a more lyrical period and the imagery of metaphor. The darkness of the cell affects the author as well as his character: both have moved from intellective description to art. Each now requires the affirmation of his sense that the mind, or its descriptive words, are not the full measure of any human dimension—that such a full measure would be a freedom exceeding the factual statement of the printed page just as it exceeds the cell that can only intensify the sense one has of it.

Camus had already recorded, in *The Myth of Sisyphus* (1942), his understanding that description can come to terms with only surfaces, but that beyond these surfaces there is something more, something that can be perceived only darkly, as through the mirror of art:

Describing—that is the last ambition of an absurd thought. Science likewise, having reached the end of its paradoxes, ceases to propound and stops to contemplate and sketch the ever virgin landscape of phenomena. The heart learns thus that the emotion delighting us when we see the world's aspects comes to us not from its depth but from their diversity. Explanation is useless, but the sensation remains and, with it, the constant attraction of a universe inexhaustible in quantity. The place of the work of art can be understood at this point. (Pp. 94–95)

The absurd work illustrates thought's renouncing of its prestige and its resignation to being no more than the intelligence that works up appearances and covers with images what has no reason. If the world were clear, art would not exist. (P. 98)

This attraction of Camus towards what he intuits as extending beyond the utmost reach of the conscious mind is similar to Dostoevsky's approval of Zosima's wisdom, whose knowledge knows that it cannot know, and which does so cheerfully though without resignation. In that splendid tension between an awareness of his limits and an awareness that there is a reach beyond those limits, Zosima achieves a greater understanding than the Bernards, who can shed only a surface light while mistakenly believing that it can illuminate all mystery. Zosima knows that only God can outreach the limits that bound him, but as a man, only Zosima possesses that awareness—and it is sublime.

An essential difference between Dostoevsky and Camus is that Camus will not settle for the peace of God however sublime or remote, but, true to a more modern tradition, prefers to maintain the state of tension that comes from removing God as the ultimate answer to the questions of men. In *The Myth of Sisyphus,* and later in *The Rebel,* Camus equates the leap of faith with the leap of death; God is philosophical *avoidance,* and what is avoided is precisely the same defining sense of which Zosima is possessed: a sense of the human contradiction born of desire and its necessary frustration.[8]

In his speculative writing, Camus alters the terms of an absurd rebellion—that simple inability of man to accept that he cannot know. Instead, Camus makes of him a blasphemer by focusing his refusal on a specific object: "The metaphysical rebel is therefore not definitely an atheist, as one might think him, but he is inevitably a blasphemer. Quite simply, he blasphemes primarily in the name of order, denouncing God as the father of death and as the supreme outrage" (*The Rebel,* p. 24). God, synonym of death, becomes the father of death, a symbol of injustice, a temptation to refuse the absurd tension. So conceived, God fathers nothing less than a death in life and becomes at least a negative *presence.* But when Camus's speculation is given the dimension of fiction,[9] the removal of that presence removes even the sense of blasphemy; the mirror of art reflects a less easily defined

8. Camus is among the first who, in emptying the void beyond man of God's occupancy, created a *space of desire,* the focus upon which claimed so much of the attention of subsequent French literary theorists. In Derrida, that space results from marginality and difference; Bataille locates in it the power of an impossible eroticism; it becomes, for feminists like Duras and Gauthier, the absence of a person—a woman—that is like a "black hole," a center of negative density within the social universe.

9. A mode Camus favored over flatly speculative fiction or nonspeculative fiction: "The great novelists are philosophical novelists—that is, the contrary of thesis-writers. For instance, Balzac, Sade, Melville, Stendhal, Dostoevsky, Proust, Malraux, Kafka, to cite but a few. But in fact the preference they have shown for writing in images rather than in reasoned arguments is revelatory of a certain thought that is common to them all, convinced of the uselessness of any principle of explanation and sure of the educative message of perceptible appearance" (*The Myth of Sisyphus,* p. 101).

play of human tensions from which the counterstating philosophical term is absent.[10]

As we have suggested earlier, the more metaphorical language of Meursault in part 2 describes a more paradoxical character: his questions bring him up against the limits of what had been an unlimited world; his discovery of a deep kinship with others effects his radical isolation; he loses the evident life of the solar absolute but will pulsate more vibrantly to the systolic rhythm of the absurd. But for this to happen, the meaningless corpse of the Arab must first come to mean death, both general and particular—an evidence of the absurd condemnation that lies upon all men, and the sense of a personal death in the intimate loss of a single man. The social peculiarities within which Meursault's trial plays itself out are either emblems of the absurd condemnation or ironical gestures enacted against the mocking evidence of a condemnatory fate.

One of the emblematic functions of the trial is to show how anxious the abstraction known as the social body (Meursault's accusers and defenders alike) is to turn Meursault into a similar abstraction: he must either be reassimilated into the social body by showing that he has strayed from it only to the extent of causing an accident to occur that repentance will suffice to efface, or he must be a figure of such absolute evil that society deems him to be amputable according to a manner that eliminates him completely but leaves no social scar either.[11] At his friendliest, the examining magistrate calls Meursault

10. It is the centrality of this tension that makes Camus reject Christian salvation, the price of which is that "sin is not so much knowing (if it were, everybody would be innocent) as wanting to know" (The Myth of Sisyphus, p. 49). Such a view removes tragedy from even the Christian stage. "Christianity plunges the whole universe, man and the world, into the divine order. There is thus no tension between man and the divine principle" (quoted by Jules Brody from Camus's "On the Future of Tragedy," in an article that derives interesting insights from the kind of language Camus uses to articulate some of these problems in his fiction: "Camus et la pensée tragique: L'Etranger," in Saggi e ricerche di letteratura francese 15 [1976]: 513–54). In contrast, "The absurd is born of this confrontation between the human need and the unreasonable silence of the world. This must not be forgotten. This must be clung to because the whole consequence of life can depend on it. The irrational, the human nostalgia, and the absurd that is born of their encounter—these are the three characters in the drama that must necessarily end with all the logic of which an existence is capable" (The Myth of Sisyphus, p. 28).

11. Camus is of two minds here. He feels strongly the dehumanizing force of the social body, but he feels as strongly that the "tender indifference" of men also derives from their necessary placement within that social body.

"Mr. Antichrist," and, once it is clear that Meursault will not "play the game," the prosecutor requires that Meursault be more than simply a man who has committed a specific action that demands his trial; he must become the very essence of criminality, even to the extent of having his guilt equated with that of the unspeakable crime:

"This same court, gentlemen, will be called on to try tomorrow that most odious of crimes, the murder of a father by his son." To his mind, such a crime was almost unimaginable. But, he ventured to hope, justice would be meted out without paltering. And yet, he made bold to say, the horror that even the crime of parricide inspired in him paled beside the loathing inspired by my callousness.

"This man, who is morally guilty of his mother's death, is no less unfit to have a place in the community than that other man who did to death the father that begat him. And, indeed, the one crime led on to the other; the first of these two criminals, the man in the dock, set a precedent, if I may put it so, and authorized the second crime. Yes, gentlemen, I am convinced" —here he raised his voice a tone—"that you will not find I am exaggerating the case against the prisoner when I say that he is also guilty of the murder to be tried tomorrow in this court." (P. 128)

Once a man begins to see his existence in ways that are not bounded by the social body, there is no telling what his private vision might be or what dangerous precedent he might set for other individuals.

In the same frame of mind, Meursault's lawyer needs to cast his client as much as possible in the role of the criminal that is most familiar and acceptable to the jury:

I could truthfully say I'd been quite fond of Mother—but really that didn't mean much. All normal people, I added as an afterthought, had more or less desired the death of those they loved, at some time or other.

Here the lawyer interrupted me, looking greatly perturbed.

"You must promise me not to say anything of that sort at the trial, or to the examining magistrate." (P. 80)

Dimly I heard my counsel making his last appeal.

"Gentlemen of the jury, surely you will not send to his death a decent, hard-working young man, because for one tragic moment he lost his self-control? Is he not sufficiently punished by the lifelong remorse that is to be his lot?" (P. 132)

None of the people involved in the trial speaks about the peculiar crime committed by Meursault, none speaks about the singularity of the participant: Meursault and his deed belong to a more general order of classification. Meursault is several times tempted to interrupt the proceedings, which seem to him to be so distinctly *outside* of him, constructing a nightmarish duplication of his crime, but one *from which he is absent*:

At one moment, however, I pricked up my ears; it was when I heard him saying: "It is true I killed a man." He went on in the same strain, saying "I" when he referred to me. It seemed so queer that I bent toward the policeman on my right and asked him to explain. He told me to shut up; then, after a moment, whispered: "They all do that." It seemed to me that the idea behind it was still further to exclude me from the case. (P. 130)

It was quite an effort at times for me to refrain from cutting them all short, and saying: "But, damn it all, who's on trial in this court, I'd like to know? It's a serious matter for a man, being accused of murder. And I've something really important to tell you." (P. 124)

But when Meursault is at last given a chance to speak, he can only begin recounting his possession by the sun. The public laughs and Meursault's attorney hastens to cut short this picture of an individual so different from what can commonly be accepted of a criminal definition.

The prison priest is guilty of an even more serious kind of reappropriation of Meursault—a reappropriation so serious, in fact, that the usually taciturn Meursault ends up by yelling his anger at him. The priest represents a death in life that mitigates the awful presence of actual death, the loss of human tension once the divine principle has been brought to this side of the unknown: "Living as he did, like a corpse, he couldn't even be sure of being alive" (p. 151). Like the judge who requires a criminal sufficiently fallen for God to redeem him, the priest believes in an absolute condemnation that transcends the peculiarities of a specific crime: "In his view man's justice was a vain thing: only God's justice mattered. I pointed out that the former had condemned me. Yes, he agreed, but it hadn't absolved me from my sin" (p. 148). Through the voice of Meursault, the voice of Camus answers that man is innocent: Meursault is not an irresponsible sinner within the will of God; he is a free man who is culpable, responsible for his crime: "I told him that I wasn't conscious of any 'sin'; all I knew was that I'd been guilty of a criminal offense. Well,

I was paying the penalty for that offense, and no one had the right to expect anything more of me" (p. 148).

Only at one moment, between deafness and anger, is Meursault able to hear the priest: "Though I didn't trouble much to follow what he said, I gathered he was questioning me again. Presently his tone became agitated, urgent, and, as I realized that he was genuinely distressed, I began to pay more attention" (pp. 147–48): Meursault hears the priest only at the moment when the priest recedes so as to disclose the man.[12] This sense of a human presence is more immediate and more intense than merely the statement of a romantic profession or a humanistic ideal: it is the humanizing consequence of a physicality that Meursault has always felt. When Camus was prefacing his *Myth of Sisyphus*, he presented it as "an absurd sensitivity [not] an absurd philosophy": this sensationism is once again stressed by Camus through the experience of Meursault; it takes over at the point where the mind becomes unavailing.

The prisoner in the dark and confining cell retains of the first Meursault an animal awareness. His inability to theorize or to imagine vouches for his particular kind of honesty. He lives through his senses: locked in an embrace with the world, he knows it only as an unmediated immediacy—he cannot *think* it. He himself confesses the debility of his imaginative faculties: "Imagination has never been one of my strong points" (p. 141). He has neither humor nor fancies. He knows what Sartre's Ibbieta (in *The Wall*) learns too late: you cannot play games.[13]

Punishment, equivalent to the metaphysical condemnation, is in the loss of the world that was once thought to be possible: the possible world is no longer measured by desire. It takes Meursault a while to grasp this irreducible truth: "There was one thing in those early days that was really irksome: my habit of thinking like a free man" (p.

12. Compare the one moment of human tragedy in the Christian parable when the figure of God turns human: "It was celebrated on Golgotha during an imperceptible instant, at the moment of the 'My God, why has thou forsaken me'" ("On the Future of Tragedy"; see Brody, "Camus et la pensée tragique," p. 551, n.31).

13. The thought is more than episodic: in his cell, Meursault finds a newspaper clipping about the return of a prodigal son who shows himself under an assumed name and is killed by his family—it is the plot of Camus's play *The Misunderstanding*, which he was to stage two years later.

95). The instinct of the caged animal is to escape: "This problem of the loophole obsesses me; I am always wondering if there have been cases of condemned prisoners' escaping from the implacable machinery of justice at the last moment, breaking through the police cordon, vanishing in the nick of time before the guillotine falls" (p. 136). Like Sisyphus, Meursault can be punished only for as long as he persists in his formerness: he must learn to know, without accepting it, that the guillotine falls inexorably: "After taking much thought, calmly, I came to the conclusion that what was wrong about the guillotine was that the condemned man had no chance at all, absolutely none. In fact, the patient's death had been ordained irrevocably" (p. 139); "No, there was no way out, and no one can imagine what the evenings are like in prison" (p. 101).

What saves Meursault spiritually is his inability to fantasize: it allows him to grasp at last that those evenings are the only ones he has. The sun has been removed from him, and with it, the sun-drenched part of his life; even Marie cannot survive in him as only a memory: "She might be ill, or dead. After all, such things happen. How could I have known about it, since, apart from our two bodies, separated now, there was no link between us, nothing to remind us of each other?" (p. 144). Marie disappeared when the taste of the sun and the sea disappeared. The senses persist, and the immediacy of their truth, however humble: no former truth, however splendid, is equal to it. The hungering is in the present, and the limits imposed upon the metaphysical prisoner are ahead of him: as long as he still lives, he remains tensed against them.

The loss of Marie represents the death of one possible life, not death itself; Meursault informs his constraint, his waiting with the tension of life:

They always came for one at dawn; that much I knew. So, really, all my nights were spent in waiting for that dawn. I have never liked being taken by surprise. When something happens to me I want to be ready for it. That's why I got into the habit of sleeping off and on in the daytime and watching through the night for the first hint of daybreak in the dark dome above. (P. 141)

He waits, tensed between the expectation of the dawn when the condemned are traditionally executed and the expectation of a reprieve: the latter expectation causes a nearly unbearable surge of life to pulse through him, "that sudden rush of joy racing through my body and even bringing tears to my eyes" (p. 143).[14] It is this intensity of expectation, of *knowing*, that keeps Meursault drawn up against the death he fears and the life whose strength surges through him so cruelly if only he allows it to; it is that same intensity of knowing that sweeps away so angrily the fairy tales about God that the priest proposes to him:

I poured out on him all the thoughts that had been simmering in my brain. He seemed so cocksure, you see. And yet none of his certainties was worth one strand of a woman's hair. . . . It might look as if my hands were empty. Actually, I was sure of myself, sure about everything, far surer than he; sure of my present life and of the death that was coming. That, no doubt, was all I had; but at least that certainty was something I could get my teeth into—just as it had got its teeth into me. (P. 151)

Meursault's sense of his own life is in his exacerbated *senses*; what he can see of the sky's luminescence, the splinters from his plank bed that he sucks while he still craves cigarettes, the voice of a man that speaks at times even in the priest. This animal life drawn to other lives, this animal awareness, was in the old Meursault as well, but it is now intensified into a new dimension. Meursault's rejection of the priest's speculative theology becomes, through its affirmation of man while he still lives his mortal life, the affirmation of a social contract. Meursault accepts men as they are—in their pettiness, their terrors, their hatred, their contrivances; he accepts even the unacceptable social apparatus that they have constructed for themselves. Meursault accepts his culpability as that apparatus determines it, as a necessary part of his belonging: "Replying to [the judge's] questions, [the witness] said that I'd declined to see Mother's body, I'd smoked cigarettes and slept, and drunk *café au lait*. It was then I felt a sort of wave of indignation spreading through the courtroom, and for the first time I understood that I was guilty" (p. 112).

The strength of the kinship that tempers the social bond is double; the sense of those living beyond the prison walls is also bound up in their sense of Meursault: it is in the depth of their awareness that Meursault becomes "just like everybody else" (p. 81). Meursault's

14. There is considerably more lyric power in the original: "cet élan du sang et du corps qui me piquait les yeux d'une joie insensée. Il fallait que je m'applique à réduire ce cri, à le raisonner."

acts and feelings attain their resonance in others; the social structure
is only the result of a sensorial identity. When Meursault is condemned to have his head lopped off, the courtroom spectators are
touched by the chill of their own condemnation—it is in their own
fear that they feel his. And the threat to their own lives, represented
by Meursault's killing of the Arab, names him criminal with a power
of awareness that neither legal classifications nor moral outrage can
achieve: their fear that erupts as hatred is the most profound assertion of a human bond: "For all to be accomplished, for me to feel
less lonely, all that remained to hope was that on the day of my
execution there should be a huge crowd of spectators and that they
should greet me with howls of execration" (p. 154).

Death is terrible for the sensationist: the entirety and the intensity
of his meaning are locked up in the moment. The priest's whole
theology is devised to counter such a terribly desperate assertion:

"Have you no hope at all? Do you really think that when you die you die
outright, and nothing remains?"

I said: "Yes."

He dropped his eyes and sat down again. He was truly sorry for me, he
said. It must make life unbearable for a man to think as I did. (P. 147)

But dying is the condition of life: its very meaning derives from the
fact that it requires facing its own extinction. This steadfast intro-
spection allows Camus to alter the tendency of Christian belief. A
century after Dostoevsky, Camus refuses to fill the void beyond
man's misunderstanding with even a name. That void is internalized:
the individual is both empty (bereft of any transcendental promise)
and turned upon himself: Camus's immediate and illusionless man is
a vital tautology, a quivering life rhythmed by its own awareness.

The death of God removes from Camus the either/or that sunders
so many of Dostoevsky's people. But it can achieve neither the serenity of a Zosima nor the madness of an Ivan for whom there are, after
all, two possibilities. But whether void or God, the terrible sense of
an incompleteness is not healed for being internalized: Meursault's
emptiness is never a vacuity. Inadequate attention has been paid to
Camus's own comments on his character, a man whom he describes
simply as being in love with the sun and who "refuses to play the
game." This character, whom so many commentators have seen only
in function of his emptiness, is full indeed: "A passion that is deep

because it is tacit animates him—the passionate desire of the absolute and of truth." And lest anyone mistake what that "truth" might be, Camus spells out its tautological, its sensory, its nonphilosophical definition: "the truth of being and feeling."[15]

Meursault goes to his death, reconciled to its inevitability and its logic, but alive nevertheless—the sense of his life heightened to the last by the final step he takes towards his death:

Almost for the first time in many months I thought of my mother. And now, it seemed to me, I understood why at her life's end she had taken on a "fiancé"; why she'd played at making a fresh start. There, too, in that Home where lives were flickering out, the dusk came as a mournful solace. With death so near, Mother must have felt like someone on the brink of freedom, ready to start life all over again. No one, no one in the world had any right to weep for her. And I, too, felt ready to start life all over again. (Pp. 153–54)

15. Preface to the American edition by Germaine Brée and Carlos Lynes (New York: Appleton, Century, Crofts, 1955).

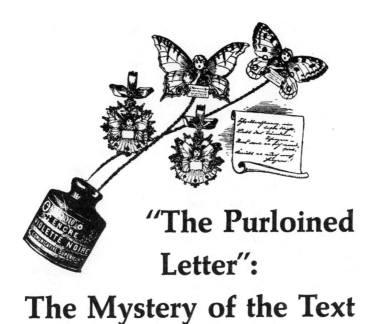

"The Purloined Letter": The Mystery of the Text

Whatever vicissitudes may have affected the recognition of Poe, the English-speaking world has not been inclined to grudge him the paternity of the detective story, a claim that rests on his "tales of ratiocination" and, in particular, the three stories that display the detective intelligence of C. Auguste Dupin—"The Murders in the Rue Morgue," "The Mystery of Marie Rogêt" and "The Purloined Letter."

It is to the first of these that we must go for our most complete presentation of Dupin—Dupin being, as we will have occasion to note later, one of the few characters in these stories who is more than simply functional. He is a young man (Poe himself was thirty-two at the

93

time) of "illustrious" lineage who has been reduced through unspecified misfortune to such poverty that he has "ceased to bestir himself in the world."[1] Drastic though his poverty may be, it is sufficiently genteel for Dupin to be a man of books ("his sole luxuries") whom the narrator meets in an "obscure" Montmartre library—both dilettantes being kindred in their search for the same "very rare and very remarkable volume."

The narrator and Dupin come to share "a time-eaten and grotesque mansion, long deserted through superstitions"; this apartment suits the "fantastic gloom" of their common temper. Inside, their seclusion is "perfect"; it is a shuttered universe within whose twilight they give themselves up to "dreams—reading, writing or conversing" (p. 180), and out of which they escape only at night.

The narrative voice speculates that Dupin is double—"the creative and the resolvent"—the latter personality being the result of "an excited, or perhaps of a diseased intelligence." The first instance of Dupin's resolvent genius shows him able—literally—to *read* his companion's mind from circumstantial evidence. "The Purloined Letter" affords us further insights into Dupin's perspicuity: it is in part psychological (the exemplary analogue is that of the schoolboy who can guess how many marbles another holds in his hand by determining the extent of the marble-holder's cunning) and in part it is due to the fact that he is a *poet*, that is to say someone who can reason from more than finite truths and general applicabilities. In this story, reasoning that is generally applicable suggests that if Minister D-- desired to hide the letter he has stolen, he would conceal it in a manner that would allow the Prefect, whose training and experience derive from the repetition of similar acceptances, to find it. The Prefect makes an erroneous assumption that the marble-collecting schoolboy avoided: the Prefect assumes that all ruses are *loyal*—cunning that is repetitive and does not depart from the expected norm. In Poe's hierarchy of symbolic callings, such low-order cunning is the mathematician's. The Minister who, because he is a villain, cannot be wholly a poet, is nevertheless a worthy opponent of Dupin to the extent of being something more than merely a mathematician ("As poet *and* mathematician, he would reason well; as mere

1. Stuart and Susan Levine, eds., *The Short Fiction of Edgar Allan Poe* (Indianapolis: Bobbs-Merrill, 1976), p. 179. All paginations of the Poe texts refer to this edition.

mathematician, he could not have reasoned at all," p. 232). Minister D-- inverts the usual ruse by turning simple concealment into concealment through display. But Dupin, at the apex of the symbolic pyramid, sees through the Minister's inversion and, for his own benefit, turns the Minister's concealment through display into display pure and simple.

Although Dupin is an astute detective, "The Purloined Letter" is not a satisfactory detective story. We know both too little and too much to enter into the usual agreement that the precarious exisence of the detective story requires.[2] We know from the very start the identity of the culprit—in fact, the culprit is given an importance equal to his crime: both are analyzed together, the definition of either being dependent on the definition of the other. But we know little about the rest of the circumstances. We will never find out what the letter contained; we can only assume the significance of its origination and the nature of its destination. In fact, we know precious little about any of the participants in this event: Dupin himself is a character nearly entirely defined by a tautology—he is the resolvent mind whom we see nearly exclusively in the exercise of his gift.

In her leisurely psychoanalytic study of Poe, Marie Bonaparte suggests that the interest of the detective story (pleasure in the elucidation of a surrogate mystery) can be related to the libido.[3] She outlines the Freudian thesis of the child's sexual fascination as an extension of the erotic pleasure first derived by the infant from oral/anal gratifications. The child soon tries to enlarge these first gratifications through apprehension of the sexual gratification of adults. The child will be twice frustrated by these selfsame adults—his parents— because of their desire to conceal their knowledge: first, within the quasi-secrecy that attempts to hide the act; second, within a similar quasi-secrecy that restricts the child's more abstract sexual education. The effect of these inhibitions is to intensify the child's fascination

2. And in virtue of which, the short story, whether Agatha Christie's or Poe's, is never as satisfactory a detective story as the full-length novel of detection because part of our agreement is *durational*: we agree to maintain our expectation of a solution (we agree to assume that there is a mystery) for a *period of time*; the short story does not quite allow us to do that: it is too close to its own articulation—a puzzle without enough of the fleshing out that is necessary to effect the illusion of a mystery.

3. Marie Bonaparte, *The Life and Works of Edgar Allan Poe*, trans. J. Rodker (New York: Humanities Press, 1971).

with the erotic mystery (in part by turning the erotic into a mystery) and to establish a subconscious ground for the pleasure of the adult, who displaces onto another object the repetition of an infantile sexual investigation, as when, for example, he eagerly follows the tracking by the detective in the mystery story.

The detective story is a poor object for the libido—a reductive surrogate of the kind that would allow the term *libido* to designate, as in Jung, any psychic charge invested in a *tension towards* (analogous to the Sartrian pro-ject). But in detective fiction, even this *tension towards* is feeble since, in addition to being a displacement object for the sexual quest, that fiction is also a displacement object for the mystery it claims to be: the most mysterious detective story can devise only the kind of mystery that contains an immanent resolution.

Though Poe may indeed be the father of the detective story, something of a cavalier attitude towards the special demands of his progeny makes one suspect that he had something else in mind. In "Marie Rogêt," he showed himself to be, like Dupin, a good resolver of a mystery whose main facts were already in the public domain. But in the first of the three stories that were to establish his reputation with reference to the genre—"The Murders in the Rue Morgue"—the reader, literally, does not have a clue: to introduce an orang-outang *ex machina* as the instrument of the crimes is hardly to play fair with the reader. Poe's mystery is of a different order from that of the detective story: the antiseptic nature of the latter is such that its aura as well as its circumstances are dissipated in its resolution. In the "Rue Morgue," Poe contrives so outlandish a resolution that it seems inadequate to dispel the very real metaphysical gloom of the story: Poe's resolvent self is as distinct as Dupin's in its separation from the author's "fantastic gloom."

"The Purloined Letter" does not even attempt to create a "mystery." Here, it is not so much that the clues are inadequate as the fact that Dupin intuits instantly what has happened; his story recounts events with which we are already acquainted: the retrospective narrative demonstrates Dupin's resolvent genius without any uncovering—no formal cover was drawn in the first place. Poe himself distinguished between the mysterious quality of his other stories and the spurious mystery (the mystery that contains its own solution) that the surface of his detective fiction evidences: in an 1846 letter to Philip Pendleton Cook, he asked "Where is the ingenuity of unravelling a web which you yourself [the author] have woven for the express purpose of unravelling?"[4] Poe's awareness of a tautology—the mystery created in order to be uncreated—confirms the suspicion of an Edgar Allen Poe who was relatively indifferent to the temporal riddle that might yield to ingenuity, and confirms, at least by implication, Poe's abiding sense of a human quandary that is less dismissible.

Why then should readers have been less prone than Poe, and for well over a century, to reject these same tales of ratiocination? A part of modern criticism has been tempted to answer that the mystery of other Poe stories, perceived by the reader as a deeper and more intimate cognition than the gothic world within which they are contained, can be found in even the least mysterious of the tales of ratiocination if one accepts that in telling a story an author in fact tells more than one story; that style, however conscious, is still idiosyncratic; that there is a more mysterious weave than the one that allows a mechanical unravelling; and if one agrees, therefore, to locate the mystery in a region situated at mid-distance between the author and his text. The game proposed by "The Purloined Letter" then becomes not so much to follow Dupin's analysis of his own resolvent faculties as to discover through the text whatever else Poe may be telling us, either consciously or subconsciously. The acrobatics of such criticism allow the formulation of more than the average reader might either formulate or wish to have formulated for him, but however audacious those acrobatics, they begin with the tenable assumption that words and their articulation usually mean more than their narrowest intent suggests; poetry, for example, is not conceivable under any other conditions.

Criticism that thus seeks to enlarge Poe's text begins by looking for traces of Poe in his text: if the word betrays more than its intent, it may indeed shift our attention to the author. For Marie Bonaparte, Dupin is the adult Poe avenging through brilliant ratiocination the failure of infantile sexual investigations. Whether or not we wish to follow the psychoanalyst that far into the author's unconscious, the fact remains that Poe invites us to see a central affinity between himself and Dupin once he has made his character represent the Poet.

4. Quoted by J. Brander Matthews, "Poe and the Detective Story," in *The Recognition of Edgar Allan Poe*, ed. Eric W. Carlson (Ann Arbor: University of Michigan Press, 1969), p. 92.

This authorial assertion invites us to pay attention to what might be other hints. The Poet, like the outlaw, is society's outcast; the Prefect (for whom Minister D-- is "not altogether a fool, . . . but then he is a poet, which I take to be only one remove from a fool," p. 228) belongs to that society. There thus develops within the game proposed by Poe a taking of sides in which Poe and Dupin are closer to the Minister than to the Prefect—closer by virtue of being the ones who will variously share in some form of knowledge and deceive others; closer to the darkness of the story than to its reader.

The triad Poe–Dupin–D-- is confirmed by other similarities between Dupin and D--. The story that Poe invents—the theft and concealment of a letter for the purpose of wielding power over the letter's former holder—is enacted by D-- and then, in exactly the same way, by Dupin. The Dupin–D-- link encourages a critic like Richard Wilbur, for the purpose of an allegorical reading, to see D-- as the unprincipled double of Dupin, and the queen whom Dupin frees from D--'s hold "is that sense of beauty which must not be the captive of our lower natures."[5] Commenting on Wilbur's comments, Daniel Hoffman avails himself of the allegorical trampoline to delve further into Poe; Hoffman suggests that "The Purloined Letter" is a disguised love story, one in which this need to preserve beauty inviolate, untouched by physical passion or bodily decay, is compelled by Poe's own "inescapable need to master his own unspeakable secrets."[6] As critics read and reread "The Purloined Letter," the unmysterious short story leads them closer and closer to a mystery within Poe whose darkness overwhelms far more evidently so many of his other tales. This critical strategy alters the nature of, and the relationships implicit in, the original detective story of which Poe is supposed to be the father and thus enlists him in the paternity of a new form of the old genre.

We have had occasion to note the self-destructing nature of the detective story text; it is little more than a prestidigitator's handkerchief used to conceal the operation of something that is known all the while. In due time (and it is never more than a *matter of time*), the "cover" of the text is no longer required, and is removed. It is this

5. Richard Wilbur, "Edgar Allan Poe," in *Major Writers of America*, 2 vols., ed. Perry Miller (New York: Harcourt, Brace & World, 1962): 1:380.

6. Daniel Hoffman, *Poe, Poe, Poe, Poe, Poe, Poe, Poe* (Garden City, N.J.: Doubleday, 1972), p. 136.

innocuous text (innocuous as the story-disclosing text of "The Purloined Letter") that the critic sets out to redeem by making of it something more than a veil over immanent knowledge. The concealment of a letter that Poe devises as a mystery for his fictional detective to uncover contains, as a text, another mystery for the critic-turned-detective. And the fictional and textual concealments work in the same way: through openness; although the queen's letter and what Poe is telling us beyond what his story relates both require "uncovering," neither the fictional letter nor Poe's statement—his letter(s)—are in fact covered; both are in plain sight.

The question of who sees what has always been central to the detective story. Of necessity, the criminal sees nearly everything that is connected with the scene of the crime. Traditionally, the detective gradually comes to see as much as the criminal, and, additionally, his sight "takes in" the criminal and the "insignificant," but all-important, details that have escaped the criminal. Only the reader is not allowed to see as clearly—at least not for the duration of an interval (the time it takes to read the detective story) during which his knowledge will be held in *suspense* as an *expectation*. Thus the detective is traditionally an "eye" in a story about acuities of seeing. Further, he is a "private" eye inasmuch as his sight is his alone—he is not a member of a collective group with special powers of acuity. The tradition that begins with Poe generally accepts that the power of sight of the "private eye" is better than the collective eye of the official police; Dupin *sees* just about as clearly as the author, whereas the Prefect sees little indeed, even though the analysis of his "looking" is impressive in its variety and thoroughness.

But Dupin is of course a private eye *avant la lettre* as well. As Poet, he is endowed with special gifts of sight defined by an exceptional *range* of vision, mental perception, judgment, and, moreover, a power of sight beyond the range of sight—*insight*—an intuition that transcends the usual limits of perception. Dupin's modest self-appraisal as a maker of doggerel is, in fact, a reference to an abnormal intelligence, the euphemistic description of which is that it is perhaps "diseased": in any event, its powers extend considerably beyond mere ratiocination. It is the Poet who dwells in a frightful mansion, long deserted because of the superstitions of others. It is not that the Poet's "fantastic gloom" is less superstitious; but the Poet's superstition is an expectation and an understanding of the supernatural rather than a fear. The more common mortal, who leaves the mansion deserted because his lack of understanding is replaced by fear, is the evidence of a common, second-rate mind. And in the commonplace world where mental faculties are measured by mathematical criteria, the Poet, whose faculties extend into the supernatural, is more than a match for any other ratiocinator.

The private eye of the Poet is exceedingly private. His dwelling is closed to other men, defined as lesser in comparison, and their world. The Poet's dwelling is, in fact, no more than his private vision, shuttered against even the sun that makes possible the vision of others; if ever he leaves his private domain, it is at night, when other men cede him the city as well and darkness hides the evidence of their traces. This closure allows him to inform his world totally: a world of "dreams—reading, writing or conversing"—the world of the Poet, the world of the book.

It is at the point where a private vision and a "text" coincide that the psychoanalyst enters. When the text is Poe's, the psychoanalyst may be drawn in for biographical reasons that are fairly obvious: young Edgar Allan was marked, in the words of Patrick F. Quinn, by "an infantile oedipal experience of great intensity. Love for his sickly, dying, and finally dead mother became a kind of protean matrix which shaped the pattern of his life, and the recurrent themes of his tales [and] poems."[7] When the particular text has been turned into a fulfilling projection of Poe the universal solver of riddles,[8] and of Poe the theorist of revenge,[9] and when additionally Poe's text presents the more innocent face of a detective story, the psychoanalyst finds

---

7. Patrick F. Quinn, "The French Response to Poe," in *Poe: A Collection of Critical Essays*, ed. Robert Regan (Englewood Cliffs, N.J.: Prentice-Hall, 1967), pp. 73–74.

8. There is a mundane side to Poe that is fascinated by less than the Poet's connection with the supernatural; Poe is also fascinated by a world of practical jokes and mental legerdemain: "He was fond of aliases; he delighted in accounts of swindles; he perpetrated the famous Balloon Hoax of 1844; and one of his most characteristic stories is entitled 'Mystification.'" (Richard Wilbur, "The House of Poe," in Regan, *Poe*, p. 99).

9. Daniel Hoffman reminds us about the concern for revenge that preludes "The Cask of Amontillado," and that, "in his *Marginalia*, years later, Poe had mused, 'What can be more soothing, at once to a man's Pride and to his Conscience, than the conviction that, in taking vengeance on his enemies for injustice done him, he is simply to do them *justice* in return?'" (*Poe, Poe, Poe*, p. 134.)

himself in what seems to be a familiar situation. Like a patient's "text," Poe's detective story offers a text that contains and disguises him, that requires and refuses elucidation. The psychoanalyst is aware that, as fiction, Poe's detective story evidences only the spurious mystery of the genre: the author is not a genuine patient since he voluntarily discloses his ruse at the end. But the analyst, prepared as he is to accept that every text is double, is sensitive to the fact that this textual elucidation (the solution of a fictional problem proposed by the fiction) is concerned with the elucidation of a text (the problem of how to read *through* the surface of texts): the termination of a problem derived from the nature of problems terminates the statement without terminating the concern that impelled the statement. Poe locates "The Purloined Letter" in a world of books that, for him, extends mystery beyond that of superable conundrums: his fiction that resolves a resolvable mystery does so as a text which, that very text tells us, the Poet views as the natural repository of deeper mysteries in a world that is as dark and distilled as the essence of the books that inform it, whose tenants meet in bookstores that are "obscure" (most likely in both senses of the word—*dark* as should properly be the *esoteric*) in search of a "rare" and "remarkable" book. (It should be remembered that "The Purloined Letter" begins, and is presumably related, in Dupin's "little back library, or book-closet," p. 226.)

The psychoanalyst who, like Freud himself, has by now become a close reader of texts—a textual analyst—is further aware that even though Poe duplicates and falsifies the psychoanalytical couch through the contrivance of a detective story that proposes and disguises the fictional author, there is also to be found in this detective text a disguise of the author that the author himself does not know about. The spurious mystery, which a part of Poe sees as a genuine mystery, contains, on the level where Poe intuits the ultimate irresolubleness of texts, a mystery that must perforce escape his own grasp. A psychoanalyst like Marie Bonaparte is interested primarily in Poe and therefore in the unconscious statement within his fiction. She notes, for example, the repeated presence of a chimney in the Dupin stories. In the "Rue Morgue," she infers that since the room of the crimes represents the body of the mother, the chimney becomes vaginal through a not uncommon symbolic disguise; it is in this chimney that, psycho-logically enough, the body of the daughter is found, wedged as in a uterine canal, head down. There is a similarly central chimney in "The Purloined Letter," in the midst of which the letter, dangling from a clitoral knob, turns the contest between Dupin and D-- into an Oedipal struggle for the mother—or for at least a part of her.

But a psychoanalyst like Jacques Lacan is willing to grant Poe greater authorial (conscious) control over his text.[10] This willingness derives from Lacan's desire to use the text's fictional events as evidence for what he terms the insistence of the signifying chain. Lacan's investigation of the text is, in fact, an investigation of the repetition compulsion, which he turns into a running argument intended to reinterpret the Freudian assumption. In so doing, Lacan extends and projects himself into the specular complexity of Poe's text seen as an argument that, as object, demonstrates the validity of its speculation.

It is this preliminary readiness of Lacan to allow that the author constructs consciously at least as much as he does unconsciously that enables him to accept in the detective story the three levels of textual reading to which we have already referred: the deciphering of a fictional text by the fictional characters; the deciphering of the text that bespeaks the fictional deciphering for evidence of another, conscious message; and finally, as is the case with Marie Bonaparte, the deciphering by the psychoanalyst of a message that Poe did not intend consciously. Lacan relates these three kinds of perception to levels of sight and insight that correspond to the fictional behavior of the story's characters. The king and the police see nothing; the queen, and later D--, when he comes to assume a queenlike role, see, thinking erroneously that they are not seen seeing; and lastly, Dupin, whose sight possesses all—those who do not see as well as those who delude themselves in the thought that their glance controls. The intersubjective relationships of the characters shift them through these various levels—or, to use Lacan's words, the characters model their being on the moment of the signifying chain that traverses them. Their trajectory through the roles they assume is always downward, to a level of greater jeopardy; Lacan comments that as the letter falls into their possession, they are possessed by its significance.

10. We are concerned here with the first part of the "Seminar on 'The Purloined Letter,'" originally translated into English by Jeffrey Mehlman in *Yale French Studies*, no. 48, (1972), pp. 39–72.

In order for the letter to affect those connected with it, it must be slowed down in its trajectory; the letter (of the text) must be read more closely by the analyst; the letter in the fiction must be delayed in its course. For this to take place, Lacan avails himself of what he interprets as certain injunctions by Poe to read the text closely.[11] This scrutiny begins with the title: Lacan questions just how Poe's fictional letter is "purloined" since, if it has been "stolen" at all, it has been only in a special way, by a number of people, and, therefore, for never more than during short intervals that limit the significance of the word. Lacan notes that "to purloin" is a strange verb—an Anglo-French word composed of the prefix *pur* and the old French *loing* in which are recognizable the Latin *pro* ("away") and *longē* ("long"): a letter that has been *purloined* is thus one whose trajectory has been pro-longed; there is ultimately not theft here, but delay. The letter is temporarily *put aside* (according to a meaning that still exists in the archaic form "to eloign") long enough (the time it takes for the story to unfold) for the characters to play out their intersubjective roles.

Thus, like more than the incriminating document it actually is, the letter as signifier begins affecting those into whose grasp it falls, in conformity with certain Freudian concepts of repetition that Lacan refers to and amends. The queen loses her regal definition when she must resort to open concealment of the letter (the letter is exposed but the side with its incriminating content is turned face down) the moment she and it fall within the acute glance of D-- and within the blind but controlling sight of the king. Lacan views the act of concealment as peculiarly female; it is a female act in this particular case since it is a woman (the queen) who is hiding an incriminating document from a man, the king. However, when the letter falls within the possession of D--, he will not only revert to a form of open concealment that is similar to the queen's, he will also begin turning into a female. After first affecting a langorous pose of boredom before

11. It would certainly not strain the text to read Dupin's disquisition on *analysis* in that way: "If words derive any value from applicability—then 'analysis' conveys 'algebra' about as much as, in Latin, '*ambitus*' implies 'ambition,' '*religio*' 'religion,' or '*homines honesti*,' a set of *honourable* men" (p. 232). Since Poe is not speaking here about Latin but about English derivatives whose meanings have been altered slightly with the passing of time, he appears to be engaged in a philological exercise the point of which has something to do with the precise usage of words.

Dupin, he effects the details of the letter's concealment in a peculiar and interesting way. Minister D-- has once again *inverted* the letter (letters, at the time, were like our present air mail forms, a single sheet of which only one side was used for the writing of the letter that was then folded twice and sealed, with the address written on the other, blank, side). This address D-- has rewritten in a "diminutive and feminine" hand (p. 235). Lacan, close reader that he is, notes that D-- further accepts this assumption of femininity by, literally, placing his stamp on it: for reasons that are not otherwise readily understandable, the Minister has replaced the broken seal *with his own*: "The seal was large and black, with the D-- cipher" (p. 235)—an unconscious pun on the part of Poe?—this incriminating initial seems to be for the sole purpose of identifying D-- with the feminine hand: Dupin certainly does not use it as the obvious and immediate *identification of the thief* that it otherwise is. Lacan's exegesis affords an identification that refers to a submerged psychology of the character, the psychology of a character appearing in a story that is not overtly told by its author: the psychoanalyst is seen here in the process of conjuring a phantasm that has no more substance than the other fictional characters but that derives its reality from the indubitableness of its author.

At this point, the psychoanalyst has reentered the story. Within the *odor di femina* that now suffuses the office of D--, the letter is as plainly visible for him as it is for Dupin, in the center of the open, genital chimney where both he and Poe have placed it in readiness for the final rape of analysis. "The Purloined Letter," which Lacan was pleased to show not to be simply Baudelaire's "Lettre volée," (Baudelaire's title for his translation of the Poe story) has now become the "lettre violée."

Lacan thus explodes into new dimensions (that ultimately involve him) the possibilities offered by Poe in the writing of a detective story that comments on detection and places both the fiction and the comment within the world of the text. Lacan, aware that both author and patient communicate and disguise through words, knows that Poe's fictional letter is more than simply the fiction of a disguise. The letter that is both hidden and revealed, sought as mask and as elucidation, provides the substance of the fiction together with the comment on implications of that fiction, even as for the analyst it emerges as an *object*—an *instance* of what it is commenting on. The text of the letter that no one in the fiction ever reads and that is known only by its superscriptions, never its addressor or its content, is of course an emblem for the shadowy author sending intentional messages through a letter that he never wrote (what we have referred to as the second level of deciphering). But in the writing that surrounds and shapes the void of the letter, other messages appear, the margin providing for the analyst a comment that informs the blank letter it frames.

Within this *absence* of the letter (this "purloining," if you will) there appears another letter of interest to a certain kind of analyst—the typographical character, perhaps, a symbol intended to convey (part of) a specific meaning. Or it may be the epistolary intent—the intent of a personal disclosure. Or it may refer to a "man of letters," representing the more complex strategy of the author who uses these symbols. Following Saussure, Lacan notes that in any event (and all three enter into the making of "The Purloined Letter") the concept is never partitive: you cannot offer it, as you might a canapé, by saying "have some letter," since it exists only as the aforementioned absence (Saussure called it a difference without the positive terms between which difference is located), "which is why," Lacan tells us, "we cannot say of the purloined letter that, like other objects, it must be *or* not be in a particular place but that unlike them it will be *and* not be where it is, wherever it goes."[12] This absence that *is* and *is not*, that speaks through the several ways in which it *says* as well as through its refusal to say, is of course language—a defining mark of the human species and an instance of the human quandary. Returning to questions of language, we return to our point of departure, having talked around something that we can know only as a void and through our avoidance; having, like the textual margin of the missing letter, talked it *into* being through our circumlocution.

As one might expect of a "man of letters," words play an important part in Poe's world and remain conscious objects of his fiction. His tales of detection revert, sooner or later, to the detection of words—whether in the scrutiny of newspaper accounts that were analyzed (and satirized) in the writing of "Marie Rogêt," or in the inner ear of Dupin, which "hears" those hearing the words of foreign suspects in the "Rue Morgue." The way in which a writer uses his words has

12. Lacan, "Seminar," p. 54.

always been a logical and legitimate aspect of literary investigation. The modern critic is different only in that he appears *after* texts have lost their innocence. Not that texts were ever quite innocent: the word is awesome in its power to represent and overrepresent the conjuring of its users, as we have seen; but that it can work a catalytic effect on its percipient is no less awesome. The symbolic letter that brings into being the shadow of a landscape, an event, or a person, effects a feebler catalysis: that landscape, event, or person is, after all, only a shadow. But if it effects a puzzlement within the reader, it is no longer a shadow that is created but the reality of an activity. Paradoxically, the spurious detective story, with its transparent characters, enters the reader as more of a reality than does the character of a more epical fiction since it enters that reader as his stance, his expectation, his bafflement. It is hardly surprising that the psychoanalyst finds less to say about the novel that offers him "full" characters than he does about the fiction that suggests only a trajectory of shadows: it is that trajectory that he is able to inform wih the reality of his own puzzling.

The void at the center of Poe's story has the density of the reader's sense of it, and that sense is of a reality, not a fiction: the "missing" letter is real. Dupin does not exist, but the Dupin "activated" in the reader does. If, additionally, that Dupin questions his own being in relation to the text of which he is a part, the reader finds himself in a position of unexpected self-consciousness. The psychoanalyst who then puzzles out the text according to his specialized insight exhumes an even fuller reality of the character in his own person. The process entraps the analyst within the intersubjective chain to which he has just given his existential dimension. A captive of his text, Lacan is possessed by the significance of the letter no less than the queen or Minister D--, and like them, he in turn descends to a level of increased jeopardy: his own text discloses the reality of a hithertho "fictional" text, but it now reveals as well what he might not know he is concealing. The compulsion of repetition continues beyond the fiction that first evidenced it.

The average reader does not descend as deeply, but to say that these analytic processes are too far-fetched to concern him would require explaining in some other way the secret hold that still attaches him to a tale whose surface Poe himself dismissed long ago.

That surface belonged to the fiction of mystery; the words that disclose the mystery of this fiction dissipate the fiction, but they also contain the real mystery, *the mystery of fiction* that conceals several truths, some of which, like mystery itself, cannot be contained, not even by the fiction.

Pirandello: The
Mask as Evidence and Limit

Freud has examined the masochistic nature of some of our rehearsals, as evidenced for example by tragedy—our willingness to rehearse in the theater our most somber sense of downfall and destruction. This compulsion (it is more than merely a willingness) to repeat our deepest and defining trauma is, in fact, an important affirmation through which we assert our collective birth and solemnly begin to read, once again, the history of the race. The religious and dramatic expression of this compulsion, as in *Oedipus the King*, can thus contemplate only the rehearsal, the reiteration of a sense of ourselves that we have already. That reiteration is its own virtue: it does not propose to convey the rehearser beyond an intensification of his own awareness. Even though we assert our collective birth, we do not dispel its mystery.

The curative reiteration that Freud proposes for psychoanalysis is different: it is the reappropriation of a realm only partially lost—one that is far away (in the past) but attainable. Because Freud proposes penetration of, and passage through, our encircling darkness to an *accessible* place, he reads *Oedipus* knowing what Oedipus cannot know. But Oedipus, and the spectator who contemplates his effigy, can only enact the circularity of a ritual that traces the mystery's impenetrable limits.

It is necessary to specify again just how the Greek spectator *observes the ritual*. That spectator does not *see* Oedipus as intently as he *hears himself*, even though the voice of Oedipus is far more resonant than his own and his stature is greater. The Oedipal drama unfolds, in many ways, *within* the spectator. It lays open to view what has been laid open countless times before; the spectator is already possessed of the awareness the drama intensifies. But as ritual, the drama also comforts: it rhythms the completeness of an action and offers that completeness as containment for the spectator's malaise. Therefore, his cothurni and his tragic mask notwithstanding, the actual figure of Oedipus is little more than a sounding board that enhances the tragic tone, allowing it to echo more deeply within the spectator. But it derives its resonance from the emptiness it masks: the actual figure of Oedipus is an absence.

It is this eventual return of the spectator to himself, his information of symbol with self, that most clearly shows the participatory nature of ritual and drama that is, in fact, ritual: the action on the stage achieves its full dimension only in its assimilation by the participant; his "participation" is a symbiotic union through which he gives his dimension to an empty form while at the same time the form into which he projects himself affects the sense he has of himself. This "spectator" must be a *believer* since it is only his belief that enables him to inform the otherwise empty shapes on his stage. At the end of an age of faith, this believer-participant becomes a *spectator*: distance and objectivity separate him progressively from a stage that he is less willing to people, less willing to believe in. At this moment, *observing the ritual* takes on a different meaning, one that accounts for the space the spectator has now placed between himself and the dramatic action.

One might assume that with the loss of such a stage are lost as well the traditional themes of tragedy, since all refractory and fundamental questions (among which, that of mystery) would not be ones from which the spectator could separate himself—precisely because these questions remain fundamental and refractory. I will argue here, as elsewhere, that it is not so much the themes that are lost as their forms—that the very containment of tragic drama offers comforting evidence that is not compatible with the "openness" of a tragic sense (just as the containment and continuity offered by ritual, even as it describes a tragic state, contradicts that state which is perceived through a sense of disjunction and finality).[1]

Still another kind of transcendency is achieved by the absolute nature of the art form whose completeness contradicts, and may therefore alleviate, a metaphysical disquietude. Complete unto itself, that form shares in other manners of the absolute, suggesting totality, plenitude, purity—which are also attributes of truth. Moreover, that all-containing completeness contrasts absolutely with the partial world of our perceived experience and comes to stand for truth once again inasmuch as we define truth as a fundamental reality that is separate from the analysis of an incomplete perception. In an age that sets greater store by analysis than absolutes, the work of art seeks other justifications: it finds them ultimately in a phenomenology that displaces truth in favor of authenticity.

The theater is admirably suited to this kind of phenomenological assertion since it is at once an object (a tangibility made of a stage, stage properties, living actors) and its own *doubling* (in Artaud's sense) through something else which it is not. The stage is both preeminently a visible place and a place of mystery: in its simplest form, it appears as nearly a physical emblem for the metaphysical definition of mystery. Perhaps in part for this reason, the tangible presence of the stage has frequently shaped the form and affected the content of metaphysical plays for as long as there have been stages— one thinks of Shakespeare's *Hamlet*, Rotrou's *Saint Genest*, Corneille's *Comic Illusion*, Calderon's *Life Is a Dream*. But starting with Pirandello, there is a more deliberate attempt to turn the material stage into a part of the dramatist's statement, a more systematic reliance on the

---

1. This contradiction is presumably the main object of ritual, and perhaps of the tragic catharsis as well.

physical assertion of the boards rather than on words from which the metaphysical bashfulness of modern authors shies.

Pirandello was acutely aware of the shadows beyond the limits of human understanding. He believed in, and revolted against, an absurd "fate which condemns man to illusion."[2] For a writer who had seen his wife sink into madness until, after nearly twenty-five years of marriage, she had to be committed, the stage as evidence and possible representation of the darkness beyond our grasp must have been especially compelling. And on the stage of such a writer, the Oedipal tension towards a truth forever secreted within those shadows must have appeared to be a defining tendency.

Coming after the kind of drama that could elevate this human propensity by ascribing it to princes who were able to confront directly their individual gods, Pirandello found an equally acute awareness of the unknown where it had begun before its dramatic amplification—upon the more modest stage of an individual perplexity. Since the writer Pirandello was himself affected by that perplexity, the very attempt to give it the form of his art also became a speculation on the possibility and the limits of art to be the expression of a private awareness—another instance of the limitations that hem us in. In Pirandello's interpretation of the Pygmalion story (*Diana and Tuda*, 1926), the sculptor Giuncano destroys the unaging and serene statues he once created because they mock his own aging and deny the life he had infused in them. Giuncano eventually kills his young sculptor friend Sirio who has begun the cycle anew: Sirio has sacrificed the life of Tuda, whom he married only that he might preserve her as a model and so immortalize the shape of her suffering.

Diana and Tuda does not end as simply a statement of the impossibility to make *form* live: the idea is caught up in the complex forces of the dramatic process itself. Pirandello wrote the play for his own Tuda, the actress Marta Abba, his stage becoming, like Sirio's sculpture, an attempt to preserve within the work of art the Hegelian power of life as a becoming in a way that the inert and unmoving sculpture could not.[3] What Pirandello saw upon the living stage was an *action*,

2. Quoted by Guy Dumur, *Le Théâtre de Pirandello* (Paris: L'Arche, 1967), p. 46, n. 1.

3. As elsewhere, Pirandello's dialogue extends a private monologue that preceded it—in this case, a genuine obsession with the fixed quality of statues; Magda Martini quotes the text of an interview in which Pirandello remarked, "I

a phenomenological event (living people within an actual space): for
him, the stage was the rare instance of a form suffused with actual
life.[4]

Constrained by the objective dimensions of this stage, the Oedipal
quest would become the attempt of a man to decipher *surfaces* behind which an important truth hides, and the *stage* upon which this
action took place would in turn offer surfaces to be similarly deciphered by the spectator. We have said already that when Oedipus
appears on the stage of Sophocles, the mystery of which he speaks
is contained within the ritual that gives the mystery its form: the
performance allows the spectator to rehearse the feeling he has of
his own incompleteness, but that performance also heals the wound
of which it reminds the spectator through a simultaneous feeling
of completeness within the containing ritual and the sense of continuity that its repetition affords. On Pirandello's stage, the dramatic
performance is an evidence, an experience of limits even before a
concern about limits has been stated. The mysterious "doubling" of
any stage action, of any actor (the objective world of the stage that
is there and yet is, at the same time, *more* than what-is-there), ac-
tualizes words spoken by the actors about the nature of mystery—
which mystery may well be that of the stage itself as an emblem of
the metaphysical mystery.

Determining what constitutes a human identity, as in *It Is So (If
You Think So)* (1917) or *Henry IV* (1922), can thus become in a play
about theater the experience of the form that states the question.
Three such plays by Pirandello (*Six Characters in Search of an
Author*, 1921; *Each in His Own Way*, 1924; *Tonight We Improvise*,
1928) extend the difficulty of grasping the mystery of personality:
trying to perceive the reality of another, in a theater that stresses

---

would feel like saying to [Michelangelo's *Moses*], 'But why do you always hold
your beard with that hand? Hold it with the other once in a while' " (*Pirandello,
ou Le Philosophe de l'absolu* [Geneva: Labor et Fides, 1969], p. 148).

4. Pirandello's phenomenology of the stage begins with his sense of the
"fixity" of other art forms. Even as fixed form, the play in its performance is
alive and in motion, and as such facilitates the Hegelian integration of the work
of art. The point is referred to frequently in Pirandello's esthetics and is given
to many of his fictional spokesmen; it is especially frequent in *Tonight We Improvise*, where Hinkfuss articulates the thought at some length even before the
curtain rises: "If a work of art survives, it is only because we are able to release
it from its fixity—because we are able to loose that form within us in a vital act."

consciously the fact that it is part actuality, part fiction, becomes a probe of the extent to which it is possible to give *life* to the *idea* of form and life, the possibility of existential assertion, the relativism of perception and understanding. The power of this tautological experiment has not been underestimated: critics are in general agreement with Robert Brustein that "Pirandello's influence on the drama of the twentieth century is immeasurable."[5]

Of Pirandello's experimental trilogy about the stage, the play that has sustained the greatest amount of critical discussion is his *Six Characters*. As Georges Neveux noted, "The entire theater of our era came out of the womb of that play."[6] The dramatis personae are divided into two groups—the *actors* who are rehearsing Pirandello's play, *The Rules of the Game* (1918), and the *characters* who interrupt them by imposing on the stage what is termed a *commedia da fare*, a play in the *process* of being made. This division suggests various kinds of becoming: the Pirandello that is being rehearsed has not yet achieved the form it would have in its "representation." And, more importantly, the "characters" who sweep that rehearsal aside are part of a tentative unfolding, a process as new to them as it is to the spectators (on both sides of the footlights) observing them. *In fact*, the play in all of its parts is as fixed and complete as any other. The *commedia da fare* is already fully written. Its "unfolding" could occur only once—as Pirandello was in the process of writing it. For all others, it is part of a ritualistic repetition that only mimes an unfolding: even the spectator who sees the play for the first time is aware that the development he witnesses proceeds according to a prescription that is already complete.

It is this intuition of completeness that the *commedia da fare* resists. Since for Pirandello, at the moment of writing, the play has not yet turned into a fiction, and as he is fascinated by the moment

5. Robert S. Brustein, "Pirandello's Drama of Revolt," in *The Theatre of Revolt* (Boston: Atlantic, Little, Brown, 1964). Reprinted in Glauco Cambon, *Pirandello: A Collection of Critical Essays* (Englewood Cliffs, N.J.: Prentice-Hall, 1967), p. 133.

6. Georges Neveux, "Pirandello's Influence on French Drama," in Thomas Bishop, *Pirandello and the French Theater* (New York: New York University Press, 1960). Reprinted in Cambon, *Pirandello*, p. 64.

when the existential act of creation becomes the inanimate form,[7] he insistently represents his creative process as an *encounter*. In a 1904 letter to Luigi Natoli, he writes about the "importuning" of his characters as they solicit him. In "The Tragedy of a Character" ("La Tragedia d'un personaggio," in the collection *La Trappola*, 1913), he describes the necessity for the author to set aside each week a day to converse with the characters that force their way upon him. In the preface to *Six Characters*, written in 1925 (four years after the play itself), he recalls a maidservant, fantasy, "bringing to my house . . . the most disgruntled tribe in the world, men, women, children, involved in strange adventures," and, among these people, the very family of *Six Characters*. For Pirandello, the initial moment in the creative process asserts itself as surprise—an external object imposes itself upon the writer; he does not secrete that object. If he is up to his craft, his purpose as an author must be to preserve as best he can that irruptive force in his creation: his characters must strike the spectator as they first struck him.

The *commedia da fare*, a lie within the prescriptive ritual of the theater, is the truth of an action that began before the play, within the private world of the playwright. The "characters" of *Six Characters* are aware of the manner in which they first confronted the author, full-grown and separate; the Father tells the stage manager:

Our reality doesn't change: it can't change! It can't be other than what it is, because it is already fixed for ever. It's terrible. Ours is an immutable reality

7. Adriano Tilgher was the first to draw wide attention to this aspect of Pirandello's work, which he considered central (*Studi sul teatro contemporaneo* [Rome: Libreria di Scienze e Lettere, 1923]. The chapter to which we refer, "Life Versus Form," is reprinted in Cambon, *Pirandello*, pp. 19–34). But the problem of life versus form, or rather, the exacerbated intensity of the attempt to grasp the moment when the first turns into the second, is only one of the questions at the limit of human understanding through which the thought and the fiction of a modern scholasticism attempt to penetrate the mystery of the human condition (see Dostoevsky and the confrontation of the ideas of God and mystery; Camus and thought on the absurd limits of thought; or, as we shall see, Borges and the specular labyrinth that bends questioning back upon itself; etc.). To these might be added thinkers like Georges Bataille or Jacques Derrida examining aspects of a quandary that derives from the contradiction of the "closed" nature of any possession, explanation, or *écriture*, and the necessarily open "structurality" of the human situation. It is not so much the questions that are new as the exacerbation of the questioning that derives from the inhuman narrowing of the question.

which should make you shudder when you approach us if you are really conscious of the fact that your reality is a mere transitory and fleeting illusion, taking this form today and that tomorrow, according to the conditions, according to your will, your sentiments, which in turn are controlled by an intellect that shows to you today in one manner and tomorrow . . . who knows how?[8]

The fiction of the Father's speech is dissipated in the reminiscence of Pirandello.

Likewise, the "defiance" of the characters who resist fictional assimilation is a fact of the creative process as Pirandello knows it:

[. . . *the* Step-Daughter, *though she has her hand to her mouth, cannot keep from laughing.*]

Leading Lady [*indignant*]. I'm not going to stop here to be made a fool of by that woman there.

Leading Man. Neither am I! I'm through with it!

The Manager [*shouting to* Step-Daughter]. Silence! For once and all, I tell you!

The Step-Daughter. Forgive me! Forgive me!

The Manager. You haven't any manners: that's what it is! You go too far.

The Father [*endeavoring to intervene*]. Yes, it's true, but excuse her . . .

The Manager. Excuse what? It's absolutely disgusting.

The Father. Yes, sir, but believe me, it has such a strange effect when . . .

The Manager. Strange? Why strange? Where is it strange?

The Father. No, sir; I admire your actors—this gentleman here, this lady; but they are certainly not us!

The Manager. I should hope not. Evidently they cannot be you, if they are actors.

The Father. Just so: actors! Both of them act out our parts exceedingly well. But, believe me, it produces quite a different effect on us. They want to be us, but they aren't, all the same . . .

The Manager. What is it then anyway?

The Father. Something that is . . . that is theirs—and no longer ours . . .
   (Pp. 256–57)

---

8. *Naked Masks*, ed. Eric Bentley (New York: E. P. Dutton, 1952), p. 266. This "English version" by Edward Storer requires the same cautionary note as do all other English versions of Pirandello's plays (see note 10 to this chapter). This quotation is from the translation's "Act III" even though Storer has given us Pirandello's nota bene at the start of the play that specifies "The Comedy is without acts or scenes." All quotations from Pirandello's texts, unless noted otherwise, are from this edition.

The "characters" do not owe their "truth" to the accuracy of personal traits that they "embody," but to the authenticity of their *manner of being* as fiction: they are, and must be sensed to be, a *resistance*. Nor is the truth of their action to be found in the story they enact: that truth is in the event that states the tentativeness of the author prior to the moment when the trajectory of his characters is complete; the action of the characters must be seen primarily as the act of the author authoring.

Having vouched personally for the antecedent existence of his characters, Pirandello faces the task of making that antecedence manifest on his stage. As an instance of that hinge-moment when life becomes form, the Pirandellian character depends for his survival on the duality of a stage where reality and irreality merge. As part of the irreality of the stage (its fiction), the characters *speak* the problem, in the traditional manner of the *raisonneur*: we have seen how the Father articulates the problem of the character's fixity within the single possibility of his role—a dilemma that Sartre's people in the hell of *No Exit* (1944) will articulate anew for the sake of a different emphasis. Meanwhile, the fictional actors in the fictional part of the play assume the role of (the) spectators.

The Mother [*to the* Manager, *in anguish*]. In the name of these two little
    children, I beg you . . . [*She grows faint and is about to fall.*] Oh God!
The Father [*coming forward to support her as do some of the* Actors.]
    Quick, a chair, a chair for this poor widow!
The Actors. Is it true? Has she really fainted?
The Manager. Quick, a chair! Here!
[*One of the* Actors *brings a chair, the* Others *proffer assistance. The* Mother
    tries to prevent the Father *from lifting the veil which covers her face.*]
The Father. Look at her! Look at her!
The Mother. No, no; stop it please! (P. 220)

The "actors," positioned midway between the "characters" and the spectator, voice what should be perplexities of the spectator—his difficulty in determining whether the stage action belongs to the fictional or the parafictional part of the stage ("Has she really fainted?") or his difficulty in perceiving the actors behind veils that Pirandello will deliberately multiply. The pretense of the actors is that they perform within the open-ended situation in which Pirandello wants his spectator to be; that they are not the creatures of an immutable text but participants in an event that has not occurred before:

Leading Man. It's absolutely unheard of. If the stage has come to this . . . well I'm . . .

Fifth Actor. It's rather a joke.

Third Actor. Well, we'll see what's going to happen next. (P. 237)

The *raisonneur* Father has other awarenesses. As a "fiction," he knows that his "reality" is not in him but in the spectator. This knowledge allows him to turn into a like fiction others on stage who are less knowledgeable:

The Father. Now, if you consider the fact that we [*Indicates himself and the other five* Characters], as we are, have no other reality outside of this illusion . . .

The Manager [*astonished, looking at his* Actors, *who are also amazed*]. And what does that mean?

The Father [*after watching them for a moment with a wan smile*]. As I say, sir, that which is a game of art for you is our sole reality. [*Brief pause. He goes a step or two nearer the* Manager *and adds.*] But not only for us, you know, by the way. Just you think it over as well. [*Looks him in the eyes.*] Can you tell me who you are?

The Manager [*perplexed, half smiling*]. What? Who am I? I am myself.

The Father. And if I were to tell you that that isn't true, because you and I . . . ?

The Manager. I should say you were mad—! [*The* Actors *laugh.*]

The Father. You're quite right to laugh: because we are all making believe here. (P. 264)

But even that appropriation by the spectator is problematic, depending as it does on a private interiority that does not extend from one spectator to another: "The drama lies all in this—in the conscience that I have, that each one of us has. We believe this conscience to be a single thing, but it is many-sided. There is one for this person, and another for that. Diverse consciences. So we have this illusion of being one person for all, or having a personality that is unique in all our acts. But it isn't true" (p. 231).[9] And the words refer also to a

9. A few years later, Artaud locates the drama's reality principle in the same place—with the spectator: "The theater will never find itself again—i.e., constitute a means of true illusion—except by furnishing the spectator with the truthful precipitates of dreams, in which his taste for crime, his erotic obsessions, his savagery, his chimeras, his utopian sense of life and matter, even his cannibalism, pour out on a level neither counterfeit nor illusory, but interior" ("The Theater of Cruelty," First Manifesto. Reprinted in *The Theater and Its Double*, trans. M. C. Richards [New York: Grove Press, 1958], p. 92). But Artaud does not

problem connected with the esthetics of this stage: the multiplicity of spectators within each of whom each character "lives" contrasts with the rigidity of the stage character to which the Father will also refer (p. 266). This opposition is a suggestion of the phenomenology that Pirandello intends to stress in emphasizing the *thingness* of the fixed "characters" on stage.

The fiction enacted in *Six Characters* is, as that in *Oedipus the King*, incest. Today we would say near-incest: the Father has nearly seduced his Step-Daughter in Madame Pace's trysting shop. In 1921, in a less shockproof age, and in a Catholic country that did not recognize divorce, such disclaimers must have been less adequate to dispel the spectator's sense of uneasiness. But Pirandello's modernity consists in a synesthesia that will achieve this sense of uneasiness through another, and less mental, uneasiness. In writing his own play about incest and death, Pirandello remembers that the Oedipal myth is also about the act of seeing and that the theater alters the privacy of a secret contemplation through public display. In order to *display* the consequences of incest, Pirandello will choose to display the stage actor and the stage: like his dramatic comment (the "dialogue"), which he restricts to what gives the comment its dramatic form, Pirandello's dramatic action (the "idea") will be perceptible through the spectator's awareness of his own percipience.

While still within their respective fictions, the actors speak of themselves as actors, reducing a first layer of fiction since they are in fact the reality to which they refer: the "characters" are forever the playback moments of a domestic tragedy; the "actors" who observe them are ready to copy their roles in a copy of that tragedy, their authenticity as actors having been vouched for from the start when they were seen "rehearsing" an actual play by an actual author, Pirandello—that play, first performed only three years before *Six Characters*, being still in the public eye. Pirandello's reference to himself and the inclusion of his play are more than simply further parafictional references: they confirm that this is a discussion in, and about, the theater, and they open the stage further to the private speculations of the author on the creative process; the play's ante-

---

feel that the spectator's appropriation of the stage is as problematic as does Pirandello: Artaud is more concerned with the stage, less with the percipience of the spectator.

cedent life within Pirandello, to which the author attached such great importance, becomes a significant part of the play after its birth.

But this use of the actor to introduce an element of authenticity into the fiction the actor represents is extended by Pirandello in his use of the actor as a visual object. The objective quality of the six characters, which contrasts with the lifelike quality of the "actors," is stressed from the moment of their first entry on stage through the masks they wear:

Whoever wishes to attempt a scenic translation of this comedy will need to strive by all means to give the feeling that these Six Characters do not blend in with the Actors of the Company. Their respective placement as they enter, indicated by the stage directions, will doubtless help; as will a different color of the light through appropriate spots. But the best and most suitable way one might suggest would be the use of special masks for the Characters: masks expressly made of a material that would not lose its shape through perspiration yet light enough for the actors who will need to speak, worked and cut in such a way as to leave free the eyes, nostrils and mouth. The deeper meaning of the comedy will also be interpreted in this way. The Characters are not to appear as *phantasms*, but as *reality created*, immutable constructions of imagination, and therefore more real and consistent than the inconsistent nature of the Actors.[10]

The mask is both a part of the actor and a deadness. Here it is closely fitted, of a light material that affects neither the actor's breathing nor his speech. But it is also *not* the actor's flesh: it is a

---

10. My translation: these stage directions do not appear in the Edward Storer version. (My Italian text: *Maschere nude*, vol. 1 of Pirandello's *Opere*, 6 vols. [Milano: Mondadori, 1958–65], p. 76.) The unsatisfactoriness of most English versions of Pirandello is compounded by the fact that, as in this instance, the stage directions that Pirandello detailed so painstakingly are frequently mutilated or ignored altogether. Some aspects of this problem have been noted by William Herman, "Pirandello and Possibility," *Tulane Drama Review* 3 (Spring 1966): 91–111. (Reprinted in Cambon, *Pirandello*, pp. 152–72). This stage direction was given due attention by Pitoëff when he first staged the play in Paris in 1923, two years after the Italian openings. Understanding that the "characters" were supposed to be stage objects, he brought them on by means of a stage elevator—one of the mechanisms of the stage that would normally be concealed. It is said that Pirandello first resisted Pitoëff's idea, but then came to understand that the *thingness* of the "characters" was forcefully demonstrated by this device. In retrospect, the hesitation of Pirandello seems understandable: these "characters" are not out-of-character actors who might use a stage elevator; they are consciously crafted stage incarnations and, as such, belong on the front of the stage, not within its mechanisms; each is the form of an actor, made set and rigid, but an actor nevertheless: their realm is the boards, between footlights and backdrop.

materiality that underscores the actor's materiality; it turns him into a tangible, unassimilable presence. Because of their masks, the "characters" are "consistent"—the most consistent presence on this stage. And it is in that consistency that must be read "the deeper meaning of this comedy." The intention is clear: to distinguish the "characters" from the "living" actors on the same stage through a physicality, a presence—not an aura; whereas the "actors" are intended to stand for, and merge with, the spectator, the "characters" are meant to remain *surfaces* that are distinct from, and that are not to be penetrated by, the spectator. The masks do not suggest a depth psychology, they reflect no soul, they will not key the spectator's emotional response: they are the integuments of simple notions, the integument being more important than the notion and resistive to the spectator's absorption of the character as emotion.

Meditation on the mask, or forms of the mask, is frequent in Pirandello. Parts of these meditations express concerns that we have analyzed already, such as the ones derived from questions of a human identity. But it will be remembered that the awareness of the mask overspreads all of Pirandello's writing: in 1918 the earliest collection of a substantial body of his plays (the edition by Treves) was published under the title *Maschere nude*, which was retained for all subsequent collections. It has not been usual for critics to question this curious juxtaposition of terms suggesting that the *covering* (the mask) represents a *stripping away*. In *Six Characters*, disclosure cannot proceed beyond the mask: we will never see a "naked" character, since the essence of the "characters" is their surface—they are totally *realtà create*, crafted personae. Such uncovering as occurs discloses that the mask is residual. Pirandello stresses that "the masks will help give the impression of figures wrought by art and each immutably set in the expression of his own defining emotion" (*Maschere nude*, 1:76). The Mother's expression, for example, is *pain*, "with frozen tears of wax in the white of the eyes and along the cheeks, as on the carved and painted figures of the *Mater dolorosa* in churches" (*Maschere nude*, 1:76). It is indeed this *mask* that the Mother attempts to mask in the scene we have referred to previously:

[*The* Mother *tries to prevent the* Father *from lifting the veil which covers her face.*]
The Father. Look at her! Look at her!
The Mother. No, no; stop it please! (P. 220)

The drama enacted by the "characters" centers on, and derives from, the imposition of these masks; it consists in the characters' efforts to protect their masks from disclosure or in their efforts to assert them against the efforts of others who want to prevent their disclosure. The Father, whose mask is *remorse*, finds assertion difficult against the efforts of his Step-Daughter, whose mask is *revenge* and whose conformable role consists in preventing the Father from enacting his own (while conversely, the Father's success in enacting the remorse proclaimed by his mask would prevent his Step-Daughter from conforming to her own emblematic persona). The gestures of the characters and their perplexity are actualized by the spectator since, in a process that depends on the spectator's perception, it is the spectator's sight that is questioned. The drama of the characters' efforts to see and be seen consists in efforts that assist or hinder us in our own seeing, and so that drama becomes the play of our seeing. Attempting this theatrical truth—a truth that has to do with a perception of surfaces, a truth that is perceptible primarily in the spectator's effort to perceive—the spectator is drawn up to the limits of the masks. Their limits become metaphysical as the masks maintain the spectator within the perplexity of the characters, preventing him as well from knowing whether the mask, beyond which no further stripping away is possible, represents the *naked* truth or simply another masking. And in his tension towards an unknown that subverts the evidence of the *realtà create*, the spectator experiences beyond the blandishments of the fiction the darkness in Pirandello before his yet-unrealized creation.

An objective stage—a stage as object—has already prepared the spectator to *objectify* the actor. Before the spectator of *Six Characters* is shown actors rehearsing a play by Pirandello, that is to say before he has been presented an ambiguous and tautological fiction that questions, and so reduces, the distance between fiction and reality, that spectator has been shown (as he entered the theater, actually) a naked stage whose curtain is up.[11] That stage, like the masks that fol-

11. The influence of Pirandello has been such that less than twenty years after *Six Characters*, on another continent, Thornton Wilder was able to place all of *Our Town* on a stage whose functional props emphasized its naked reality. But in 1921, before this kind of experience had become familiar, the disclosure of the working stage must have made a strong impression on a spectator prepared for another kind of ritual.

low, is a real object, a final stripping down. But as that stage is caught in the ambiguous fiction of actors who are real actors performing on a stage that is a real stage, it becomes, like the masks, an obstacle rather than simply a surface—a *limit* with the compelling suggestion of *another side*, of something *beyond*.

Other factors contribute to the ambiguity of this kind of stage and staged world. Early in his *Journal* (August 1893), Gide notes a form of composition that will be of lasting fascination to him—the so-called "composition en abîme," which he finds in Memling's mirrors, *Hamlet's* play within the play, the marionette scenes in *Wilhelm Meister*, etc.[12] The simplest image for this figure of Heraldry is the box of Quaker Oats with the figure of a Quaker holding an identical box—one whose identicality requires that the figure perpetuate itself *ad infinitum*. The reality of the Quaker's image occurs at the moment when, coming out of interreflecting depths, the sequence is broken: when the last image of the Quaker is not held by another Quaker but by the beholder who holds the box. Yet the second figure of the Quaker (the figure held by the figure on the box that is held by the beholder) exists in virtue of a reference that is *real*—the actual box of Quaker Oats. That second figure reverses the process of reality and fiction by containing the reality of the first figure within itself, whereas the first figure (the one on the *actual* box) refers only to a fiction. In a similar way, any play within a play is less fictional than the play that contains it since it claims to be only what it is: like the second Quaker, its fiction is its reality; it turns the referentiality of the fictional play that contains it into the genuineness of an authentic reference. But, like the second Quaker as well, it is caught, in fact, within an oscillation.

For all of its implications, the Quaker on the box is only an image. The stage complicates that image: its actors are at once images and actual people; unlike the Quaker on his box, they are *in motion*, that is to say, *alive* within their fiction.[13] When that life is constrained by

---

12. Andé Gide, *Journals*, 4 vols., trans. J. O'Brien (New York: A. A. Knopf, 1947–51), pp. 29–30.

13. This "life"—the mortality of the actor within his role—provided reflections for later playwriting theorists like Cocteau. But for Pirandello, attention to the actual life that can be preserved within the artifact became a metaphysical focal point. We have seen that concern in the relatively late *Diana and Tuda*; it can be found as well in Pirandello's earlier reflections on the cinematographic process (see, for example, *Shoot!*, 1915, reworked and reprinted as *The Notebooks of Serafino Gubbio*, 1925, an analysis of the play of forces around the objective

the mask (Bergson's "mechanical" imposition upon the living force), it serves to emphasize the mask: though they are "alive," the masked "characters" are reduced to a tautological motion—they can signify only their surfaces. But the actors who play the "actors" arrayed between the "characters" and the spectators serve the economy of a play about a play by allowing Pirandello to emphasize further the extent to which *Six Characters*, like *Oedipus the King*, is a play about the intensity and the limits of human sight.

We have said that the drama of the "characters" derives from their efforts to assert the meaning of their mask. Again like Sartre's people in *No Exit*, they envy the infinite flexibility, the multiple possibilities, of those who are "alive," those who are not fixed as they are in a single role, those who are free to alter their significance. Bound by their definition, they are not only constrained to be what they are, but they cannot avoid the continual patterns of conflict into which their individual definitions engage them. Those patterns of conflict result from efforts at *staging*: like the unhappy actors they are, they are forced to perform constantly a single role before a singularly skeptical audience. The central figure, the Father, must find a way to *represent* what a Father is; he must find ways to convince the others, and the spectators, that he is what his mask claims him to be. His difficulty derives, as it must in the theater, from the fact that he is forced to perform before *witnesses*—the other "characters," the critical "actors," the spectators. If one were to assume that the Father felt only the emotions of a father towards his stepdaughter, and if they were alone, he could counter with mere silence her assertion that he is not a Father but a seducer. But as soon as her accusation is made before witnesses—and this particular fiction as well as the nature of the theater make this witnessing necessary—the Father is compelled to *enact* the role he claims: he becomes because of that fiction what its form requires him to be.[14] And so, in the magnificent

eye of the camera that is positioned between the subjectivism, which it records, and the eye of the cameraman, which is itself affected by the objectivity of the camera eye and its own subjectivities).

14. A public definition that creates an individual personality provides Pirandello with many of his plots, the most famous of which is most likely *It is So (If You Think So)*. It is noteworthy that he returned to the same theme as soon as he was through with that play, staging the same year *The Pleasure of Honesty*. The curiosity of a small town that invents relationships for a family that withdraws itself from its collective gaze, or the "honesty" that is vouchsafed a woman through the role she is given to play, are analogues through which Pirandello

economy of Pirandello's play, actors enact actors acting out a story about the keenness of human sight and the imposition of public judgment, while the necessary relation of the spectator to the stage makes him the measure of that visual acuity and, at the same time, the judging eye. The stage coerces the actual participation of the spectator for the understanding of its fiction: the spectator, through his *spectation*, enacts what the play invites him to reflect on.

This play of surfaces is all the theater gives us. Traditionally, the drama strives to efface those surfaces so as to return the spectator from the illusory reality of the stage to the reality within him. The dramatic revolution of Pirandello consisted in turning the process around, establishing the materiality of the actor/object on stage and tensing the spectator towards that object. The drama Pirandello devised for the object emphasized through frustration the spectator's movement towards the stage, making of the stage object an impenetrable limit that rehearses the spectator's need and his inability to transgress such absolute limits. The nature of that theater extended for Pirandello his intuition that what we see of people is only the mask that hides, transforms, interprets a human truth that is itself affected by the selfsame mask, our own reaction to that mask, our masking of our own reaction. The playwright Pirandello sensed that what the theater can precipitate of an actual existence, regardless of the "story" it tells, is the (genuine) pathos of the *attempt* to give the inner truth a face: the theater—a mode of showing—can demonstrate this failure to show.

Others, like Genet, carried Pirandello's revolution further, balancing their drama even more acutely on the line between seeming and being. When Genet writes a play whose understanding is conditioned by the racial whiteness of its spectator and the racial blackness of its actor, or when he turns his stage into the room of a brothel whose clients are the fictional voyeurs on stage or the actual voyeurs on the other side of the footlights, he allows reality to alter his fiction and project the spectator within its performance.

But Pirandello was more deeply touched by the gravity of the

---

rephrases his private questionings. But once the analogue is given the dimensions of the stage, it draws the spectator into the quandaries of mystery and decipherment.

mystery. On his deathbed, he thought he had solved the ending of what was to remain his unfinished *Mountain Giants*; according to his son, the resolution had something to do with an olive tree: "In the middle of the stage, there is an old Saracen olive tree; between it and the wall, a rope is stretched upon which the curtain is pulled."[15] That olive tree was of some concern to Pirandello; his son recalls, " 'There is,' he said to me smiling, 'a large Saracen olive tree in the middle of the stage: with that, I have resolved it all.' And as I did not understand well, he added, 'To pull the curtain.' "[16] One wonders. So much symbolism attaches to the olive tree, the gift of Athena to the city that was so grateful to her that it took on her name; the branch that was a symbol of peace even before Christian times because of its curative values; Noah's first sign that the Deluge was about to end. But these symbols are *internalized* by the spectator who sees the cardboard tree on stage (assuming that he is able to read them all): that "tree" is as *unreal* as are its cultural investments. But the rope that is drawn from it, and the stage curtain that it supports, are real indeed, and twice real for being this stage's actual stage and the one upon which the play's heroine/actress, Ilse, will perform. If this reading is correct, Pirandello's last questioning was still focused upon the intersection of an idea and its materialization on stage, the point to which he had so frequently attempted to draw his spectator— in this case, somewhere between the illusory, symbolic tree and the real stage it helps improvise.

In one of his plays about the theater, *Each In His Own Way*, Pirandello uses an image for this new kind of dramatic experience; it is an image he has used before—that of the shattered mirror. Coming to the theater at a time when the mirror of the stage no longer provided a satisfactory reflection, he was not only able to shatter that mirror, but he was able to show that when the mirror is shattered, the reality of the broken pieces becomes more significant an *object* than the illusion of the reflected "image." This altering of our perception helped bring into being a new age of fiction, of fictionalizing— making the fictional object an object of our awareness sufficiently acute to contain the essential mystery that Zosima perceived in whatever could be looked at, in whatever could be *seen*, with intensity.

---

15. *Maschere nude* (1965), 2:1373.
16. Ibid., 2:1371.

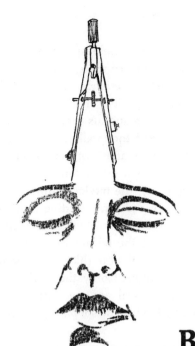

Borges: The
Dream Dreaming the Dreamer

Increasingly, the author's sense of an encompassing mystery has penetrated modern writing, blurring the distinction between existential speculation and the fiction into which it is cast. Yet at the same time there has been a turning away from fiction as a way of speculating on the "idea" of mystery, if only because such fiction would be an instance of control, a denial of its premise: to be able to write about (to be able to describe through fiction) what Dostoevsky's Zosima referred to as the divine mystery of the world is a drastic reduction, a nonsensical act that attempts to enclose what is limitless and unfathomable within the containment of a realized fiction. Dostoevsky's solution

127

was to shift his focus from the mystery to the desperate perplexity of the one who confronts it. But for the modern writer, even such a shift from fictional commentary to fictional experience fails to break free from a kind of romanticism—the dissipation of a *sense* within the words that it occasions. Moreover, as Poe and his exegetes told us, the words themselves have become a part of the modern perplexity.

Abandoning commentary, since commentary can only evidence the resistance of mystery to speculation (the mystery remaining inviolate even as it is absorbed by the comment), the modern author gives his writing as an *instance* of that mystery and turns reading into another encounter with the unknowable. The discredited mind, otherwise comforted by the inherent structure of the terminable novel, is disquieted by a writing that resists assimilation (like mystery itself), providing in lieu of description or comment only the feeling of that disquiet. As the source of a metaphysical anxiety with which the reader is already acquainted, that fiction becomes a parafictional object and/or experience.

Jorge Luis Borges has noted how nearly akin is his writing to his "other" self, that private world of anxiety, desire, and perplexity. It is not simply, as he has written in "The Reaches of My Hope," that, in the end, all writing is autobiographical; the act of writing is more like the splitting of self into sentience and commentary that he describes in "Borges and I," ending, "I do not know which one of us has written this page"[1]—a conclusion that stresses the problematic nature of the act. Borges's inner anxiety, which intends to escape from the containment of his fiction, derives from a sense of the absolute nature of the unknown that may be analyzed as the mystery of time ("I can't get rid of my obsession with time"[2]), of the infinite (in a 1965 radio interview with Georges Charbonnier, Borges spoke about the dual nature of his stories as "two sides of the same coin, one comprising the intellectual possibilities of a cosmic idea, the other the emotions of anguish and perplexity in the face of an endless universe"[3]), or of the refusal of the unknown to be reduced to either

---

1. In *Labyrinths: Selected Stories & Other Writings*, ed. D. A. Yates and J. E. Irby, (New York: New Directions, 1964), p. 247. Collection henceforth referred to as *Lab*.

2. *Borges on Writing*, ed. N. T. di Giovanni, D. Halpern, F. MacShane (New York. E. P. Dutton, 1973), p. 51. Henceforth referred to as *BOW*.

3. James E. Irby, "Borges and the Idea of Utopia," in *The Cardinal Points of Borges*, ed. L. Dunham and I. Ivask (Norman: University of Oklahoma Press, 1971), p. 42. Collection henceforth referred to as *CPB*.

coherence or permanency ("If the characters of a fictional work can be readers or spectators, we, its readers or spectators, can be fictitious"[4]).

The possibility of a *reality* emerging from the printed page through more than the symbolism of its words (as well as the special place that books occupy in Borges's cosmogony) derives in part from the fact that Borges is himself a bookish creation. He describes his existence, in which "life and death have been lacking," as "infested with literature' (*BOW*, p. 6). The first part of the statement is subject to caution: there is indeed a coldness and a distance in the Borges pages that talk about blood and death that gives those pages a metallic and artificial quality. But the anxiety that suffuses so many of the stories is evidence of the many ways in which a sense of life and death has affected Borges. And his references to metaphysics and philosophy are ironic reminders that before their specialized analyses became academic, metaphysics and philosophy belonged to religion, and their purpose was to help cope with the ambient darkness of a human life. Borges returns the parlor game to its original function even as he preserves the ludic part of the exercise: "I am quite simply a man who uses perplexities for literary purposes: the dead ends of philosophy and metaphysics."[5]

A book is an ordering; we have stressed throughout this discussion how its very being denies, and will convey less than adequately, the structureless and unpronounceable chaos, the infinity of space and formlessness that extends beyond man's ability to measure and to shape. Nevertheless, Borges is concerned with that sense of chaos in much of his writing and so he faces the technical problem (which may also be a metaphysical problem) of articulating that sense through his fiction, without that fiction becoming, for him or for his reader, a surrogate ordering.

The temptation the book represents as the Absolute Book, as perfect order, or as "The God's Script" is one of the pervasive influences on the thought and fiction of Borges: if such an absolute ordering were possible within a book, then the unknown, the "god," would be manifest within it. But the perverse nature of books, like the nature of the unknown, is that their ordering is never more than partial and that their most forceful disclosure about mystery is that it cannot

4. "Partial Magic in the Quixote," *Lab*, p. 196.
5. Quoted by Donald A. Yates, "The Four Cardinal Points of Borges," *CPB*, p. 28.

be disclosed. "Tlön, Uqbar, Orbis Tertius" describes "a labyrinth devised by men, a labyrinth destined to be deciphered by men" (*Lab*, pp. 17–18). Tlön begins as only the thought of men, and its only tangibility, at first, is the spurious tangibility of texts: "I had discovered, in a volume of a certain pirated encyclopedia, a superficial description of a non-existent country" (p. 7). Founded by Berkeley and other members of a "benevolent society" (p. 15), it is intended as a realm of human control. Even though this "complete idealism invalidates all science" and its very order is an epistemology where things "tend to become effaced and lose their detail when they are forgotten" (p. 14), ideas do, in fact, multiply, and sciences, religion, letters, metaphysics ("derivations of their language," p. 8), "do exist, and in almost uncountable number" (p. 10). Eventually, the language of Tlön that resists formulation ("Every mental state is irreducible: the mere fact of naming it—i.e., of classifying it—implies a falsification," p. 10) invades the earth as tangible evidence: the letters around the edge of a compass. And the book devised by benevolent humanists who intended it as a replacement for the unfathomable labyrinth of god becomes just one more divine Script, wholly impenetrable, and about which men can only speculate: "One of the schools of Tlön [theorizes] that the history of the universe—and in it our lives and the most tenuous detail of our lives—is the scripture produced by a subordinate god in order to communicate with a demon" (p. 10). The book, in its exacerbated desire to become the sum and the ordering that will eclipse all mystery, may go as far as to create the objects of a new world, but it will do so only in order to renew, once again, the frustration of attempting to achieve that sum and that ordering.

"I owe the discovery of Uqbar to the conjunction of a mirror and an encyclopedia" (p. 3); the mirror, the perfect Berkleyan instrument that contains nothing but shows everything that is *seen in it*, also inverts reality (or the illusion of reality): the encyclopedia, in which men had hoped to establish an ordering of all things reduced to their symbols (the symbol, like the mirror, is a container only by virtue of our willingness to grant it a thing contained), ends, in "Tlön, Uqbar, Orbis Tertius," by returning to our world nonsymbolic and mysterious objects—the compass tremulously seeking an unknowable North, or "small, very heavy cones (made from a metal that is not of this world) [which] are images of the divinity in certain regions of Tlön" (p. 17). After the failure of reflecting symbols, the hermetic object returns and is deified as the latest avatar of the unknowable.

The mirror also multiplies: "For one of those gnostics, the visible universe was an illusion or (more precisely) a sophism. Mirrors and fatherhood are abominable because they multiply and disseminate that universe" (p. 4); the mirror image is the equivalent of a world that is illusory or it is an adequate image for a world whose quintessence cannot be apprehended. The mirror's image, which is not spatial, renders accurately of a spatial world only what is not in that world: it is thus an emblem for the unavailing mind that cannot ever fully grasp its object, while at the same time it is the ironic counterpart of that object—a negation of the original negation.[6] In Tlön, one of the metaphysical hypotheses ("They judge that metaphysics is a branch of fantastic literature," p. 10) proposes "that while we sleep here, we are awake elsewhere and that in this way every man is two men" (p. 10). The fantastic literature of Borges, which is sometimes a kind of metaphysics, occasionally prescribes such a trajectory for his character: it represents yet another avatar of the mirror when, as in Tlön, the reflection becomes flesh. At such times, Borges suggests a lunge at the unknown that is of such desperate power as to carry the lunger to the other side of the metaphysical barrier without having been able to penetrate it (a sense often present in the fiction of Cortázar, who may have derived it from Borges): the insubstantial reflection of the mirror becomes the image (even as it begins to devise fictional structures of its own) of this failure.

Dreams and time are similarly attempted and with as little success. The character in "The Circular Ruins" dreams a creature into being (even though he is "troubled by the impression that all this happened before," *Lab*, p. 49), only to understand at the end "that he too was a mere appearance, dreamt by another" (p. 50). The dream dreams the dreamer dreaming and, as in Tlön, which was the climactic effort of (philosophical) idealists to construct a controllable universe, the discouraged mind ultimately suspects that all being, all creation, is

---

6. Compare with André Gide, *The Notebooks of André Walter*, trans. W. Baskin (London: Peter Owen, 1968): "Last night, looking into the mirror, I contemplated my image. As if it had emerged from darkness, the fragile apparition takes shape and becomes rigid; . . . my soul hovers uncertainly between this double illusion, dazed, and wondering which is the phantom" (p. 112).

someone else's communication—the reference to a "subordinate god" suggesting that the process is infinitely recessive, like that of the mirror, and thus contrives simply one more image or sense of the infinite.

This vision of cyclical time and a cyclical return, associated by a number of critics with the Nietzschean concept,[7] appears to be still another instance in which the fictional event attempts to pattern itself on the metaphysical concept in order to show the ineffectuality of concepts. Nietzsche emphasized the *Übermensch's* exhilaration in the knowledge of an identical rebirth because of the possibility of escape from a Judeo-Christian morality of enslavement confined to the present cycle, stressing the extent of the condemnation imposed by an awareness of such recurrences on the slavish mind. Borges, on the other hand, telescopes time and duplicates personality without exultation, as coldly as the mirror whose interreflections occur within a wholly closed space, however deep their illusory space might be. Borges believes that while metaphysics develop freely within the self-containment of the mind, they founder in their actualization within the *seeming* they intended to dissipate: the metaphysical speculation is an act with no extension, and the actual act that extends from it becomes a dream with no more substance than the thought that was its impetus.

An act attempted is likely to be dissipated in the ineffectuality of the dream since Borges suggests on more than one occasion that the percipient of the idea is likely to be created by the idea. In "The End of the Duel," Borges contrives without a shudder a story of murder and abomination. His explanation leaves us somewhat dissatisfied: "You're given the impression, I hope, of a rather grim country where the kind of story I'm going to tell is thought of as a joke" (*BOW*, p. 23). The authorial voice cannot separate itself as clearly as the commentator from participation in this kind of "joke." In order not to be contaminated, in order not to sound as harsh and inhuman, the authorial voice must be subsumed within a vaster joke—a metaphysical joke, in fact—where no blood actually flows because the substance of the joke concerns the problematic substance of personality and the problematic nature of its description. The faceless creatures of Borges

7. For example, Ana María Barrenechea, *Borges the Labyrinth Maker* (New York: New York University Press, 1965), p. 2; or Jaime Alazraki, *Jorge Luis Borges* (New York: Columbia University Press, 1971), p. 36.

bleed less for being the figures of an equation written on the lunar surface of his landscapes. The extent to which those surfaces are reinvested with human depth as they "create" the reader (or author) who creates them remains to be analyzed, as do the ways in which that reverse creation is attempted.

Borges is both the victim and the perpetrator of his joke. His fiction, so consistently woven out of speculative essays,[8] confirms the judgment of "The Immortal" that "there is no pleasure more complex than that of thought" (*Lab*, p. 115); but the uneasiness Borges feels at being adrift in a chaotic and timeless universe becomes dismay (serious or ironic) when he considers the efforts of those who attempt to encapsulate the unknowable within their theories. Not infrequently, Borges makes his ironic point by projecting a character into the realized world of such theory and watching that character founder within substitute shadows that grow into a surreal intensification of the darkness that the rational construct was meant to reduce; as Jaime Alazraki has remarked, "Human intelligence cannot reconstruct an order which does not exist, or if it does is ruled by divine laws which are inaccessible to men."[9] As in Tlön, men have only words, and they become as unsatisfactory as mirrors: a world that cannot be *penetrated* is only *reflected* by symbols that are no more than another part of the illusion. Still, the words spill over: in the same way that the fiction enlarges and echoes for Borges a private uneasiness, his fictional comment is extended into an existential multiplicity of interviews, discussions, postfaces about his stories, and these in turn spur the critical comments of others (the comment sometimes bearing an uncanny resemblance to its fictional object[10]). The peripheral commentary has long since exceeded the internal one; Robert L. Fiore's tentative bibliography of writings on Borges between 1923 and 1969

8. Borges goes as far as labeling his early stories "hoaxes and pseudo-essays" ("An Autobiographical Essay," in *The Aleph and Other Stories*, trans. N. T. di Giovanni [New York: E. P. Dutton, 1970], p. 239, henceforth referred to as *Aleph*). The question is whether the label would be less appropriate to a number of the later stories.

9. Alazraki, *Jorge Luis Borges*, p. 10.

10. For example, Ronald Christ, especially his "Modest Proposal" (*CPB*, pp. 7–15). Yates, "Four Cardinal Points of Borges," which borrows the author's famous compass for its structure. Or again, Néstor Ibarra's interview in *L'Herne* (partially translated in *Prose for Borges* [*TriQuarterly*, no. 25 (Fall 1972), pp. 88–99]; collection henceforth referred to as *PB*), where the interviewee turns into the same kind of semifictional construct as does the Borges of "Borges and I."

runs in excess of twenty pages (*CPB*, pp. 83–105): as in the case of
Mark Twain's weather, words and ideas create palliative activity
within a world that denies the possibility of deeds.

Up to this point, Borges loses the game, even though his ironic
Weltanschauung may benefit from the loss: fictional commentary (intended to be more than an instance of the metaphysical failure), that
evidences such exuberant health as it spills out of the book, requires a
metafictional comment in order to remain within the author's control and the limits of his original intent. It is evident that Borges has
been a ready contributor to this metafictional commentary. But he has
also tried to make his fiction oscillate between the text's containment
and the reader's parafictional world in ways that are more complex.

Tlön is a planet perplexed by language, evidencing a genetic pe-
culiarity that links it, beyond fiction, to the book (Borges's) that
creates it as a literary fiction about a literary fiction. Since the limits
of language are an instance of human limitation, the writer in search
of his form-ulation provides an instance as well as an emblem for man
in quest of a structuring answer. In the story about the revelatory
power of a mystical object, "The Aleph," Borges encounters the difficulty of presenting its magical simultaneity (that is to say, total and
unequivocal revelation) through language, man's inadequate instrument, which is perforce sequential and partitive: "I arrive now at the
ineffable core of my story. And here begins my despair as a writer.
All language is a set of symbols whose use among its speakers
assumes a shared past. How, then, can I translate into words the limitless Aleph, which my floundering mind can scarcely encompass?"
(*Aleph*, p. 26). In the end, the fictional voice of "The Aleph" will
doubt both possibilities—the possibility of the magical realización
within the fiction as well as the possibility of the actual transcription
to suggest a fictional realization: "Does this Aleph exist in the heart
of a stone? Did I see it there in the cellar when I saw all things, and
have I now forgotten it? Our minds are porous and forgetfulness
creeps in" (p. 30). But this discouragement, because it is so pervasive
and because it is the state of mind of the author Borges attempting
this story, this sense of failure begins the process of linking two
worlds that are utterly different in kind—the world of the fiction and
the world of the reader in which the fiction may attain an entirely new
dimension.

Before this discouragement, a postscript to the "ineffable core" of the story provides what the fiction claims as parafictional evidence—documentation that would establish the fact of a nonfictional Aleph and thereby cast doubt on the reality of the fictional one. Through a clever and ironic play of fictional mirrors (mirrors in fiction, such as Spenser's *Faerie Queene*, III, 2:19—with the suggestion that the Aleph is, in fact, another of those special mirrors—as well as mirroring structures of fiction: fictional tricks used like a system of mirrors) Borges offers the evidence of the parafictional world to stress the fraudulence of his fiction. The rejection of the fiction as truth rehabilitates that fiction at another level, since the "real" world cannot comment on the devising of a fiction (that is, something that does not exist in "reality") without being itself fictionalized: the evidence of a real Aleph outside the referential fiction of Borges invalidates his Aleph (it is only a fiction) but requires that fiction for its own claim to reality, without which it cannot invalidate its fictional mirror.[11] The interplay of these fictional (and parafictional) reflections begins to give "The Aleph" the dimension of an Aleph—the story becomes a special kind of revelatory mirror.

A part of the interreflections of these mirrors leaves the printed page. Still, Borges wants their very substance to be caught in the same oscillation between the spurious world of the story and the actual world of the reader. In the same way as did Sartre two years earlier (in *Nausea*, 1938), Borges attempts the leap from fictional to phenomenal object through the tangible hybrid the reader holds in his hands.[12] In "The End of the Duel," Borges begins with an autobiographical note that commits the subsequent story: "It's a good many years ago now that Carlos Reyles, the son of the Uruguayan novelist, told me the story one summer evening out in Adrogué" (*BOW*, p. 15): at this point, the story might well be simply an expansion of the biographical fact. Later, in a Columbia University seminar (now in print),

11. A device for springing free of the fiction not unlike Gide's "composition en abîme" discussed in my chapter on Pirandello.

12. The book that Roquentin *will* write—the gap between the undated pages and the first Journal entry—is the book that the reader, as he finishes reading it, holds in his hands, tangible evidence of his experiencing Roquentin's experience. Irby adds an interesting footnote for those who did not read the Borges story when it first appeared in *Sur* and shows the extent of Borges's concern with the story as *object*: at first, "the opening words of the postscript where 'I reproduce the preceding article just as it appeared in number 68 of *Sur*—jade green covers, May 1940,' i.e. the very issue the reader held in his hands" ("Borges and the Idea of Utopia," CPB, p. 44, n. 2).

Borges absorbs both the prefatory note and the story itself within the web of his explication:

Well, this is a mere statement of what actually happened. I got the story from somebody else as well, but since it would have been awkward to mention two names and have two characters, I left out my other friend. Adrogué means a great deal to me because it stands for my boyhood and for my youth. It was the last place my father went before he died, and I have very pleasant memories of it. Adrogué was once quite a fine little town, to the south of Buenos Aires, but now it has been spoiled by flats, garages and television. But in its time it was full of *quintas,* with large gardens, and was a fine place to be lost in. Adrogué was a kind of maze, and there were no parallel streets. Reyles was the son of a famous Uruguayan novelist. (P. 22)

This is a way, not uncommon for Borges, to either stress the autobiographical part of his fiction, or turn the fiction into a form of autobiography (see the collection called, in its English translation, *The Aleph and Other Stories,* where each story is given a postscript—a "commentary"—that makes it an *event* in the life of the author). Borges knew that he had at least one illustrious predecessor in these attempts—Cervantes. When the author of the first *Quixote* became aware of the pirating of his work, he hastened the completion of a second *Quixote.* But he also gave an added reality to his original work—a compensation for what it had lost at the hands of plagiarists —by making it the object of a commentary in the second work: those comments were no longer simply "fiction" since they referred to an actual object, and both books thus acquired a parafictional dimension that the author enlarged by having the minor characters of the second book encounter principals that now existed in two worlds.[13] This was the hybrid literary object that Borges chose to weave into his "Pierre Menard, Author of the *Quixote,*" a commentary meant to be read as fiction. The story, which Borges calls "a halfway house between the essay and the true tale," (*Aleph,* p. 243) is essentially a reading of three lines of *Don Quixote* in book 1, chapter 9. Since the fiction tells about a Pierre Menard who has been able, by dint of effort, to write

---

13. "Although [Sansón Carrasco] had read the First Part of the history, he never would have believed that the squire was as droll as he was depicted there. But as he now heard him . . . he was convinced of the truth of it all" (II, vii); what the bachelor "hears" is the phenomenological evidence of the book that now exists as an object; similarly, the reader "trusts" that object more through reading *about* it in volume 2 than when he first read it as fiction.

a *Don Quixote* identical to that of Cervantes, the difference between the two texts will be determined by the way in which Borges's reader reads them. In order to determine those differences, the reader must first become a fictional character—the one who reads Cervantes (alongside Menard) through a genuine historical distance so as to inform the lines with their seventeenth-century modernity. It is only then that he will be able to note in the identical lines of the modern Menard an archaism of tone and idea (especially as it pertains to the nature of history). Inserting the phenomenological object that is the Cervantes text within his fiction, Borges coerces from his reader the performance that the fiction requires of that reader—understanding the archaic text as a modern one and then understanding the selfsame text, when the fiction claims it to be modern, as if it were archaic.

This fiction that oscillates between the worlds of parafictional commentary and those of its making, because of the insertion of a text that had already been placed within such an oscillation by Cervantes, emerges as commentary alongside the other commentaries that Borges has made on the curiously hybrid nature of the *Quixote*. In the essay called "Partial Magic in the *Quixote*," Borges is reminded that in the now parafictional object, a parafictional wedge in the form of a fictional object had already been introduced by Cervantes, whose own *Galatea* is found in the Don's library and upon which the "barber, a dream or the form of a dream of Cervantes, passes judgment" (*Lab*, p. 194). And in the "Parable of Cervantes and the *Quixote*," Borges notes how time has changed the nature of the original fiction in a way that is identical to the intent of his own fictional tricks and those of Cervantes, though Borges, through sheer perversity, confirms the equation by inverting it. Recalling the reality of the Spanish region of La Mancha, Borges remarks that the original story juxtaposed and contrasted "the unreal world of the seventeenth century" (*Lab*, p. 242). But by now, that "ordinary" world has ceased being part of *our* "everyday" and has receded for us as far as the unreal world contrived by books of chivalry. One "unreal" is now as "unreal" as the other and, in the fullness of time, the once-real La Mancha has become as mythical as the mythical Montiel. What Borges does not tell us here, but what his belief in the dream dreaming the dreamer allows us to infer, is that the real La Mancha, now buried within the depth of centuries, reacquires phenomenological presence as the myth that focuses our comment.

The specular interreflection is thus an image that turns into a process relating a reader and a text—a reading that obtrudes an *object* into the world of the reader even as it absorbs that reader into its own. The "object" created by the specular mechanism of "Pierre Menard" is the reader made for the purpose of reading "Pierre Menard," in a devising that subverts the expectation of control that such a reader would otherwise bring to his text. Within the infinite recession of the dream dreaming the dreamer dreaming (a maze extended through the comments of the commentator being commented on by the commentary), the reader is thrust through the fiction into a confrontation with the unknowable that creates the existential sense that the fiction is investigating. In "Tlön, Uqbar, Orbis Tertius," the author despairs of knowing a reality that his fiction is also in the process of subverting: "It is useless to answer that reality is also orderly. Perhaps it is, but in accordance with divine laws—I translate: inhuman laws—which we never quite grasp. Tlön is surely a labyrinth" (*Lab*, p. 17).

A labyrinth created so as to be decipherable would lack the defining essence of god's labyrinth—its nondecipherable nature. In order for the design of "Tlön" to be like god's, it loses those who venture into it. Several labyrinth stories of Borges instance and discuss how the text becomes an accurate labyrinth. In "The Two Kings and Their Two Labyrinths" (which purports to be a trope for another story, "Ibn Hakkan al-Bokhari, Dead in His Labyrinth"), the chronicler quoted by the fictional voice records that "in former times there was a king of the isles of Babylon who called together his architects and his wizards and set them to build him a labyrinth so intricate that no wise man would dare enter inside, and so subtle that those who did would lose their way. This undertaking was a blasphemy, for confusion and marvels belong to God alone and not to man" (*Aleph*, p. 89). The "isles of Babylon" remind us that the city in Shinar where the famous tower was to have been constructed was indeed Babylon and that its purpose, to reach heaven, was defeated by the confusion of tongues.[14] A lesson of Babel is that the word that cannot penetrate the unknown can at least lose its user in such a way as to give him a sense of the unknown. The author thus becomes an ultimately futile

14. The symbol appears often, as in the explicitly titled "The Babylonian Lottery" or "The Library of Babel"—the latter story confirming the wordlike nature of the labyrinth.

intercessor but one who is nevertheless lustered with some of the mystery that he attempts; and Borges, faithful to his way of populating his fiction with aspects of his own quandaries, is likely to turn his victims into such unavailing intermediaries dwelling at the outer limits of the unknown and on whom some of the mystery rubs off. These ambiguous figures, like that in "The Circular Ruins," are mere appearances, as distant from the unknowable as those for whom they mediate the unknowable, but who, like their author, distill some of its flavor through proximity or concern.

The labyrinth of "Tlön" is a device of language; its failure to reach the unknown is a failure of language.[15] For the author, that failure is both confirmation of his participation in the human condition and an unacceptable evidence that his writing attempts to cancel. But, as we have seen, it is the specular and speculating part of the fiction that contaminates speculation, entrapping not only the commenting Borges but his own commentators as well. Monegal, who appears as an episodic character in "The Other Death" (a part of the maze through which the narrator tries to get to the story he is attempting to tell[16]), notes how "Pierre Menard" devises even a critic of its own making; referring to Gérard Genette's article, he writes: "It is possible to attempt another reading of these texts, and of the famous 'Pierre Menard,' and instead of taking literally the conclusions of those critical articles, or the ironies of the story, perhaps to see in these short pieces the foundation of another aesthetic discipline, based not on the creation of the literary work but on its reading."[17] These parafictional and concentric expansions of the fiction provide Borges with an enlargement of the maze, extending it like the interreflections of the mirror over two worlds through which Borges moves, now as the writer entrapped within his fiction, and again as the "I" who escapes from it, and forcing the reader who follows him to go through similar

15. A continuing part of the author's meditation, as well as his experimentation, has been on language (for example, El idioma de los argentinos [Buenos Aires: Gleizer, 1928], or El lenguaje de Buenos Aires [Buenos Aires: Emecé, 1963]).

16. Thus causing the commentator who will expand the maze to be also a part of the maze that he expands, and implicating the critic's difficulty in "telling about" in the author's difficulty of telling.

17. "Borges: The Reader as Writer," PB, p. 105. The Genette article appears in Figures, vol. 1 (Paris: Seuil, 1966).

avatars.[18] At one level, the reader confronts, instead of his fictional object, another existent—Borges, engaged in the process of writing. But if the reader attempts that passage out of the maze, Borges fictionalizes himself, reentering, from the opposite end as it were, his specular construct.

The philistine mind will conclude that these speculations and specula, these alternations of the reader and his reading, the modification of the author and his object in their respective functions, are only mental postures—and Borges would most likely not disagree: however doggedly the human mind attempts the unknowable, it is always thrown back upon itself, it contrives only another posture. If metaphysics is ultimately, as in Tlön, only another form of fiction, a branch of fantastic literature, then Borges will gentle the exacerbation of the metaphysical quest through the irony and the games of his fiction. In time he will reduce the whole metaphysical quandary to a detective (short) story—though even this ultimate reduction will be approached cautiously: "The solution of a mystery is always less impressive than the mystery itself. Mystery has something of the supernatural about it, and even of the divine; its solution, however, is always tainted by the sleight of hand" ("Ibn Hakkan," Aleph, p. 123); this last intercessory fiction—the detective story—failing like the others in its intercession, is interesting (like the others) especially because of the mysterious aura that it acquires in the usual manner of intercessors.

About "Death and the Compass," Borges has said that it is a "nightmare version of the city [Buenos Aires]" (Aleph, p. 268), a work that "should stand or fall by its general atmosphere, not by its plot" (p. 269)—as ever, in Borges, the statement merits some reflection. Even if one excludes the H. Bustos Domecq stories that Borges began writing in the early forties in collaboration with Adolfo Bioy Casares, much of Borges's writing could be thought of as detective

18. Monegal reminds the uninitiated that in his preface to A Universal History of Infamy, Borges "calls his stories 'exercises in narrative prose' and indicates the general sources: 'my rereadings of Stevenson and Chesterton, and also from Sternberg's early films, and perhaps from a certain biography of Evaristo Carriego.' In his eagerness to acknowledge other people's inventions, he forgets (or prefers not to say) that Carriego's biography was written by him in 1930" (art. cit., p. 115). The "exercise" as well as the fictional disguise of the commentator are further detours in the maze that sometimes leads the reader into fiction and sometimes into parafiction.

story-writing: one need only allow an unallowable departure from the strict definition of the genre—the fact that the riddle proposed by Borges is seldom resolved in his resolution. A labyrinth successfully traversed is a labyrinth no more, and the Borgesian labyrinth must remain a labyrinth at the end of even a detective story. That persistent labyrinth accounts for both the detective nature and the "atmosphere" of Borges's stories.

One way of reducing the detective story to its simplest definition is to say that it concerns a detective who is looking for a name—the identity of the culprit (identity that is, in a genre not overly concerned with identity, little more than a name). So defined, the quest reminds Borges that the mystery for which god is a substitute concept also becomes, as any enduring mystery must, the object of an exacerbated quest: "I learned that the holy fear of uttering God's Name had given rise to the idea that that Name is secret and all-powerful. I learned that some of the Hasidim, in search of that secret Name, had gone as far as to commit human sacrifices" ("Death and the Compass," *Aleph*, p. 77).

The Tetragrammaton hides the four mystical consonants of God's Name. When, during the Middle Ages, the Tetragrammaton is in danger of yielding its secret, the Masoretes disguise the disguise by altering the original consonantal Hebrew under sets of vowel markings. Thus protected, the secret preserves the power of the unspeakable Name, reserved as always for the few who consider themselves initiates. The Tetragrammaton is an object, not an idea. God creates his world out of the alphabet's letters, and those who decipher his world do so by reading the evidence of God's text in the very symbols that create his text. I have had occasion already to point out how the peculiar economy of Borges requires him to create a text about (and ultimately as undecipherable as) the "Book of God" (for example, in "The Circular Ruins"). "Death and the Compass" is perhaps the most explicit of such Borgesian exercises, even though, as the trajectory that contrives a detective story, it appears to be considerably less than that.

Again in the simplest terms, "Death and the Compass" is about a criminal's vengeance on a detective: Lönnrot has arrested and "put away" the hood Scharlach's brother. Seriously wounded, "Red" Scharlach mulls an exemplary revenge during the nine days of his delirium. His opportunity comes when, one day, through treachery and a mistake, one of his men kills the Talmudic scholar Marcel Yarmolinsky. Since Talmudic scholars and detectives are decipherers of tangible signs, the Borgesian Scharlach sees in this conjuncture the possible form of a retribution to be exacted from Lönnrot, and one his delirium had suggested to him before ever the opportunity arose: what could be more devilish than to entrap a detective within the web of a maze of his own making? Or, from the point of view of a devilish story-writer, what could be more devilish than to entrap a reader within the expectation of a resolvable mystery? (Both detectives and their readers live within a similar expectation.) Accordingly, Borges devises a "Jewish" story (*Aleph*, p. 269), in which the four-parted Tetragrammaton and the four-pointed compass conceal a mystery whose *events* will have a resolution to the extent that this is a detective story—even though the mystery itself will not be dissipated: the Tetragrammaton does not yield the mystery associated with it.

The first murder, Rabbi Yarmolinsky's, allows Borges to place his story within the world of the book: once again, the text of the story is about a text and its elucidation is about the elucidation of a text. Yarmolinsky brings with him to the Talmudic congress "His many books and his few suits of clothes" (p. 66). Among these, two are of special interest. One, the *Vindication of the Kabbalah*, is in fact an essay by Borges himself,[19] who thus lends his reality to his fiction (while stating, at the same time, his own parafictional interest) with an expectation of the consequences that we have previously described in this kind of Cervantine ploy. The other book is the *Sefer Yetzirah*. I am indebted to Jaime Alazraki for an analysis of the "thirty-two secret paths of wisdom"[20]—the *Sephirot*, or ten primordial numbers, and the twenty-two letters of the alphabet out of which God "produced everything that is and everything that will be": these are among the revelations of the books in which Lönnrot will steep himself as he gradually becomes a part of the case he is investigating. But in becoming a Kabbalist (for the Kabbalistic texts, which Lönnrot also reads, derive from the *Sepher Yetzirah*), Lönnrot falls not only into a Borgesian posture, but into that of the Borges who falls into the posture of God for whom the world is a text: "For the Kabbalists, the letters of the Torah are the mystical body of God, and from this it

19. *Discusión* (Buenos Aires: Emecé, 1964).
20. In an intriguing article, "Borges and the Kabbalah," *PB*, pp. 240–67.

follows that the Creation is just a reflection or emanation of the Holy text."[21]

Lönnrot finds himself trapped in a Jewish story where murder appears to be ritualistic: Rabbi Yarmolinsky is killed on the night of the third day of December; his death is followed by that of his assassin on the third night of January; another mystery occurs on the third night of the following month; and so on. Lönnrot, who "thought of himself as a pure logician, a kind of Auguste Dupin" (though Borges specifies in the first line of his story that Lönnrot's is a "rash mind" and that he has in him "a streak of the adventurer and even of the gambler," p. 65), Lönnrot is provided with a number of Kabbalistic signs. The Kabbalah is also a game of signs; it seeks its occult meaning as much in the evidence of its signifiers as in their symbolic translation: it reads its texts as letters, numbers, and positionings because those texts are not only an idea of God but also one of His objects. It is therefore logical for a Kabbalistic detective to be presented with a world he must decipher as the tangible signs of a book, within a Jewish story that is, in fact, a Jewish joke on him.

Lönnrot's "rash mind" distinguishes him from Inspector Treviranus. The latter's professional intuition allows him to make throughout the case shrewd guesses about what is happening, and one might have expected similar intuitions from Lönnrot had he not been corrupted by fascinations of the mind. Early on, Treviranus tries to warn Lönnrot —while at the same time demonstrating an instinctual distrust of the number *three*—by telling him "We needn't lose any time here looking for three-legged cats";[22] he has inferred fairly correctly that "everyone knows the Tetrarch of Galilee owns the world's finest sapphires. Somebody out to steal them probably found his way in here by mistake. Yarmolinsky woke up and the thief was forced to kill him" (p. 66). But Lönnrot has already taken Scharlach's bait and become the creature he was fated to be. "Possible, but not very interesting," answers Lönnrot, "I'd much prefer a purely rabbinical explanation" (pp. 66–67).

In a story that turns out to be circular, coincidences are part of a necessary linking: the first of Lönnrot's signs is a sheet of paper in

---

21. Alazraki, "Borges and the Kabbalah," p. 247.
22. An expression whose awkwardness in English points up the importance of the original Spanish.

Yarmolinsky's typewriter with the words *"The first letter of the Name
has been uttered"* on it. Each crime is similarly numbered, though
Lönnrot will be provided with double clues so that he might read
through the "inaccurate" disguise to the hidden meaning—a response
more to be expected of a "rash" mind than of a Kabbalistic one: the
third "crime" misleadingly announces that *"The last letter of the
Name has been uttered"*; here, as elsewhere, Lönnrot reads *four*, as
he was expected to, through the *three* that he is shown, because of the
evidence of the four-lettered Tetragrammaton. When, after the first
crime in the Hôtel du Nord, followed by a second at "the city's western reaches" (p. 68) and a third on the waterfront (the *east* of Buenos
Aires), the Tetragrammaton indicates the missing point of the compass—the south: the last letter has *not* been uttered. The four-sided
rhombus that appears as the lozenges on the paint store where the
second crime is committed and in the dress of the harlequins who
stage the third, leads Lönnrot to the diamond-shaped panes in the
windows of Triste-le-Roy. Further, Scharlach conveys to him a copy
of the 1793 edition of Leusden's *Philologus Hebraeo-Graecus* (in a
text about books, even the hoods are erudite bibliophiles), in which
Lönnrot learns that the Jewish day begins at sundown and ends at the
following sundown—a further invitation to read *four* in the date of
each crime, instead of the Christian three that is proposed.[23]

But, as Borges points out, the Tetragrammaton is a recent awareness of Lönnrot's (p. 72): he reads with the haste of a neophyte, or
perhaps with the haste of someone hurried, and hurrying on, to his
destiny. In a text about the phenomenological evidence of text and
world, and of world through text, Lönnrot makes the mistake (which
is perhaps part of an ultimate plan) of reading with his mind objects
that are more arcane than their symbolism. The logical process of his
deductions speeds him to the southern part of the city and the villa
Triste-le-Roy. In his recent Kabbalistic learning, Lönnrot has discovered that "Tradition [the meaning of the Hebrew word *Kabbalah*]
lists ninety-nine names of God; Hebrew scholars explain that imper-

---

23. The three that turns into a four can be found in still other parts of the
story and most significantly where Lönnrot turns the North-West-East triangle
on his map into a South-seeking rhombus by *doubling* it. John Sturrock (*Paper
Tigers: The Ideal Fictions of Jorge Luis Borges* [London: Oxford University Press,
1977]) adds to these the *Tre* of *Treviranus*; the rabbi who arrives on the third
day to attend the Third Talmudic Conference; the thirty-third chapter of the
Philologus Hebraeo-Gracecus that contains the clue; etc., etc. (p. 130).

fect cipher by a mystic fear of numbers; the Hasidim argue that the missing term stands for a hundredth name—the Absolute Name" (p. 68). As Lönnrot now hurries to Triste-le-Roy, Borges notes that the "mystery seemed almost crystal clear. He felt ashamed for having spent close to a hundred days on it" (p. 73): but the absolute name that is to be revealed within a perfect cipher is meant to elude him.

Lönnrot has already become a piece of the puzzle he is fitting together (he was more than just one of the symbolic "people of the Book" when Treviranus had previously encountered him, a very Jewish figure with, in his hands, Leusden's *Philologus Hebraeo-Graecus*: "Lönnrot, not even bothering to take off his hat, began reading," p. 71). At Triste-le-Roy, where the "two-faced Hermes [that casts] a monstrous shadow" (p. 74) is but a symbol of the doublings that, like images caught within facing mirrors, turn the villa into an issueless labyrinth, Scharlach is waiting to kill Lönnrot. And the red thread that has been running through the blood splattering previous corpses, coloring "the garish sunset" (p. 69) that helps number correctly the appointed days, through the crimson of the prophetic lozenges, that thread suddenly draws together, in their respective names, Lönnrot (whose last syllable means *red* in German) and "Red" Scharlach (whose name in German means *scarlet*). Remembering the interreflecting mirrors of Triste-le-Roy and the straight-line maze of Zeno the Eleatic, Lönnrot tells Scharlach: "When in another incarnation you hunt me down, stage (or commit) a murder at A, then a second murder at B, eight miles from A, then a third murder at C, four miles from A and B, halfway between the two. Lay in wait for me then at D, two miles from A and C, again halfway between them. Kill me at D, the way you are going to kill me here at Triste-le-Roy" (p. 78). And Scharlach, who all along has been well aware of circularities, answers, "I promise you such a maze, which is made up of a single straight line and which is invisible and unending."

The awareness of another incarnation, of a reversal of this particular hunt (though it is hard to say with certainty who is the hunter and who the hunted), the similarity of the thought that has enabled Scharlach to think Lönnrot thinking his way to the center of the maze at Triste-le-Roy, these make of Lönnrot and Scharlach the same man at point D of a straight line maze that has already been drawn as inescapably as the infinite line of images caught in the facing mirrors of the villa.

This much Borges himself is willing to confirm (*Aleph*, p. 269). But there is a third man as well at point D, the one who entered the story earlier as the author of the *Vindication of the Kabbalah*—Borges himself. For Triste-le-Roy is a part of the author's private maze. It is the "beautiful name invented by Amanda Molina Vedia [to whom the story is inscribed]." Furthermore, it "stands for the now demolished Hotel Las Delicias in Adrogué. (Amanda had painted a map of an imaginary island on the wall of her bedroom; on her map I discovered the name Triste-le-Roy)" (*Aleph*, p. 268). We know of Adrogué already, which Borges confirms in "An Autobiographical Essay" to be indeed "some ten or fifteen miles to the south of Buenos Aires" (p. 212). Adrogué is the place of Borges's childhood summers, to which he returned for many years thereafter, the stuff of "so many memories" of his (p. 269) and about which he wrote "a longish elegy" by the same name. What dies at the point of the circle called Triste-le-Roy is not only the possibility for Lönnrot-Scharlach to decipher the criminal's name, but, deep within the intimate memory of Borges, the possibility for him to inscribe within his fiction the Absolute Name out of which, as out of God's Torah, the world is made.

"For the Kabbalists, the letters of the Torah are the mystical body of God, and from this it follows that the Creation is just a reflection or emanation of the Holy text."[24] At the melancholy point named Triste-le-Roy where the author and his characters merge within a Kabbalistic story that preserves, as in a maze, the mystery that is the mirror of a deeper Mystery, the tale of this particular Tetragrammaton ends: its fourth letter remains unknown, and with that missing letter, the unutterable remains unuttered. Like other unsanctified intercessors, Borges has stolen from the mystical sign only an amulet, and his power—like theirs—is only the distillation of a Kabbalistic flavor, a sense of the unknown and the unknowable, within the text of a story concerned with the mystery, the power, and the limits of texts. And the modern reader, reading with his head because the head can best control the metaphysical shudder, confronts an object that is wholly closed and refractory, a *thing* of the author's making, which, like the four mystical consonants of the Tetragrammaton, becomes a physical epitome of all mystery. And so, the reader's head notwithstanding, the shudder returns.

24. Alazraki, "Borges and the Kabbalah," p. 247.

Kafka:
Structure as Mystery (I)

The fate of Oedipus hinges on a misreading. The oracle speaks unambiguously but through force of conditioning. Oedipus tries to read *into* the signs traced out by the gods. The gods know that, one way or another, Oedipus is fated not to understand. His quick wit and impetuousness notwithstanding, Oedipus is turned into a plodding and awkward interpreter. His exacerbated attempt upon the limits of human understanding is reduced, like any other such attempt, to a questioning of the impediment. As in a fluoroscopic process, what cannot be penetrated contrives the only possible picture of the impenetrable. For Oedipus, the veil that hides the unknown is a *text*.

It is the possibility for his text to be this kind of veil that causes Borges to turn his text into a *reflecting* surface, a mirror that keeps his reader out even as it talks to that reader about him and his problematic world. The reader's desire to penetrate the Borgesian surface makes of him a different kind of reader—a reader conscious of reading. And when the fiction, within whose surface text the reader is birdlimed (the text as labyrinth, as palimpsest), also speaks about the efforts of a man (as often as not a reader) to progress beyond metaphysical entrapments, the story makes its appeal to the self-conscious part of the reader created by the text; the fiction of Borges is then transubstantiated as it reawakens the reader in a moment of his metaphysical dilemma.

Through an interesting coincidence, the surface of the text happens to be already the special province of a particular sort of critic who is less likely to be engaged by the author's purpose than by the way in which the author went about achieving that purpose. The superficial eye of this kind of critic (like that of a tailor for whom the cowl does not make the monk, or the painter for whom pigment does not turn into a landscape) has the virtue of making its object *real* which, at a greater depth, would be only a semblance: all surfaces, whatever intent is vouchsafed them, have in common this substantiality. When the critic has been encouraged by authors like Borges to look for the substance of the work within its surface, he is the more likely to read the surface of other texts as intention, as Lacan in the case of Poe. But the deciphering of a textual surface that is intentionally indistinct from other phenomenological evidence returns the reader/critic to the existential perplexity of Oedipus. At the ultimate extension of this process, the critic is a psychoanalyst questioning the man (the author) through the utterance of his fiction. When that has happened, the unaffected mystery is located once again, after its avatars as fiction, at its nonfictional source.

A century after Poe, what might have been his private nightmares have become considerably less private. Much of the century's writing assumes that the reader feels less comfortable in a world that seems more alien even as it is better known. When Kafka takes his turn as chronicler, he does not describe the aberration of a single consciousness; rather, he describes the aberration of a world that mocks the obdurate sanity of a single consciousness. The reader recognizes Kafka's strange world in his own familiar malaise, but that very familiarity is strange—it is unable to allay the reader's sense of estrangement. Evolution from the private world of Poe to the public world of Kafka suggests that the specialized probing of the psychoanalyst has become less necessary for an understanding of the author behind his text: Kafka is closer to his reader by virtue of what has happened to that reader since Poe. The affinities between author and private awareness, which the fiction of Poe may well mask for the lay reader, appear on the surface of Kafka's text. Kafka has no story to tell; he conveys a mood, an anxiety—*his* anxiety. He does not comment on the mystery: he and his book are a part of it. In the deceptive hints given him, Oedipus reads a text that alludes to the unknown only through such hints as preserve that unknown. When, for once, the god of the oblique speaks straight, he demonstrates that the impossibility of knowing is in Oedipus: Oedipus, the fumbling reader, is seen fumbling before an obliging text. When Kafka contrives a text that discloses Kafka rather than a fiction, he shows again that the impossibility of knowing is within the one who wants to know. And, like Apollo, he does it for a captive reader. Without the benefit of Borges's mirrors or Poe's psychoanalyst, the reader reads himself in the man writing because even after the veil of Kafka's fiction has been thinned into evanescence, the mystery is still not disclosed—only the author stands revealed as another kind of text to be deciphered within the unending process of reading.[1]

Blanchot, who is not necessarily in disagreement with this "reading" of Kafka, begins nevertheless with a challenge:[2] since the art of writing creates at best a surrogate self, are we not indulging in loose talk when we substitute the man writing for his text? How can I write "I am unhappy," asks Blanchot, without turning misery into *calculation* through the contrivance of a text that *states* my misery? An answer (though not quite the one Blanchot proposes) is that a wholly

---

1. In the subheading of a chapter (appropriately called "Literature As Exorcism"), Franz Kuna notes that Kafka evidenced "a compulsive interest in fictional works of a strongly autobiographical kind (Goethe, Dostoevsky, Strindberg, Grillparzer, Kleist, Kierkegaard)": *Kafka: Literature as Corrective Punishment* (Bloomington: Indiana University Press, 1974), p. 20. I reserve for later confirmation the fact that Kafka (always according to Kuna) evidenced a like interest in biblical exegesis.

2. Maurice Blanchot, *La Part du feu* (Paris: NRF, 1949).

impersonal contrivance by the author is just as impossible. The least personal statement—the most fictional—is an idiosyncrasy: the voice of the writer is in his words whatever those words say. Blanchot, who concludes that writing can only sham life, also concludes that writing is impossible: the writer's voice, as that voice, cannot sham. And Kafka writes stories whose only subject is Kafka.[3]

The paradox begs the question of Kafka's intent; Kafka is not just an anxious man transcribing an anxiety: no act of transcription is innocent. However much the man Kafka is caught up in his act of transcription, that transcription remains a conscious strategy that is distinct from the intimate sense that impels it. That strategy is affected by the strange persistence of the reader's hope—the reader's desire for his text to have a meaning (that is to say an *end*) that corresponds to his need for his world to have a meaning, to *signify*. The modern reader appears to remain as thralled by his expectation as did previous readers who could assume more legitimately that the book might finally be *closed* and its truth contained, though so much of modern fiction subverts the possibility of closure, resists the possibility of a metaphysical assertion even within the boundaries provided by the physical space of the text.

The success of that strategy can be seen in *The Trial*, a text about the confusion of critics and other readers that adroitly confuses critics and other readers. *The Trial's* story (before Kafka finally wears out the veil of the story) looks like those of the most fraudulent, and hence the most comforting, of fictional appropriations of mystery— the mystery story. Even when his predicament cries out for K. to ask "why?" he insists on asking, as any ordinary detective might, "where?" or "who?": condemned by a perverse metaphysics, the victim argues all aspects of his case except the metaphysical. We recall from our discussion of Freud that this refusal to internalize is necessary for the dissemination of the "unheimliche": Kafka is conjuring not a metaphysics, but its climate.

That climate results from a world described as a surface (the resistance to interiorization begins in this kind of description): it is a staged, artificial, but generally nonsymbolic world;[4] it has the partially

3. Ibid., pp. 27, 34, 29.
4. If details of the story connote a particular symbolism, they never do so through the main thrust but only in episodic and unimportant moments, as when K.'s lamp goes out in the cathedral.

comic, partially frightening rigidity of any nonhuman imitation of life. The staged artificiality suggests a self-consciousness, the felt presence of an observer. "One fine morning," when the day begins as innocuously as any other for K., he notes among many familiar reminders "the old lady opposite, who seemed to be peering at him with a curiosity unusual even for her."[5] K.'s angered exclamation at the presence of the warders confirms their being and their presence as a dominative intrusion: "It occurred to him at once that he should not have said this aloud and that by doing so he had in a way admitted the stranger's right to superintend his actions" (pp. 4–5). The strangeness of K.'s circumstances results from his attempt to enact everyday gestures on what is becoming more and more definitely a stage: "The old woman, who with truly senile inquisitiveness had moved along the window exactly opposite, in order to go on seeing all that could be seen" (p. 5). "At the other side of the street he could still see the old woman, who had now dragged to the window an even older man, whom she was holding round the waist" (p. 11). "In the window over the way the two old creatures were again stationed, but they had enlarged their party, for behind them, towering head and shoulders above them, stood a man" (p. 15).

K.'s sense that the gaze of another is on him represents largely his altered perception of the world around him; he now subjects what would be otherwise an unperceived continuation in his existence to the disjunction of analysis so that what should seem natural appears to be contrived, as when he hears the intimate talk between Leni and Block: "K. had the feeling that he was listening to a well-rehearsed dialogue which had been often repeated and would be often repeated" (p. 241). Only very occasionally does the strangeness of this staging derive from an actual alteration of K.'s world, as when the warders first appear in his bedroom, or when, walking along a hall in his bank, K. discovers those same warders being whipped in a closet.

Because the event is staged, it *contains* the actor and limits him. The metaphysical constraint is forever being echoed in the comic reductiveness of functional gestures that have become problematic— as when K. tries to hurry his loud and indiscreet uncle out of the bank: " 'I thought,' said K., taking his uncle's arm to keep him from

5. Franz Kafka, *The Trial*, trans. Willa and Edwin Muir (New York: Vintage Books, 1969), pp. 3–4. All references are to this edition.

standing still, 'that you attach even less importance to this business than I do, and now you are taking it so seriously.' 'Joseph!' cried his uncle, trying to get his arm free so as to be able to stand still, only K. would not let him, 'you're quite changed' " (p. 120). But the implications of this comic constraint extend into the implication of a menace: any attempt at a disengagement from this constraint, however successful the attempt appears to be, leads only to further constraint. Direct confrontation of the impediment may cause it to recede, not to disappear:

"Here's a fine crowd of spectators!" cried K. in a loud voice to the Inspector, pointing at them with his finger. "Go away," he shouted across. The three of them immediately retreated a few steps, the two ancients actually took cover behind the younger man, who shielded them with his massive body and to judge from the movements of his lips was saying something which, owing to the distance, could not be distinguished. Yet they did not remove themselves altogether, but seemed to be waiting for the chance to return to the window again unobserved. (P. 18)

The futility of even modest gestures to achieve an intended purpose demonstrates through comic reduction the metaphysical verdict of the Court that Titorelli spells out for K.: he is "provisionally free" (p. 197); definite acquittal is out of the question; only the possibilities of ostensible acquittal and indefinite postponement can sustain the balance of hope and frustration that define the victim once he has begun to question his circumstances.

The comic quality of this artificial world eventually turns into what it was all along—the horror of inhuman motion, a supreme illogicality resulting from the only logic that is possible: somewhat in the manner of Munch's cry frozen within the silence of his canvas, Kafka arrests within the frieze of his denouement K. moving at an ever accelerated pace, and finally at a run, to his own death. What accounts for the comic and the horror is the man at the center, K., not simply an initial but an anthropocentric obduracy, the persistent belief in a world that cannot be subverted "one fine morning" by agents of the unknown; a world in which a sense of boundaries and control makes the question "where?" possible and gives it meaning—along with all other aspects of existence. K. is more than the evidence that Kafka assumes the same expectations in his readers: K. is the encouragement for them to persist, as does K., in those expectations.[6] Kafka's whole strategy of disquietude depends on his ability to counterstate the obdurate normalcy of K. and of a reader who, like K., obdurately requires that normalcy. Kafka thus presents and subverts simultaneously the reassuring surfaces of a familiar world. Henry Sussman notes that this duality reaches the heights of irony in K. himself, whose everyday existence absorbs within its unvarying pattern the magnitude of the abnormalcy that has invaded it: K. goes as far as to abet the conspiracy of which he is a victim whenever he can.[7] K.'s outburst to Frau Grubach (an exclamation later reinterpreted by Groucho Marx) is a comic synopsis of the duality that acknowledges his victimization even as he makes an attempt at self-assertion by assuming the point of view of the victimizers: " 'Respectable!' cried K., through the chink in the door; 'if you want to keep your house respectable you'll have to begin by giving me notice' " (p. 29).

The power of any self-assertion is ultimately sexual. For K., sex represents, like the rest of his life, the evidence of both a process that continues and its subversion. His desperate need for the familiar, normative world is, in part, libidinal—this is one way of reading K.'s assault on Fräulein Bürstner: " 'I'm just coming,' K. said, rushed out, seized her, and kissed her first on the lips, then all over the face, like some thirsty animal lapping greedily at a spring of long-sought water" (p. 38). His staged world stresses both the reality of closure and the possibility of transcending it, and as a part of him intuits that both the definition and the desire are located within him, he is desperately attracted towards others; communication is a way of transcending, and sex is a way of communicating. But on the unnatural stage, that truth becomes, like all others, constrained and misshapen. When the Court usher's wife leads K. to a part of the Law's library, he discovers obscene books instead of the revelatory texts he had hoped for—and

6. Many critics have remarked on these victims' utter lack of surprise at their fate: they enter their staged world as if it were indistinct from the normal world they have forever left. Note, for example, Michel Dentan: "On a souvent relevé le manque absolu d'étonnement des personnages kafkéens devant l'étrangeté de leur sort. Ils ne s'étonnent pas de ce qu'ils sembleraient en droit de considérer comme une injustice ou une catastrophe, ou une condamnation scandaleuse et incompréhensible" (*Humour et création littéraire dans l'oeuvre de Kafka* [Geneva: Droz, 1961], p. 20).

7. "The Court as Text," *PMLA* 92, no. 1 (1977): 41.

they themselves are emblematically marred, artificialized out of even their erotic meaning:

> He opened the first of them and found an indecent picture. A man and a woman were sitting naked on a sofa, the obscene intention of the draftsman was evident enough, yet his skill was so small that nothing emerged from the picture save the all-too-solid figures of a man and a woman sitting rigidly upright, and because of the bad perspective, apparently finding the utmost difficulty even in turning toward each other. (P. 65)

This stage stunts its actors: when she thrusts herself on K., the usher's wife cannot of course allay the malaise to which her ministrations contribute. She is a part of the circumstances that invert K.'s libidinal assertion: the females around K. turn into hungry, uterine mouths.[8] Montag, Leni, the girls in Titorelli's studio, are sexually aggressive, and the threat of the aggression is magnified by the flawed quality of the pleasure they promise: all have more or less startling physical deformities; Fräulein Bürstner's second incarnation— Fräulein Montag—limps; Leni's two middle fingers are webbed; the girl at Titorelli's who pursues K. most closely is hunchbacked, though "scarcely thirteen years old" (p. 177).[9] The womb that is the promise

---

8. Ruth Tiefenbrun has analyzed in some detail Kafka's writing with a view to developing the hypothesis that he was a homosexual. *Moment of Torment: An Interpretation of Franz Kafka's Short Stories* (Carbondale: Southern Illinois University Press, 1973).

9. Heinz Politzer (*Franz Kafka: Parable and Paradox* [Ithaca, N.Y.: Cornell University Press, 1962]) has noted the similarity of Kafka's views with those of the Viennese philosopher Otto Weininger (1880–1903), whose dissertation *Sex and Character* was among the first to equate the categories of mother and whore. Politzer believes that the female characters in *The Trial* amount to a separate appendix of Kafka's general indictment of the world and that Kafka saw them as agents of evil; Politzer notes that in his "Reflections," Kafka wrote: "One of the most effective means of seduction that Evil has is the challenge to struggle. It is like the struggle with women, which ends in bed" (p. 200). Rather than showing women as instruments of a moral wrong, this passage would seem to confirm them as the frustrating intercessors positioned at a boundary that appears to yield but does not in fact allow penetration. Martin Greenberg (*The Terror of Art: Kafka and Modern Literature* [New York: Basic Books, 1968]) is able to read a moral lesson in part of this negative view of women: "Unlike K., Fräulein Bürstner is 'shameless' and therefore beyond the reach of the warders of a court of alienated conscience" (p. 130). Greenberg believes that when K. kisses her like a thirsty animal, what he thirsts for is her freedom. The point is that K.'s thirst, for a sexual object or for the metaphysical absolute of which sex is an emblem, can never be slaked.

of selfhood recovered, the ultimate possession of self through possession of another, but that becomes instead a threatening vortex, corresponds to a necessary law of gravity that replaces on this stage the lost possibilities of a motion that might have been willed and effective. The Law is the central evidence of such a process; instead of being a dialectical object contained within the mind, it functions as a kind of monstrous tropism—another form of the vortex: "Our officials," the warder explains, "never go hunting for crime in the populace, but, as the Law decrees, are drawn towards the guilty and must then send out us warders" (p. 10). Its mode describes the sort of process that draws K. into its working from the moment he begins dressing for his part even as he refuses to play his role:

"What are you thinking of?" [the warders] cried. "Do you imagine you can appear before the Inspector in your shirt? He'll have you well thrashed, and us too." "Let me alone, damn you," cried K., who by now had been forced back to his wardrobe. "If you grab me out of bed, you can't expect to find me all dressed up in my best suit." "That can't be helped," said the warders, who as soon as K. raised his voice always grew quite calm, indeed almost melancholy, and thus contrived either to confuse him or to some extent bring him to his senses. "Silly formalities!" he growled, but immediately lifted a coat from a chair and held it up for a little while in both hands, as if displaying it to the warders for their approval. They shook their heads. "It must be a black coat," they said. Thereupon K. flung the coat on the floor and said—he did not himself know in what sense he meant the words —"But this isn't the capital charge yet." The warders smiled, but stuck to their: "It must be a black coat." (Pp. 13–14)

In the force of this strange gravitational pull, the reader senses the presence of an alien world—however familiar its surfaces might be. But Kafka is not satisfied with such reminders. What marks him as a modern author is his refusal to let the reader find refuge within that last perimeter of his control—the book. Like Borges or Poe, Kafka replaces the *idea* of an alien world with the objective *evidence* of a text. This inhibiting and contrived world is, after all, a real book that rehearses, within the one who wants to know, the impossibility of fully knowing. The reader cannot *contain* Kafka's text even though it presents itself as the form (the mystery story) that most readily contains mystery.

The evidence of the text is confirmed by the central image: the Law is a world of books; K. is convinced that if he could read them, he would win his case—possession of the Word being, perhaps, less problematic than possession of an other: K. responds to the sexual blandishments of the Court usher's wife in order to possess the books that are in the library of the Law (only to find in their stead, as we have seen, further instances of an unappealing and frustrating sexuality). These books are not, of course, available to K.: those behind whom the Law hides are the sole repositories of a textual secret. The Examining Magistrate has, as his only distinguishing prop, a single notebook:

But the Examining Magistrate did not seem to worry, he sat quite comfortably in his chair and after a few final words to the man behind him took up a small notebook, the only object lying on the table. It was like an ancient school exercise-book, grown dog-eared from much thumbing. "Well then," said the Examining Magistrate turning over the leaves and addressing K. with an air of authority, "you are a house painter?" (P. 50)

Writing is a lingering activity, even within the deserted Court offices: "Some of the offices were not properly boarded off from the passage but had an open frontage of wooden rails, reaching, however, to the roof, through which a little light penetrated and through which one could see a few officials as well, some writing at their desks" (p. 78). Because he is a part of the Court, Titorelli is the scribe of a tradition, even though he is a painter. Because he uses a different language, he *paints* Court legends:

[W]e have only legendary accounts of ancient cases. These legends certainly provide instances of acquittal; actually the majority of them are about acquittals, they can be believed, but they cannot be proved. All the same, they shouldn't be entirely left out of account, they must have an element of truth in them, and besides they are very beautiful. I myself have painted several pictures founded on such legends. (P. 193)

What Titorelli's paintings have in common with other texts that represent the Law is that they cannot be grasped, that they possess no efficacy, no firm or reliable substance; like the very text given the reader, the texts of the Law are adequate only to sustain for a while the hope of the one who inquires of them, not to reward that hope.

But texts persist in the persistence of the decipherer's hope of possessing his text: one of the many ways K. is tempted to join the world of his persecutors is by turning into a writer of his own script—creating the arcane document that will *stand for him*:

The thought of his case never left him now. He had often considered whether it would not be better to draw up a written defense and hand it in to the Court. In this defense he would give a short account of his life, and when he came to an event of any importance explain for what reasons he had acted as he did, intimate whether he approved or condemned his way of action in retrospect, and adduce grounds for the condemnation or approval. The advantages of such a written defense, as compared with the mere advocacy of a lawyer who himself was not impeccable, were undoubted. (P. 142)

Writing would represent a new aspect of the same quest for K.: it would be a way for the patient reader, which the victim—K. or Block —has already become, to seize his text, instead of being reduced, like Kafka's own reader, to read those reading (writing), unable as he is to read the text those readers read (or write).

Whatever object the quest may posit, through whatever subterfuge, that object remains elusive. The word *God* is absent from Kafka's fiction, but the Jewish mystical tradition (upon which Borges also draws) equates for Kafka the impossible revelation and the revelatory letter:[10] it is within scripting signs that the unknowable shows and conceals itself. The word, as mystical mediator, as initiate, is caught up in the dialectical process that affects the way in which all initiates are perceived: it can only state its failure to reveal but in so doing is suffused with intimations of the mystery it has attempted. The Kabbalah believes in the occult meaning of the letter, the presence of God in the sign of His word: instead of making God apprehensible, this presence makes the letter awesome. We have noted in our reading of Borges how, in time, this awesome signifier becomes little more than an amulet, a container suggesting a reversal of the original denial by offering as *possible* the appropriation of a final and absolute mystery. But a sacredness attaches to even the ineffectual amulet (it is for that reason that no amulet is wholly ineffectual).

In Kafka's fiction, the missing term *God* is replaced by His letter, the Law, an ironically scripted form of the absolute, in the same way

10. Johannes Urzidil (*There Goes Kafka* [Detroit: Wayne State University Press, 1968]) refers, like Borges, to the *Yetzirah*, the earliest of cabalistic works, and its conjecture about the possibility of informing matter (clay: *golem*) with life. Urzidil is mindful of the fact that cabalists believed it possible, under certain circumstances, to bring life to *golem* (in the famous legend of that name associated with the figure of a man) by affixing to it the scripted symbol of the divine name, the *shem* (p. 130).

as the letter of this text is informed by the presence of its own *deus absconditus*—Kafka. "Everyone strives to attain the Law" (p. 269): K.'s hope, and the reader's, are sustained by an awareness—the importance of the part of themselves that is concealed by the fiction of their text. For both, the integument of the mystery that cannot be uttered (as cannot be uttered the name of God) will be the *parable*, the traditional reduction of that mystery as allegorical fiction.

The parable, a mode in which Kafka showed an abiding interest, acknowledges intellectual slippage, a failure of the mind to apprehend its object. The parable is a *substitute*, a simile. The German word *Gleichnis* also means simile; its root, *gleich*, evidences the perplexity of knowing: it means both *same* and *resembling*—that is to say, identical and different. It is not improbable that Kafka favored the parable because he was most intent on demonstrating this slippage, on making the reader experience the impossibility of locating his world anywhere else but in this slippage. In his *Parables and Paradoxes*, he says, "All these parables really set out to say is merely that the incomprehensible is incomprehensible."[11] The parable also contains the tone, the tradition, and the manner of the failure of the hidden god to become manifest. And when the parable comments on the failure of the parable, it merely returns to literature a traditional concealment of god as text.

Long before Kafka turns formally to the parable, he has already constructed a fiction that proves, in the multiple instances of its own slippage, to be more than a mere fiction. And in this endeavor, he is seconded by an ironic fate: none of his major fiction is complete in the form we have of it; in *The Trial*, the very ordering of the chapters is not necessarily Kafka's. It is on this shifting ground that contrives the deceptive revelation of a parable whose magnitude is equal to the totality of the fiction that Kafka establishes a central parable that his fiction treats as a problematic text—a parable whose lesson is the doubtful nature of parables.

Since the parable is a *likeness* that discloses and disguises a more distant truth, what will be the central parable of *The Trial* does not disturb the innocuousness of other events: the self-consciously moral fiction develops within the continuation of an apparently conventional

11. New York: Schoken Books, 1961 (German and English texts), p. 11.

fiction. An influential Italian customer of the bank where K. still works is visiting town and K. is appointed to squire him. Like all other episodic and trivial events within K.'s life, this one contains in germ the mood of, and what might be read as emblems for, something more than the story that those episodes contrive. K's encounter with the Italian visitor in the office of the Manager suggests the inevitable continuation of the perverse law proclaiming that everything that can go wrong will. K.'s knowledge of Italian is tenuous, the Italian speaks fast and lapses frequently into a southern dialect, a bushy moustache conceals the motion of his lips: the problem of understanding signs, of trying to solve the unintelligible, becomes once again a preoccupation of K., within the similar but overriding preoccupations that already perplex him. Once more, K. is outside an event that concerns him but that he cannot penetrate.

The visitor wants to visit the town's Cathedral, where K. agrees to meet him later in the morning. While waiting for that meeting, K. continues within a life whose normalcy has already become an annoying irrelevance. Now, additionally, that normalcy mocks the urgency of an event: a new puzzlement has thrust itself into a pattern whose ordinariness has long since been subverted by K.'s other predicaments. K. is now three times baffled: the routine at the bank prevents him from refreshing his Italian, which he will need for his encounter with the incomprehensible visitor; and the visitor, for whom he must perfect his Italian, provides an additional distraction from K.'s obsessive need to give all his time to his "case." This tiered frustration leads him to believe that "they're goading me" (p. 255): as usual, K. creates an otherness in which to place his dilemma.

K. arrives punctually for his appointment at the Cathedral, but his visitor is of course not there. Since the central question revolves around the possibility of *understanding*, K. wonders whether he is in possession of the correct facts: was the visitor supposed to be there at all? The day is rainy, the Cathedral dark. A few candles have been lit, emblematic objects that do not cast sufficient light to see clearly by; their only true clarity is in their emblematic significance. To their half-light, K. adds the inadequate light of his own pocket lamp. It picks out of the gloom the strange figure of a knight in a canvas against one of the walls. For a moment, the incongruity of the figure holds K.'s attention. When he moves his light over the rest of the canvas, it discloses a conventional Sepulture of Christ and he loses interest. In this rare instance, the normative world dissipates the question, and K. is no longer able to be held by a normative world.

K. catches sight of a verger who is making signs to him that he cannot understand: the verger is enacting a role for the benefit of K. but it is one that K., once again, cannot fathom. The Cathedral is full of such signs, among them a light over a small side pulpit that is hardly larger than a niche for a statue. K. is drawn to the pulpit: the light over it would be "the usual sign that a sermon was going to be preached" (p. 260). Is a sermon going to be preached there—will there be a religious discourse delivered for the sake of instruction? The answer is that a religious discourse will be delivered indeed: the pulpit has the attributes of height and sanctity from which an absolute truth is traditionally handed down. But whether instruction will be handed down as well, or what exactly the form of that instruction will be, is problematic: instead of the sermon's instruction, Kafka will insert here the ambiguity of the parable.

In the house of God, and in the accepted manner of any solemn handing-down, a voice calls K. from the pulpit: the ultimate mystery, like lesser ones, states clearly its relation to its object and little more. The voice acquires its resonance not only from the spiritual acoustics of the Cathedral but because it belongs to a young priest who knows K.: he is connected with the Court. Intuiting the ambiguity of what will follow, K. responds only when he has been able to make the unequivocal summons seem ambiguous:

But if he were to turn round he would be caught, for that would amount to an admission that he had understood it very well, that he was really the person addressed, and that he was ready to obey. Had the priest called his name a second time K. would certainly have gone on, but as everything remained silent, though he stood waiting a long time, he could not help turning his head a little just to see what the priest was doing. (Pp. 262–63)

With comic obduracy, and true to his mode, K. tries to reduce the intrusion of a transcendental revelation to the mundane level of his everyday life: "I came here to show an Italian round the Cathedral" (p. 263). So K. must be told what the reader knows already, that this normalcy is "beside the point." The point is that K. is presumed guilty. For one of the few times in his life, K. rebels: if he is guilty, then no man is innocent: "If it comes to that, how can any man be called guilty? We are all simply men here, one as much as the other" (p. 264). The priest acknowledges this similarity but reminds K. that this is nevertheless the talk of guilty men; the condition is not circumstantial and is therefore not subject to rational rejection. The *trial* (in German, *der Prozess*), which is never a trial but simply a *process*, turns into guilt as part of the process: "The verdict is not suddenly arrived at, the proceedings only gradually merge into the verdict" (p. 264). In the *process* of our existence, our *arrest* is nothing more than our awareness, our *trial* the result of that awareness.

This concomitance denies the possibility of melioristic gestures and human contact. The priest is supposed to bring comfort, but however good his intentions, he is likely to harm K. Still, K. is drawn to this figure of good: "With you I can speak openly" (p. 267). The priest's answer is ambiguous: "Don't be deluded"; it may refer to what K. was saying previously, it may refer to what K. has just said. K. attempts to clarify the ambiguity; in response, the priest delivers Kafka's parable, the similitude that instances an *otherness*, the periphrase whose elaboration confuses.

The parabale reinforces within this context notions of mystery, elevation, and final revelation. In a story about the impossibility of passing beyond, the Door (the traditional gateway to a supernatural realm) and the Law loom (like the word of God) before the man from the country. For the reader, the parable also borrows biblical cadences in order to tell about the Door—the uttermost extension of the human possibility, informed with the terrible mystery that it proclaims and protects.

The doorkeeper is the traditional intercessor similarly haloed (though here in a comic mode) by his proximity to the unknown and, in the manner of all intercessors, utterly ineffectual. The doorkeeper, like the Door itself, like the priest who tells the story, like the very story of which that story is a part, is on *this side* of the impenetrability: he can only be a distracting focal point. Moreover, he does not keep out the man from the country, and the door is always open; the inability to enter is in the one seeking admission. The priest's critical analyses may be confusing in their catholicity, but they are not necessarily wrong:

He allows the man to curse loudly in his presence the fate for which he himself is responsible. (P. 272)

The man from the country is really free, he can go where he likes, it is only the Law that is closed to him, and access to the Law is forbidden him by only one individual. (P. 274)

There is no lack of agreement that the doorkeeper will not be able to shut the door. (P. 275)

It is the necessary ineffectiveness of the intercessor that allows him even to be kind: "The doorkeeper gives him a stool and lets him sit down at the side of the door" (p. 268); "The doorkeeper often engages him in brief conversations, asking him about his home and about other matters" (p. 268). The kindness of the doorkeeper, like the consolation of the priest, are of the same order as the impediment that may be forced temporarily to recede, but not to disappear, or the human gesture that achieves an immediate end mocked by the metaphysical dilemma that constrains it.[12]

The man from the country can do only what man has always done before the unknowable: fasten on the figure of the intercessor. Like Oedipus, like Block, like K. himself, the man becomes a close reader of the surface of an impenetrable text: "In his prolonged study of the doorkeeper he has learned to know even the fleas in his fur collar" (pp. 268–69). As the mystery asserts its impenetrability, man acknowledges his failure to know by deifying the unknown: in an ultimate and self-deriding attempt to contain what cannot be contained, he makes of the mystery God: "In the darkness he can now perceive a radiance that streams inextinguishably from the door of the Law" (p. 269).

But Kafka is concerned, of course, with an entirely different text— there is no man before the Door: there is only a reader, Kafka's, before *his* text. The parable that complicates the complex fiction within which it is set will now be turned into an object lesson—literally, a parafictional object on which the reader will perform the exercise suggested by the fictional characters. The priest, who belongs

12. Sartre has discussed this aspect of Kafka (*Being and Nothingness*, trans. H. E. Barnes [New York: Citadel Press, 1964], pt. 3): to the extent that K.'s acts are related to cause and effect, he is able to perform them satisfactorily ("actes réussis"); he can predict their result as it affects his objective world, but the truth of their meaning escapes him; he is a being-in-the-world for others, experiencing total opacity within what appears to be total transluscence. The parable makes this point explicit for K.: the man from the country may bribe the doorkeeper but he cannot change him into a compliant instrument.

to the Court, has charitably entertained all of K.'s unanswerable questions; the priest, as critic of the text, will entertain sufficiently numerous and contradictory interpretations to show the impossibility of reading.

The "scripture" related by the priest is both holy and full of holes: it is given as the comfort of a truth recaptured, an absolute that can be comprehended. But modern fiction, perhaps starting with Kafka, opens fiction unto the unknown deliberately, offering itself as experience rather than imitation. The priest is not content to set forth a parable about the impossibility of knowing; he will not lose the reader within the diverse and contradictory possibilities afforded by the genre. Though he is the only speaker of the parable, he cautions K. against hasty interpretations: "Don't take over someone else's opinion without testing it" (p. 269). But there is no "someone else": K. has only the priest's text, just as the reader has only Kafka's; the suggestion is inescapable: though the priest has told "the story in the very words of the scriptures" (p. 269), the very text as text is suspect.

Once doubt has been cast on the body of orthodoxy, its absolute assertion is no longer commensurate with absolute revelation. Any interpretation is possible: "The commentators note in this connection: 'The right perception of any matter and a misunderstanding of the same matter do not wholly exclude each other'" (p. 271). The scripture therefore invites a gloss that is supposed to provide further steps towards the unknown. But as the gloss is the intercessor of an intercessory text, it represents in fact a step back, a greater distance from the inaccessible truth. Even though K. was admonished by the priest because he had "not enough respect for the written word" (p. 270), that "disrespect" comes from the only posture that is possible before the text: utmost respect; through overly close scrutiny, K. has analyzed the only surface allowed him into meaninglessness. It is through this same kind of gloss-making that the priest now leads Kafka's reader. As the reader is drawn through the maze of the text, he is drawn through another part of his awareness; forced to proceed tentatively through the text, he rehearses the tentative nature of his being, the tentative nature of an existential process of which the book he is reading is now only a part.

For neither K. nor the reader can there be any ultimate revelation. There is only description, necessity: "I don't agree with that point of view," said K., shaking his head, "for if one accepts it, one must accept as true everything the doorkeeper says. But you yourself have sufficiently proved how impossible it is to do that." "No," said the priest, "it is not necessary to accept everything as true, one must only accept it as necessary." "A melancholy conclusion," concludes K., "It turns lying into a universal principle" (p. 276). But such "lying" results only from a confrontation with the absolute; the priest is more philosophical and relativistic—he is, after all, only a part of the shifting boundaries that defeat the possibility of any human grasp.

K.'s light, which the priest gave him to hold, has long since gone out; small loss: it was more limiting than revelatory. Kafka snuffs it out three times: in the cathedral, in the death of K. (our confused eye within this particular text), in the text itself. Like K., and for the duration of the fiction we share, we have been kept at arm's length from something that is important to us and that we can sense only by circling around it. But in our circling we have become K., and we also have been reading about ourselves reading—hopelessly. Starobinski notes a similarity between Dostoevsky and Kafka in that the characters of each no longer have a "chez soi"—they have been expelled from their rightful home, they are in exile from themselves.[13] Kafka's purpose is to make us aware of our own exile, but in the process we have entered his book, we have entered into his sense of the unenterable: *we* now inform the pale surfaces of his story as he first did.

13. Jean Starobinski, "Kafka et Dostoievski," *Cahiers du Sud*, no. 304 (second semester, 1950), pp. 466–75.

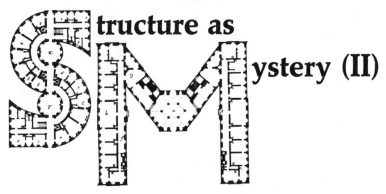

Robbe-Grillet:
Structure as
Mystery (II)

We end where we began, with the story of Oedipus, with the implications of the myth. In his first novel, *The Erasers* (1953), Robbe-Grillet attempted nothing less than to cast the archetype in a new idiom. So new was the idiom that it obscured for some the author's purpose, substituting one kind of obscurity for another. Robbe-Grillet's most astute readers pointed out that he made too much of the myth for his references to be taken seriously and that his exegetes frequently made too much of those clues to really understand them.

A "prière d'insérer" by Robbe-Grillet for the first edition of *Les Gommes* summarizes the story:

It is about a precise, concrete, essential event: the death of a man. It is an event of a detective nature—that is to say, there is an assassin, a detective, a victim. In a sense, their roles are even respected: the assassin fires on the victim, the detective *resolves* the question, the victim dies. But the relationships that bind them are not as simple, or rather, are not as simple until the last chapter is ended. For the book is precisely the story of the twenty-four hours that elapse between this pistol shot and this death, the time the bullet required to travel three or four meters—twenty-four hours "in excess" ["en trop"].

Thus, according to Robbe-Grillet, we also return to the detective story —though, as might be expected of a detective story over which falls the Oedipal shadow, this is a detective story of a peculiar kind. For if, "in a sense," the rules of that fiction are "respected," the clear implication is that, in another sense, they are not. The very sequence that Robbe-Grillet presents in his summary—"The assassin fires on the victim, the detective *resolves* the question, the victim dies"—is indeed that of the events in *The Erasers*, but it does not correspond to the expected linearity of the detective story, which would normally have the assassin fire, the victim die, and *then* the detective's solution. It is this inversion that casts doubt on the meaning of Robbe-Grillet's italicized "resolution." In turn, that doubt questions the possibility of there being a "last chapter" after which the relationships will become (retrospectively?) simple.

Whatever these twenty-four hours "in excess" may mean, they belong to "special agent" Wallas—it is through them that he enters the story. He does so, without nationality or credentials,[1] in order to bring the suspension of time to an end rather than to "resolve" any questions: Garinati, the political hit man, shoots Daniel Dupont but misses; Wallas, called in to "resolve" the series of killings that led to the attempt on Dupont's life, arrives as his watch stops running; twenty-four hours later, he kills Dupont by accident, his watch starts off again, and, after an epilogue, the novel comes to a close. The fictional twenty-four hours during which we concentrate on Wallas

---

1. But as a definite echo—that of Edgar Wallace (even though de-Anglicized), whose thrillers sold up to 5 million copies a year at the height of his popularity, not a few of them disseminated in France.

are a hiatus with reference to the killing of Dupont—it is the time during which *something else* happens.

If this hiatus is of a "detective nature," then that "detection" is different in kind from those to which we are accustomed: the presumption of a synthesizing eye through which we define the sleuth in detective fiction is replaced here by the evidence of sight fragmented. We are dealing with an utterly different kind of detective: the private eye of the more usual kind is his own privacy; he is not our sight— our sight is his unperceptive sidekick's, and our questions, funneled through that Watson, remain unanswered: we do not know but we are confident that we will. The significant clues, which the traditional detective always reads with smug elation and little else by way of commentary, concern us to the extent that they bolster our confidence in the detective. But in *The Erasers*, Wallas *is* our private eye: he picks up no clues for himself and serves mainly to confuse our vision. We do not see, and we gradually come to understand that we never will.

To that end, the principal purpose of Wallas during the span between prologue and epilogue is to encounter for us intimations of the Oedipal myth. He encounters them in the motifs of the lace curtains behind certain of the city windows: "At one ground-floor window, the curtains are decorated with a mass-produced allegorical subject: shepherds finding an abandoned child, or something of the kind. . . . Again, open blinds and that cheap net curtain: under a tree, two shepherds in classical costume give ewe's milk to a tiny naked baby."[2] They appear in the city's monuments and public thoroughfares: "In the middle of the square, on a low pedestal protected by an iron fence, stands a bronze group representing a Greek chariot drawn by two horses, in which are standing several individuals, probably symbolic, whose unnatural positions are out of harmony with the presumed rapidity of their equipage" (p. 58); "At the same time, he has had the waitress explain the most convenient way to get to the Rue de Corinthe. Passing once more in front of the statue that decorates the Place de la Préfecture, he has approached it to read, on the west side of the pedestal, the inscription carved in the stone: 'The Chariot of

2. Pp. 45, 46. Unless otherwise specified, pagination for *The Erasers* refers to the translation by Richard Howard (New York: Grove Press, 1977).

State—V. Daulis, sculptor.' "[3] These Oedipal hints are echoed, appropriately enough, by a drunkard who is given a new form of the traditional riddle: "What animal is parricide in the morning, incestuous at noon, and blind at night?" (p. 226); less appropriate are the drunk's references in a story that has nothing direct to say about parricide or incest. But of note is the fact that the question is no longer a riddle about prophetic feet: it is now a synopsis of the myth, part of a game that Robbe-Grillet extends in the same scene through a discussion of the (Loxian) oblique:

The manager serves the three men at the bar another round. The other two have resumed their argument; it is the meaning of the word *oblique* that is in dispute. Each man is trying to prove he is right by shouting louder than the other.

"Are you going to let me talk?"

"That's all you do is talk!"

"You don't understand: I said I can go straight ahead while still taking a direction that's oblique—oblique in relation to the canal."

The other man thinks a moment and remarks calmly:

"You're going to fall into the canal."

"Listen, Antoine, you can say whatever you want, I'm not changing what I said: if you walk obliquely, you don't go straight ahead! Even if it's in relation to a canal or anything else." (P. 224)

The focal point of Wallas's Oedipal quest is an eraser: Wallas is looking for a particular object: "A soft, crumbly eraser that friction does not twist but reduces to dust; an eraser that cuts easily and whose cut surface is shiny and smooth, like mother-of-pearl. He has seen one such, a few months ago, at a friend's but the friend could not tell him where it came from" (p. 126); the description is familiar: not even wartime shortages could have dissipated its memory. The reason why Wallas cannot find that kind of eraser is that it exists here only as a tenuous emitter of Oedipal signs: "It looked like a yellowish cube, about an inch or two long, with the corners slightly rounded—maybe

---

3. Pp. 79–80. Retention of the French street names in this translation is unsatisfactory: it makes the unspecified town too much like a French place, and it contrasts markedly with the author's intention. Just as he has de-Anglicized "Wallace" into "Wallas," Robbe-Grillet is careful not to allow any nationalisms to personalize or render more familiar the places through which Wallas moves. And the intent of Corinth Street is clearly not that conveyed to an English reader by the French "Rue de Corinthe."

by use. The manufacturer's brand was printed on one side, but was too worn to be legible any more: only two of the middle letters were still clear: 'di'; there must have been at least two letters before and perhaps two or three others after."[4] That eraser is important, nevertheless, in its contaminating function. As Wallas on his quest enters a stationery store, he notes the window display:

A dummy, dressed in a paint-spotted smock and whose face is hidden under a huge "bohemian" beard, is hard at work in front of his easel; stepping back slightly to see both his work and the model at the same time, he is putting the finishing touches on a carefully drawn landscape—which must actually be a copy of some master. It is a hill with the ruins of a Greek temple among cypress trees; in the foreground, fragments of columns lie scattered here and there; in the distance, in the valley, appears a whole city with its triumphal arches and palaces—rendered, despite the distance and the accumulation of buildings, with a scrupulous concern for detail. But in front of the man, instead of the Greek countryside, stands instead of the setting a huge photographic reproduction of a modern city intersection. The nature of this image and its skillful arrangement give the panorama a reality all the more striking in that it is the negation of the drawing supposed to represent it; and suddenly Wallas recognizes the place: that house surrounded by huge apartment buildings, that iron fence, that spindle-tree hedge, is the corner of the Rue des Arpenteurs. Obviously.[5]

This is a vision that recurs, transposed, as the negative/positive moments of a photograph (two ways of *seeing into* what is not actually there).

The ruins of Thebes.
On a hill above the city, a Sunday painter has set up his easel in the shade of cypress trees, between the scattered shafts of columns. He paints carefully, his eyes shifting back to his subject every few seconds; with a fine brush he points up many details that are scarcely noticeable to the

---

4. Page 126. The eraser is all too legible: the reader's deciphering within this purposeful context spells out "Oedipus." Since this is the stuff of which critical games are made, any number of critics have already pointed out that the French name Didier would be a more likely brand. (See, for example, Leon Roudiez, cited by Bruce Morrissette: *The Novels of Robbe-Grillet* [Ithaca, N.Y.: Cornell University Press, 1975]; p. 63. Also, Morrissette himself, pp. 63ff.)

5. Pages 124–25. Too obviously: the world of Wallas flows in and out of mythical and literary allusions. The Surveyors' Street reminds us of another character lost within a labyrinth of the author's making—the surveyor in Kafka's *Castle.*

naked eye, but which assume a surprising intensity once they are reproduced in the picture. He must have very sharp eyes. One could count the stones that form the edge of the quay, the bricks of the gable-end, and even the slates in the roof. At the corner of the fence, the leaves of the spindle trees gleam in the sun, which emphasizes their outlines. Behind, a bush rises above the hedge, a bare bush whose every twig is lined with a bright streak where the light hits it, and a dark one on the shadow side. The snapshot has been taken in winter, on an exceptionally clear day. What reason could the young woman have for photographing this house? (Pp. 168–69)

The "reason" for that photograph is merely that it is one more emitter in this orchestration of Oedipal signs: the house is Dupont's; the young woman is likely his wife; the photograph will be Wallas's lure to the selfsame house where he will shoot Dupont. It is part of this landscape informing, or informed by, Wallas's eyes alone: the nameless city in which Wallas is lost is the composite nightmare of his recollections, his frustrated eye, his circular returns. This landscape that contrives in a fleeting moment a vision of the myth—

The oil slick finishes off a grotesque clown's face, a Punch-and-Judy doll.

Or else it is some legendary animal: the head, the neck, the breast, the front paws, a lion's body with its long tail, and an eagle's wings. The creature moves greedily toward a shapeless prey lying a little farther on. The corks and the piece of wood are still in the same place, but the face they formed a moment ago has completely disappeared. The greedy monster too. (Pp. 32–33)

—is the one that Wallas enters also through the intimacy of his own childhood recollections—recollections that will be "Oedipal," by virtue of fictional and other necessities:

The scene takes place in a Pompeian-style city—and, more particularly, in a rectangular forum one end of which is occupied by a temple (or a theater, or something of the same kind), the other sides by various smaller monuments divided by wide, paved roadways. Wallas has no idea where this image comes from. He is talking—sometimes in the middle of the square—sometimes on stairs, long flights of stairs—to people he cannot distinguish from one another but who were at the start clearly characterized and individual. He himself has a distinct role, probably a major one, perhaps official. The memory suddenly becomes quite piercing; for a fraction of a second, the entire scene assumes an extraordinary density. But what scene? He has just time to hear himself say:

"And did that happen a long time ago?"

Immediately everything has vanished, the people, the stairs, the temple, the rectangular forum and its monuments. He has never seen anything of the kind.

It is the agreeable face of a dark young woman which appears in its place—the stationery saleswoman from the Rue Victor-Hugo and the echo of her little throaty laugh. Yet her face is serious.

Wallas and his mother had finally reached the dead end of a canal; in the sunlight, the low houses reflected their old façades in the green water. It was not an aunt they were looking for: it was a male relative, someone he had never really known. He did not see him that day either. It was his father. How could he have forgotten it? (Pp. 230–31)

We have already drawn comparisons between the Oedipal story and the detective story. But in a broader sense, every fictional text is, for every reader, a quest for a quest, the interrogation of a symbol that stands for interrogation. In that sense, every story repeats through variations a form of the Oedipal concern—the detective story being simply the mode that reduces the question as much as possible to simply its form. But if the detective and the Oedipal stories are similar because their questioning is so central and so little disguised, they are also at antipodes from each other because the intrinsic and unanswerable nature of the Oedipal question can only emphasize the anxiety that prompts it, whereas the detective question derives from knowledge that has never been put in doubt or thought to be inaccessible. The figure of the Oedipal quest is a circle: the myth is a retracing of what has already come to pass because there are no answers; the answer "Man" is more than even a tautology—it is because Oedipus *is* Man that he has *already* killed his father and slept with his mother: the end of his story will not alter the definition of the spectator. If the circle is able to construct the comforting limits of a ritual, it is only because the rehearsal of the human dilemma is its only possible answer. The closure of the detective story represents a circle of a different kind: it constructs a false circle, a circle with an end. When an author, Faulkner in *Sanctuary* or Robbe-Grillet in *The Erasers*, allows the myth's more primal questioning to enter the detective story, he is contriving a deliberate subversion of the genre.[6]

6. It was André Malraux who spoke of the intrusion of Greek tragedy in the detective story, in a preface to a French translation of *Sanctuary* in 1933. For a more extended discussion of these particulars, see Ben F. Stoltzfus, *Alain Robbe-Grillet and the New French Novel* (Carbondale: Southern Illinois University Press, 1964), pp. 67ff.

The unanswerable nature of the Oedipal question allows it to retain its power even as a question, as a posture of the mind: it is sufficiently close to the shadows where the mind fails not to be absorbed in the manner of lesser dilemmas. The questions of Oedipus put *in* our mind what our mind desires to expel: we are contaminated by a questioning that escapes so unseemingly from the fiction that should contain it; we know, after all (and the very thought is awesome), that the answers Oedipus seeks are hidden within the symbolic depths of the Pythia: as Otto Rank surmised, Oedipus finds his truth only in the final accomplishment of the circle, within the womb, in death—when he is at last engulfed by the darkness that must not, and cannot, be penetrated.

But we also *talk* about the myth. The circularity of the unanswerable that first creates our myth creates the comfort of our own repeating. And that repeating extends into our every repossession of the myth through the further reductiveness of our commentary. Every reference to Oedipus leads us back to ourselves even as it leads us out into a world of "meanings": *Oedipus* is also what Jean Alter has called 'un mythe pourri des significations.'[7] As a philosopher and as a practicing writer, Robbe-Grillet is aware of the dulling effect that results from too much "meaning," and he has directed a large part of his polemic writing against this cultural burden. An article like his "Nature, Humanism, Tragedy," whose title itemizes the categories of that burden, is typical of his strategy.[8] The nature of his attack is twofold: it contains a philosophy and a program—two different concerns that critics have usually lumped together.

The strategic part of Robbe-Grillet's argument resists an anthropocentrism that renders vision tautological, allowing the beholder to see only himself in the world that he informs through the act of his perception. The philosophical part of his argument, borrowed from Sartre (whom Robbe-Grillet assails in his tactical argument), rejects a like information of the "neutral" world around us by the beholding eye, which the Humanist considers to be "tragic."[9] To specify that

---

7. *La Vision du monde d'Alain Robbe-Grillet* (Geneva: Droz, 1966), p. 8.

8. In *For a New Novel*, trans. Richard Howard (New York: Grove Press, 1965).

9. In his theoretical writing, Robbe-Grillet is skittish about even such terms as *indifferent* or *absurd* when a Sartre uses them to designate the outer world that *is there*; he sees a persistent anthropocentrism seeping through such designations and therefore prefers the term *neutral*.

such an assimilation of the "neutral" world by the reader should be resisted through the author's "neutral" style is quite different from the philosophical assumption that the reader will be able to accept such an askesis: the absorption of even Robbe-Grillet's "neutral" world will be effected through individual and private filterings—what Robbe-Grillet might specify for himself is unlikely to match the effect of the reader's prior conditionings. It is doubtful whether, even with the benefit of the author's theoretical writing and the amplification of his exegetes, the reader of Robbe-Grillet perceives that world as neutral; one would guess that he perceives it to be generally grim and, not unlikely, tragic.[10] Robbe-Grillet elaborated his literary theory after *The Erasers;* but even a later novel like *La Maison de rendez-vous* (1965) shows that the absolute purpose of his theory represents a program and an approach and, as such, only takes into account a part of his own novels. In choosing to work his first novel around the most primal of all mythical structures, Robbe-Grillet could not have been ignorant of certain consequences that his theoretical program does not envisage.

The critic who nevertheless accepts Robbe-Grillet's antitragic premise without questioning the applicability of the theory to this particular myth is forced to read *The Erasers* as an ironic piece, a deconstruction of the myth.[11] Aside from the fact that such a deconstruction presupposes acknowledgment of the myth, there is sufficient evidence to show that Robbe-Grillet intended a more limited destruction, that *The Erasers* is meant to shatter only the overly familiar *surface* of the myth that shields us from its dangerous core. In talking about the novel, Robbe-Grillet spoke of his desire to tell a story that would self-destruct as it went along:[12] to choose a myth with such a

10. Even though there are many parts of the "tactical" Robbe-Grillet that show his knowledge of theoretical phenomenology and, specifically, of Merleau-Ponty, the "philosophical" Robbe-Grillet slights certain key reservations of Merleau-Ponty. Following Koffka, Merleau-Ponty writes: "The light of a candle changes its appearance for a child when, after a burn, it stops attracting the child's hand and becomes literally repulsive. The vision is already inhabited by a significance which gives it a function" (*Phenomenology of Perception*, trans. Colin Smith, [London: Routledge & Kegan Paul, 1962], p. 52); and he concludes: "Nothing is more difficult than to know precisely *what we see*" (p. 58).

11. For example, Olga Bernal, *Alain Robbe-Grillet: Le Roman de l'absence* (Paris: Gallimard, 1964), or Stoltzfus, *Alain Robbe-Grillet and the New French Novel*.

12. Quoted by M. Chapsal (*L'Express*, 12 January 1961).

heavy overlay of cultural signification, while wishing at the same time to undo the story that avails itself of and contributes to that overlay, aims the undoing at the cultural overlay. If we are correct, Robbe-Grillet's strategy is complex, dependent as it is on the reawakening of certain intimate echoes in the reader that require the destruction of certain overly familiar reminiscences.

Many truths are spoken through the drunkard's words: taken together, those words become an ironic synopsis of the myth's disintegration:

He speaks slowly, so as not to get his words confused:
"Tell me what animal is a parricide in the morning . . ."
"That's all we needed was this goon here," Antoine objects. "You don't even know what an oblique line is, I'll bet . . ."
"You look pretty oblique to me," the drunk says mildly. "I'm the one around here who asks riddles. I have one here just for my old pal . . ."
The two adversaries move away toward the bar, seeking new partisans. Wallas turns his back on the drunk, who goes on nevertheless, his voice jubilant and deliberate:
"What animal is parricide in the morning, incestuous at noon, and blind at night?"
At the bar the discussion has become a general one, but the five men are all talking at once and Wallas can hear only snatches of their remarks.
"Well," the drunk insists, "can't you guess? It's not so hard: parricide in the morning, blind at noon . . . No . . . blind in the morning, incestuous at noon, parricide at night. Well? What animal is it?" (Pp. 225–26)

Within its disjointed fragments voiced by the drunkard, the Oedipal myth subsists as echo but disappears as *meaning*; in a similar way, the fragments of the myth surface throughout the story, but with too much coyness and too little reason to construe meaning. If those fragments instanced only a failure to mean, the story would be indeed a parody, and purposeless. But to read *The Erasers* as only parody is to neglect the purpose and the effect of their surfacing.[13]

13. The critic who insists on doing the reverse, on preserving within the fragments their full cultural content, is restricted to playing a game on the surface of the text. Morrissette picks up the inscription on the symbolic statue and notes in the sculptor's signature, V. Daulis, "a name containing an anagram for Laïus" (*Novels of Robbe-Grillet*, p. 56). Daulis, in the original, suggests the French preposition used for origination and the town *from which* the Greek fleet left for Troy: *d'Aulis*—meaning that this reference, like the Trojan epic itself, has Aulis as its starting point. Aulis as a simple memory jog is more

Once the name "Oedipus' is dropped in our ear, we are given a certain orientation: along with other intimations, we know "how things will come out." That awareness affects our analysis of the moments that precede the ending: each moment loses some of its distinctness because of its linkage with that ending. And the quality of each is further affected by our sense of the ending; that awareness (because it is an *awareness*) is perforce more philosophical, more reflective, more soothing, than would be our jagged motion through disjunctive events of whose outcome we would *not* be sure. Robbe-Grillet comes at a time when the metaphysical author knows that metaphysics slight a metaphysical sense: he knows that the synthesis contrived by the crafted artifact (the novel) must be purposefully disarticulated if it is to be more than a comment on existence that we experience as *analysis*, as a groping through perilous discontinuities. Robbe-Grillet's text *is* the unchartered road that the Oedipal comment only *describes*: his reader is allowed to experience in the vortex of the text the groping towards a text that the myth relates.

This shift from mind to eye, from control to groping, begins with the disappearance of narrative control. Unlike Borges, Robbe-Grillet pretends *not* to be in his story. In a first breaking up of the unitary nature of the fictional text, the reader is allowed to "follow" the path of the novel only through the eyes of a protagonist whose vision has been deranged. That derangement is of a peculiar kind: it derives from a tautology within the fiction—a break between the character's perceptive powers and the mental control that would normally result from that perception. The character's eye is variously demented through an exacerbation of questioning and anxiety resulting from his halting efforts to right himself inside a disarticulated world. The questioning and the anxiety may be sexual (*Jealousy*, 1957), the result of a feverish illness (*In the Labyrinth*, 1959) or of an obsession rooted in criminal guilt and sexual need (*The Voyeur*, 1955), or again, as in *The Erasers*, the protagonist's eye may be simply obsessed with Oedipal clues.

Wallas's round within the vortex of these clues is reminiscent of

---

than sufficient: the fact that Aulis is also the perfect anagram for Laius is just a bit of fortuitous luck on the part of Robbe-Grillet, as was presumably the unnumbered page 88 between parts 1 and 2 in the original edition of *Le Voyeur*, a novel that details the obsessed double circuit of Mathias through his island and contrives repeated reminders of the figure "8."

the repetition compulsion that Lacan traces through Poe's "Purloined Letter."[14] But in *The Erasers*, that repetition is on the surface—it *is* a surface, that of a shifting and perverse text. Wallas proceeds on his way through a set of instructions left by Garinati and written by Bona for Garinati. At a bridge, Garinati anticipates himself arriving at that bridge; or, in a rearrangement of the scene, Garianti anticipates the arrival of Wallas at the bridge. Wallas "penetrates"—as he might the photograph itself—the positive and negative images in the displays of the stationery store that invert the photographic use of Dupont's house, before Wallas, drawn by yet another reproduction of that photograph, penetrates the same house in order to kill Dupont. These repetitions cause the movement that they describe to break down, to become pure analysis: the circle repeats itself, leads nowhere. And sometimes, as in the slow motion of a nightmare, action itself comes to a halt:

Suddenly the limpid water grows cloudy. In this setting determined by law, without an inch of land to the right or left, without a second's hesitation, without resting, without looking back, the actor suddenly stops, in the middle of a phrase. . . . He knows it by heart, this role he plays every evening; but he refuses to go any farther. Around him the other characters freeze, arm raised or leg half bent. The measure begun by the musicians goes on and on. . . . He would have to do something now, speak any words at all, words that would not belong to the libretto. . . . But, as every evening, the phrase begun concludes in the prescribed form, the arm falls back, the leg completes its stride. In the pit, the orchestra is still playing with the same vigor. (p. 19)

Wallas's eye, like other points of opening onto Robbe-Grillet's fiction, "takes in" poorly and affects the reader's sight, which is given no other point of reference. In fact, that eye does not "take in": it only *sees*; it is drawn to an *out there* that it cannot assimilate. The author never allows that glance the security of dwelling on its object: the disjunctive moments are kept brief (or deliberately frozen) so as to be perceptual immediacies that create the sense of what would be otherwise an idea (a fiction) about a *groping towards*. Robbe-Grillet's novel is not about "neutral" moments: it is a novel of *nausea*, in

14. D-- becomes "feminized" after appropriating the queen's letter when Dupin's appropriation of the letter forces D-- to assume on several levels the role of the queen.

Sartre's use of the word, about the coercive assertion of moments that have become objects.

When the movement breaks down, we are left with the image. But it too is separate, alone, bereft of the meaning that it might have derived from motion or transversal linking. As in a de Chirico painting, where we recognize the statues, the façades, the skyline, the clouds, that recognition of familiar surfaces does not compose a familiarity: a failure of the objects to relate to each other, to their setting, forces us to see them as they are, independent of each other, irrelevant, preventing their absorption into each other, into *us*, and causing our malaise. The spyglass hero of Robbe-Grillet, through whom we attempt to focus on his world, is at fault: it is he who cannot render his world familiar; he allows it to break down into a number of objects, or into a single object, which his obsessed vision cannot appropriate. The cube/eraser that Wallas *knows* but cannot see is an exemplary instance of his world—a shifting of transitory moments, inadequate stimuli, confusing reminders, problematic inversions: the *grasp* is always frustrated.

This primacy of the eye over the mind is a strength of the eye, an exacerbation of sight. Its acuity sees angles rather than curves, sharp planes rather than shadows.[15] That eye also counts: there are twenty-one steps leading to Dupont's study (or so many banana plants in *Jealousy*): in all of its apperceptions, the eye is keen but cannot derive meaning.[16] And through that eye, the reader confronts a world of disjunctions, of fragmentary scenes that compel his own questioning. The Oedipal reminders, unable to construct a myth, contrive

15. There is adequate cause for the eraser to remain a cube through the metamorphoses that bring it into being as something else: just as the photograph becomes negative/positive, the cube/eraser becomes the cube/paperweight on Dupont's desk ("A kind of cube, but slightly misshapen, a shiny block of gray lava, with its faces polished as though by wear, the edges softened, compact, apparently hard, heavy as gold, looking about as big around as a fist; a paperweight? It is the only trinket in the room," p. 21), which is itself subject to further metamorphoses: a keenly perceived object is maintained before the eye but remains evanescent in its trenchancy.

16. Robbe-Grillet's novel invites comparison with other "flat" forms of representation. See, for example, Elly Jaffé-Freem: *Alain Robbe-Grillet et la peinture cubiste* (Amsterdam: Meulenhoff, 1966). For reasons like the ones we have analyzed, Jaffé-Freem feels more comfortable comparing the "surfaces" of Robbe-Grillet and those of cubism. Because he does not acknowledge a *mood* resulting from either the worlds of Robbe-Grillet or cubism, he tends to reject comparison with a painter like de Chirico (p. 159).

only an aura: they hint to the reader about the loftier name he might give his malaise.

There are twenty-one steps for the eye to count because a cipher tells us nothing about the stairs. Within the words of the text, the alienation of the reader results from an echo break. Robbe-Grillet has spoken at some length about a tactical depersonalization of language, a rejection of what he terms our pack of animistic or domesticating adjectives.[17] The words he uses, like the surfaces he shows us, are plain, bare, and intend to refer only to themselves. They resist metaphoricity or synonymy, attempting no more than the aggregate creation of an *object*, a refractory "cube" that cannot be appropriated by the reader, into which no meaning can be read: in the same way the image is voided of its motion, the word is voided of its echo. Its function is to keep the reader in the alienated world of the character.

And so, Oedipus and Wallas walk their appointed, circular routes to discover an order of circularity: they are the perpetrators of the crime into which they inquired. Their crime *becomes* the answer to their question about the crime. The answer that cannot stay the question is in us from the start. The grim virtue of the Oedipal story is its economy: its understanding requires the exercise it describes. That return to self is achieved in Robbe-Grillet's version of the myth through a similar economy: he is aware that both Oedipus and the reader are given a text to decipher. The reader's special agent in that deciphering, Wallas, will give him for his exercise an Oedipal eye, with Oedipus's acuity and his ultimate blindness. That this undecipherable text is that of our own being will be stated only by the coincidental nature of the reader's foundering within the reminders of a former grandeur—the scattered shards of what was once the myth.

The epigraph for *The Erasers* is drawn from *Oedipus*: "Time that sees all has found you out against your will"; in Sophocles, there is a "fullness" of time within which all things are "found out." This is the gift of Sophocles to his spectator, but it is not the private world of that spectator. For Oedipus, the terrible blindness of having eyes is replaced, at last, by the comforting darkness of his knowledge. The

17. "A Future for the Novel," in *For a New Novel.*

moment of his most awful revelation *closes*, with his eyes, the moment of a still more awful innocence. But the spectator is not granted Oedipus's termination, and he must begin anew his own questioning since that questioning has only been stayed through the duration—the fullness of time—of the ritual play. The epigraph at the start of Robbe-Grillet's text merely ironizes, and the reader is so informed within the first page that follows the epigraph:

Soon unfortunately time will no longer be master. Wrapped in their aura of doubt and error, this day's events, however insignificant they may be, will in a few seconds begin their task, gradually encroaching upon the ideal order, cunningly introducing an occasional inversion, a discrepancy, a confusion, a warp, in order to accomplish their work: a day in early winter without plan, without direction, incomprehensible and monstrous. (P. 7)

Time, the "closure" of a day, of twenty-four hours during which the fictional event occurs, is fictional—*in excess*. Time has become yet another *thing*: within its circling, its reminiscences, its halting, its inversions, it "finds out" nothing. Or rather, it finds out what the myth has always told us: that we cannot find out.

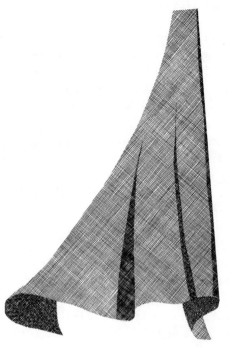

Conclusion:
Job and the
Unendurable Mystery

We keep reinventing our gods: we cannot entertain for long the thought that our limits are limits, that god is our ultimate script for the unknown. We acknowledge the awareness in brief epiphanies but move on quickly to the greater comfort of dialectical possibilities. The exacerbation of this awareness of our non-awareness and our refusal to accept it is as old as the race. Our wisdom literature records it perhaps as early as the seventh century B.C., certainly no later than the fourth: we are the recalcitrant progeny of Job. But Job also shows us the poignancy of the dilemma.

It is not God who proposes to test Job, the "blameless and upright" man: it is one who is still a son of God, though already a skeptic—Satan. Job, or his legend, was known before the recording of his story: he was "the greatest of the people of the east" (1:3); his 7,000 sheep, his 3,000 camels, his 500 yoke of oxen and 500 she-asses raise the question whether rewards attend the virtuous man on earth or in some other realm. It is through his possessions that Satan first strikes Job and Job responds as the Lord expects him to: "In all this Job did not sin or charge God with wrong" (1:22). After this initial failure, Satan argues that a man will not be moved by adversity until he is stricken in his flesh: accordingly, the Lord allows Job to be afflicted with particularly loathsome sores. The sight of this torture is so agonizing that Job's wife urges him to put an end to his misery: "Curse God and die" (2:9). Job refuses and bears his ordeal in exemplary fashion: "In all this Job did not sin with his lips" (2:10). But the torture has not yet reached full intensity; three friends of Job now descend on him.

To them, Job sums up his dilemma: "Why is light given to a man whose way is hid, whom God[1] has hedged in?" (3:23); if Job has the power to qeustion, why can he not *know*? The first of Job's friends, Eliphaz the Temanite, begins discourse with him. He argues that surely no mortal man can be righteous in the eyes of God: "Can a man be pure before his Maker?" (4:17): there must be a *reason* for the mystery of Job's curse. Eliphaz advises that if he were Job, he would accept the chastening of the Almighty. Job rejects the applicability of this doctrine (*muscar*) to his case: it is he, Job, who is *experiencing* the agony, not Eliphaz:

> O that my vexation were weighed,
>   and all my calamity laid in balances!
> For then it would be heavier than the sand of the sea;
>   therefore my words have been rash.
> For the arrows of the Almighty are in me;
>   my spirit drinks their poison;
>   the terrors of God are arrayed against me. (6:2–4)

Job knows that such retribution is incommensurable with his presumed guilt. His unendurable suffering might turn him into an unwilling blasphemer—a man cannot be brought up with such force against the limits beyond which God is concealed: "Is my strength the strength of stones,/or is my flesh bronze?/In truth I have no help

---

1. Here named in His terrible omnipotence—Eloah.

in me,/and any resource is driven from me" (6:12–13). No human sin can justify the kind of rack upon which his mind fails—certainly not his sin:

> If I sin, what do I do to thee, thou watcher of men.
> > Why hast thou made me thy mark?
> > Why have I become a burden to thee?
> Why dost thou not pardon my transgression
> > and take away my iniquity?
> For now I shall lie in the earth;
> > thou wilt seek me, but I shall not be. (7:20–21)

Now comes the turn of Bildad the Shuhite. In his pious haste to justify God, Bildad suggests that there must be guilt in either Job or his children:

> Does God pervert justice?
> > Or does the Almighty pervert the right?
> If your children have sinned against him,
> > he has delivered them into the power of their transgression.
> If you will seek God
> > and make supplication to the Almighty,
> if you are pure and upright,
> > surely then he will rouse himself for you
> > and reward you with a rightful habitation. (8:3–6)

The zeal of Bildad either sweeps away his logic or condemns Job: Bildad urges Job to implore grace but argues that salvation awaits the just. Job responds that it is mockery to confront limited human perception and so irreducible a mystery: "How can a man be just before God?" (9:2). "Behold, he snatches away; who can hinder him?/Who will say to him, 'What doest thou'?" (9:12): if God is a thief of man's power to know, who can point out the monstrousness of that thievery to the power that wrought it? Who can fathom the monstrousness of that thievery when the knowledge that it removes is required to endure the magnitude of the theft? Only the sufferer knows the extent to which his suffering is compounded by his failure to be able to attach a *reason* to it. Job is pinioned upon the extremity of a dilemma, held fast within so absolute a grip that dialectical motion is impossible: "There is no umpire between us,/Who might lay his hand upon us both" (9:33).

But for those who do not experience the agony of that extremity, the problem is relative: it is contained within theoretical and legal categories. The third friend, Zophar the Naamathite, speculates that the punishment implies the crime: "Know then that God exacts of you/less than your guilt deserves" (11:7). Job's suffering measures the distance between such effortless words and the acuity of his dilemma:

> But I would speak to the Almighty,
> and I desire to argue my case with God.
> As for you, you whitewash with lies;
> worthless physicians are you all.
> Oh that you would keep silent,
> and it would be your wisdom! (13:3–5)

Before the absolute equipoise of the reach that cannot avail and an unknown that remains silent, the words of the others must be empty for as long as those words are void of that terrible tension. Their very piety reduces their moral force, unbalancing as it does the absolute equilibrium of the dilemma. That categorical piety supposes, moreover, that a rhetorical tautology can resolve the problem. In fact, the three friends speak in the name of an unknown they cannot fathom and thereby repeat, without being aware of it, the acuteness of the dilemma. Only Job knows—and God, who knows all:

> Will you speak falsely for God,
> and speak deceitfully for him?
> Will you show partiality toward him,
> will you plead the case for God?
> Will it be well with you when he searches you out?
> Or can you deceive him, as one deceives a man? (13:7–9)

Because there can be no communication between the theorist and the sufferer, Eliphaz now repeats his argument, and so does Bildad. Both repeat words: "What is man, that he can be clean?/Or he that is born of a woman, that he can be righteous?" (15:14), and Job knows that his friends cannot understand, "How long will you torment me,/and break me in pieces with words?" (19:2). Unable to escape the prison of God's irreducible argument, Job pleads for pity in his solitariness—

> Have pity on me, have pity on me, O you my friends,
> for the hand of God has touched me!
> Why do you, like God, pursue me?
> Why are you not satisfied with my flesh? (19:21–22)

—and for a *text* of his misery that will allow at least its *reflection* to escape:

> Oh, that my words were written!
>   Oh that they were inscribed in a book!
> Oh that with an iron pen and lead
>   they were graven in the rock for ever! (19:23–24)

In this dialogue of the deaf, the friends continue to repeat themselves with a passion that weakens further the logic of their reasoned premise in proportion as mere logic becomes circular and self-contradictory. And now, as if to evidence another sign of God, the very scripture begins to break down. What may have been the third discourse of Zophar is now spoken by Job (24:18–25). Job's response to Bildad (26:5–14) sounds more like the continuation of Bildad's response to Job, and may be an interpolation of the text. But within this cacophony of meaning rises a hymn on the failure and inaccessibility of human wisdom (28:1–28). At last, all words fail: "So these three men ceased to answer Job, because he was righteous in his own eyes" (32:1).

Now a new voice is heard, that of Elihu the Buzite. He argues that the ways of God are ultimately just. A man cannot conceive the mystery that is God, the very attempt betokens a hint of unseemly scorn:

> Behold, God is great, and we know him not;
>   the number of his years is unsearchable. (36:26)

> The Almighty—we cannot find him;
>   he is great in power and justice,
>   and abundant righteousness he will not violate.
> Therefore men fear him. (37:23–24)

Awareness of that impossible awareness and the refusal of that awareness is a passion demonstrable only through an intensity of suffering like Job's. Lesser wisdom is mere scorn, and God scorns such scorners: "He does not regard any who are wise in their own conceit" (37:24). If Elihu does not represent simply the late addition of a bridge between the argument that has gone before and the revelation of God, Elihu's escape from the wrath of God that condemns the three friends is due to the fact that he speaks of acceptance, not of causal relationships. Elihu does not reduce Job's anguish of awareness to the simplicity of moral categories.

Having made His point, God appears. He first rebukes all users of words—including Job: "Who is this that darkens counsel by words without knowledge?" (38:2). But there is a difference: in his agony, Job has given evidence that he knows how absolutely irresoluble the irresolubility is. His excessive words are less of a sin: they are the inverse of a glibness that reads its texts with too little effort. It is ultimately these glib readers who are smitten by God for misreading Him, for thinking they could read Him: "The Lord said to Eliphaz the Temanite: 'My wrath is kindled against you and against your two friends; for you have not spoken of me what is right, as my servant Job has'" (42:7). And Job, for having experienced the inexperience-able, is restored twofold into his possessions. (Even so, God may not be wholly satisfied with the result of Satan's experiment; too acute a sense of the divine impenetrability is of itself something too much like a penetration of the divine: nothing is said about clearing up Job's skin.)

Job represents a sublime thrust, the furthest extension and frustration of the human will to understand. Thereafter, Western thought will be tempted by weaker doctrines of consolation: they will "humanize" the mystery; that is to say, they will place before its void what human experience can recognize, turning the awesome limit into a god of acts, or hastening to people the nothingness of Sheol—desperately trying to a-void the vision of visionlessness.

In his pain, Job cries out for a reduction of his awareness to a *text*, even as he knows that the three learned critics who already read him as a text have not read him at all. Job is desperate for an echo, a witness, even though he has ample proof that one text is much like another and that one can only hope that the quality of the reader may improve: Job's cry that he might be duplicated as a text is deep evidence of his despair.

This disparity between the metaphysical anguish that prompts the fictional comment, and its necessary betrayal by that comment, will preoccupy fiction-makers for centuries to come. Today, when meta-physical despair is less intense for being more common, that com-monness discovers for itself the fictional trick that turns the very text into simply another moment of an unspecified despair.

There remains the reader. When all is said and done, the three friends, Elihu, and Job say exactly the same thing: each affirms that knowledge is impossible, and in the mouth of each, all arguments become appropriately circular. In the end, the only distinction between these voices is their *tone*: Job and his text are looking for a reader. The better text cannot better that reader; but the better reader who has found his adequate text—any text—can rehearse within it the part of him that is Job.

Bibliography

Aeschylus. *Seven against Thebes*. Translated by Anthony Hecht and Helen H. Bacon. New York: Oxford University Press, 1973.

Alazraki, Jaime. *Jorge Luis Borges*. New York: Columbia University Press, 1971.

Alexander, Lloyd, see Sartre (*Nausea, The Wall*).

Alter, Jean. *La Vision du monde d'Alain Robbe-Grillet*. Geneva: Droz, 1966.

Artaud, Antonin. *The Theater and Its Double*. Translated by Mary C. Richards. New York: Grove Press, 1958.

Bacon, Helen H., see Aeschylus.

Barnes, Hazel E., see Sartre (*Being and Nothingness*).

Barrenechea, Ana María. *Borges the Labyrinth Maker*. New York: New York University Press, 1965.

Barthes, Roland. *The Pleasure of the Text*. Translated by Richard Miller. New York: Hill and Wang, 1975.

Baskin, Wade, see Gide (*The Notebooks of André Walter*).

Bataille, Georges. *Death and Sensuality*. New York: Ballantine Books, 1962.

Bentley, Eric, see Pirandello (*Naked Masks*).

Beowulf. Edited by Charles L. Wrenn. London: G. G. Harrap, 1958.

Berdiaev, Nicolai A. *Dostoevsky*. New York: Meridian Books, 1957.

Bernal, Olga. *Alain Robbe-Grillet: Le Roman de l'absence*. Paris: Gallimard, 1964.

Bishop, Thomas. *Pirandello and the French Theater*. New York: New York University Press, 1960.

Blanchot, Maurice. *La Part du feu*. Paris: NRF, 1949.

Bloom, Harold. *Poetry and Repression: Revisionism from Blake to Stevens*. New Haven, Conn.: Yale University Press, 1976.

Bonaparte, Marie. *The Life and Works of Edgar Allan Poe*. Translated by John Rodker. New York: Humanities Press, 1971.

Borges, Jorge Luis. *The Aleph and Other Stories*. Translated by Norman T. di Giovanni. New York: E. P. Dutton, 1970.

————. *Borges on Writing*. Edited by Norman T. di Giovanni, D. Halpern, F. MacShane. New York: E. P. Dutton, 1973.

————. *The Cardinal Points of Borges*. Edited by Lowell Dunham and Ivar Ivask. Norman: University of Oklahoma Press, 1971.

————. *Discusión*. Buenos Aires: Emecé, 1964.

————. *El idioma de los argentinos*. Buenos Aires: Gleizer, 1928.

————. *Labyrinths: Selected Stories & Other Writings*. Edited by Donald A. Yates and James E. Irby. New York: New Directions, 1964.

————. *El lenguaje de Buenos Aires*. Buenos Aires: Emecé, 1963.

————. *A Universal History of Infamy*. Translated by Norman T. di Giovanni. New York: E. P. Dutton, 1972.

Bower, Anthony, see Camus (*The Rebel*).

Brée, Germaine, see Camus (*L'Etranger*).

Brooks, Peter, see Kernan.

Brustein, Robert S. *The Theatre of Revolt*. Boston: Atlantic, Little, Brown, 1964.

Cambon, Glauco. *Pirandello: A Collection of Critical Essays*. Englewood Cliffs, N.J.: Prentice-Hall, 1967.

Camus, Albert. *Caligula and Three Other Plays (The Misunderstanding; State of Siege; The Just Assassins)*. Translated by Stuart Gilbert. New York. A. A. Knopf, 1958.

————. *L'Etranger*. Edited by Germaine Brée and Carlos Lynes. New York: Appleton-Century-Crofts, 1955.

————. *The Myth of Sisyphus and Other Essays*. Translated by Justin O'Brien. New York: A. A. Knopf, 1955.

————. *The Rebel*. Translated by Anthony Bower. Rev. ed. New York: A. A. Knopf, 1971.

————. *The Stranger*. Translated by Stuart Gilbert. New York: A. A. Knopf, 1946.

Carlson, Eric W., ed. *The Recognition of Edgar Allan Poe*. Ann Arbor: University of Michigan Press, 1969.

Cawelti, John G. *Adventure, Mystery and Romance*. Chicago: University of Chicago Press, 1976.

Christie, Agatha. *At Bertram's Hotel*. London: Collins, 1965.

———. *Curtain*. New York: Dodd, Mead, 1975.

———. *Murder on the Calais Coach*. New York: Pocket Books, 1940.

———. *The Mysterious Affairs at Styles*. New York: Bantam Books, 1940.

Cruickshank, John. *Albert Camus and the Literature of Revolt*. New York: Oxford University Press, 1960.

Darwin, Charles S. *The Origin of Species*. New York: Oxford University Press, 1951.

Delcourt, Marie. *Oedipe ou La Légende du conquérant*. Paris: Droz, 1944.

———. *L'Oracle de Delphes*. Paris: Payot, 1955.

Dentan, Michel. *Humour et création littéraire dans l'oeuvre de Kafka*. Geneva: Droz, 1961.

Derrida, Jacques. *Marges de la philosophie*. Paris: Minuit, 1972.

Di Giovanni, Norman T., see Borges *(The Aleph; Borges on Writing; A Universal History of Infamy)*.

Dostoevsky, Fyodor. *The Brothers Karamazov*. Edited by Ralph E. Matlaw. New York: W. W. Norton, 1976.

———. *The Diary of a Writer*. 2 vols. New York: Charles Scribner's Sons, 1949.

———. *The Idiot*. Harmondsworth, Middlesex: Penguin Books, 1955.

———. *Notebooks for the Brothers Karamazov*. Edited and Translated by Edward Wasiolek. Chicago: University of Chicago Press, 1971.

———. *Notes from Underground*. New York: E. P. Dutton, 1960.

———. *The Possessed*. New York: Modern Library, 1963.

Dumur, Guy. *Le Théâtre de Pirandello*. Paris: L'Arche, 1967.

Dunham, Lowell, see Borges *(Cardinal Points of Borges)*.

Duras, Marguerite, and Cauthier, Xavière. *Les Parleuses*. Paris: Minuit, 1974.

Earle, M. L. *The Oedipus Tyrannus*. New York: American Book, 1901.

Else, Gerald F. *Aristotle's Poetics*. Cambridge: Harvard University Press, 1957.

Freud, Sigmund. *Beyond the Pleasure Principle*. New York: Liveright, 1950.

———. *Studies in Parapsychology* ("The Uncanny"; "Dreams and Telepathy"; "Neurosis and Demoniacal Possession"). New York: Collier Books, 1971.

———. *Totem and Taboo*. New York: W. W. Norton, 1962.

———. "Das Unheimliche," see *Studies in Parapsychology*.

Gauthier, Xavière, see Duras.

Genette, Gérard. *Figures*. Paris: Seuil, 1966. Vol. 1.

Gide, André. *Dostoevsky*. London: Secker & Warburg, 1949.

———. *Journals*. Translated by Justin O'Brien. 4 vols. New York: A. A. Knopf, 1947–51.

————. *The Notebooks of André Walter*. Translated by Wade Baskin. London: Peter Owen, 1968.

————. *Oedipus* and *Theseus*. Translated by John Russell. London: Secker & Warburg, 1950.

Gilbert, Stuart, see Camus (*Caligula; The Stranger*); Sartre (*No Exit*).

Girard, René. *Dostoïevski: Du double à l'unité*. Paris: Plon, 1963.

Gould, Thomas, see Sophocles.

Green, André. *Un Oeil en trop*. Paris: Minuit, 1969.

Greenberg, Martin. *The Terror of Art: Kafka and Modern Literature*. New York: Basic Books, 1968.

Grossvogel, David I. *Limits of the Novel*. Ithaca, N.Y.: Cornell University Press, 1968.

Halpern, D., see Borges (*Borges on Writing*).

Hecht, Anthony, see Aeschylus.

Heidegger, Martin. *Being and Time*. Translated by John Macquarrie and Edward Robinson. New York: Harper & Row, 1962.

Herodotus. *Works*. 4 vols. Cambridge: Harvard University Press, 1931–40.

Hesiod. *Works*. Cambridge: Harvard University Press, 1936.

Hoffman, Daniel. *Poe, Poe, Poe, Poe, Poe, Poe, Poe,* Garden City, N.J.: Doubleday, 1972.

Hoffmann, E. T. A. *The Best Tales of Hoffmann*. Ed. E. F. Bleiler. New York: Dover Publications, 1967.

Holquist, Michael J., see Kernan.

Howard, Richard, see Robbe-Grillet (*The Erasers; For a New Novel; In the Labyrinth; Jealousy; La Maison de Rendez-vous; The Voyeur*); Todorov.

Howe, Irving. *Politics and the Novel*. New York: Horizon Press, 1957.

Irby, James E., see Borges (*Labyrinths*).

Ivask, Ivar, see Borges (*Cardinal Points of Borges*).

Jaffé-Freem, Elly. *Alain Robbe-Grillet et la peinture cubiste*. Amsterdam: Meulenhoff, 1966.

Kafka, Franz. *The Castle*. Translated by Willa and Edwin Muir. New York: A. A. Knopf, 1941.

————. *Parables and Paradoxes*. New York: Schoken Books, 1961.

————. *The Trial*. Translated by Willa and Edwin Muir. New York: Vintage Books, 1969.

Kernan, Alvin B.; Brooks, Peter; and Holquist, Michael J., eds. *Man and His Fictions: An Introduction to Fiction-Making, Its Forms and Uses*. New York: Harcourt, Brace, Jovanovich, 1973.

Koffka, Kurt. *The Growth of the Mind*. New York: Harcourt, Brace, 1924.

Krieger, Murray. *The Tragic Vision*. Baltimore, Md.: The Johns Hopkins University Press, 1973.

Kuna, Franz. *Kafka: Literature as Corrective Punishment.* Bloomington: Indiana University Press, 1974.

Lee, H. D. P., see Plato.

Levine, Stuart and Susan, see Poe.

Lévi-Strauss, Claude. *The Elementary Structures of Kinship.* Boston: Beacon Press, 1969.

————. *Structural Anthropology.* 2 vols. New York: Basic Books, 1963–76.

Lupoff, Richard A. *Edgar Rice Burroughs: Master of Adventure.* New York: Carnaveral Press, 1965.

Lynes, Carlos, see Camus (*L'Etranger*).

Macquarrie, John, see Heidegger.

MacShane, F., see Borges (*Borges on Writing*).

Martini, Magda. *Pirandello, ou Le Philosophe de l'absolu.* Geneva: Labor et Fides, 1969.

Matlaw, Ralph E., see Dostoevsky (*The Brothers Karamazov*); Turgenev.

Merleau-Ponty, Maurice. *Phenomenology of Perception.* Translated by Colin Smith. London: Routledge & Kegan Paul, 1962.

Miller, Perry, ed. *Major Writers of America.* 2 vols. New York: Harcourt, Brace & World, 1962.

Miller, Richard, see Barthes.

Morrissette, Bruce. *The Novels of Robbe-Grillet.* Ithaca, N.Y.: Cornell University Press, 1975.

Muir, Edwin and Willa, see Kafka (*The Castle; The Trial*).

Murray, William, see Pirandello (*To Clothe the Naked*).

O'Brien, Justin, see Camus (*The Myth of Sisyphus*); Gide (*Journals*).

Pachmuss, Temira. *F. M. Dostoevsky: Dualism and Synthesis of the Human Soul.* Carbondale: Southern Illinois University Press, 1963.

Pausanias. *Guide to Greece.* 2 vols. Harmondsworth, Middlesex: Penguin Books, 1971.

Pirandello, Luigi. *Mountain Giants and Other Plays.* New York: Crown Publishers, 1958.

————. *Naked Masks (Liolà; It Is So (If You Think So); Henry IV; Six Characters; Each in His Own Way).* Edited by Eric Bentley. New York: E. P. Dutton, 1952.

————. *Opere.* 6 vols. Milano: Mondadori, 1958–65.

————. *To Clothe the Naked and Two Other Plays (The Rules of the Game; The Pleasure of Honesty).* Translated by William Murray. New York: E. P. Dutton, 1962.

————. *Tonight We Improvise.* Translated by Samuel Putnam. New York: E. P. Dutton, 1932.

Plato. *The Republic.* Translated by H. D. P. Lee. Harmondsworth, Middlesex: Penguin Books, 1955.

Poe, Edgar A. *The Short Fiction of Edgar Allan Poe*. Edited by Stuart and Susan Levine. Indianapolis: Bobbs-Merrill, 1976.

Politzer, Heinz. *Franz Kafka: Parable and Paradox*. Ithaca, N.Y.: Cornell University Press, 1962.

Proust, Marcel. *Remembrance of Things Past*. Translated by Charles K. Scott-Moncrieff. 2 vols. New York: Random House, 1941.

Putnam, Samuel, see Pirandello *(Tonight We Improvise)*.

Rank, Otto. *The Trauma of Birth*. New York: Harcourt, Brace, 1929.

Regan, Robert, ed. *Poe: A Collection of Critical Essays*. Englewood Cliffs, N.J.: Prentice-Hall, 1967.

Richards, Mary C., see Artaud.

Robbe-Grillet, Alain. *The Erasers*. Translated by Richard Howard. New York: Grove Press, 1977.

———. *For a New Novel*. Translated by Richard Howard. New York: Grove Press, 1965.

———. *In the Labyrinth*. Translated by Richard Howard. New York: Grove Press, 1960.

———. *Jealousy*. Translated by Richard Howard. London: J. Calder, 1965.

———. *La Maison de Rendez-vous*. Translated by Richard Howard. New York: Grove Press, 1966.

———. *Les Gommes*. Paris: Minuit, 1953.

———. *Le Voyeur*. Paris: Minuit, 1955.

———. *The Voyeur*. Translated by Richard Howard. New York: Grove Press, 1958.

Robinson, Edward, see Heidegger.

Rodker, John, see Bonaparte.

Rosenfeld, Andrée, see Ucko.

Russell, John, see Gide *(Oedipus)*.

Sartre, Jean-Paul. *Being and Nothingness*. Translated by Hazel E. Barnes. New York: Citadel Press, 1964.

———. *Nausea*. Translated by Lloyd Alexander. New York: New Directions, 1969.

———. *No Exit* and *The Flies*. Translated by Stuart Gilbert. New York: A. A. Knopf, 1947.

———. *The Wall*. Translated by Lloyd Alexander. Norfolk, Conn.: New Directions, 1948.

Scève, Maurice. *Oeuvres complètes*. Paris: Mercure de France, 1974.

Scott-Moncrieff, Charles K., see Proust.

Smith, Colin, see Merleau-Ponty.

Sophocles. *Oedipus the King*. Translated by Thomas Gould. Englewood Cliffs, N.J.: Prentice-Hall, 1970.

Stoltzfus, Ben F. *Alain Robbe-Grillet and the New French Novel.* Carbondale: Southern Illinois University Press, 1964.

Sturrock, John. *Paper Tigers: The Ideal Fictions of Jorge Luis Borges.* London: Oxford University Press, 1977.

Tiefenbrun, Ruth. *Moment of Torment: An Interpretation of Franz Kafka's Short Stories.* Carbondale: Southern Illinois University Press, 1973.

Tilgher, Adriano. *Studi sul teatro contemporaneo.* Rome: Libreria di Scienze e Lettere, 1923.

Todorov, Tzvetan. *The Poetics of Prose.* Translated by Richard Howard. Ithaca, N.Y.: Cornell University Press, 1977.

————. *The Uncanny.* Translated by Richard Howard. Ithaca, N.Y.: Cornell University Press, 1975.

Turgenev, Ivan S. *Fathers and Sons.* Translated by Ralph E. Matlaw. New York: W. W. Norton, 1966.

Ucko, Peter J., and Rosenfeld, Andrée. *Paleolithic Cave Art.* New York: McGraw-Hill, 1967.

Urzidil, Johannes. *There Goes Kafka.* Detroit: Wayne State University Press, 1968.

Vernant, Jean-Pierre. *Mythe et pensée chez les Grecs.* Paris: Maspéro, 1966.

Wasiolek, Edward, see Dostoevsky *(Notebooks).*

Watson, Colin. *Snobbery with Violence.* London: Eyre and Spottiswoode, 1971.

Wilder, Thornton. *Our Town.* New York: Harper & Row, 1960.

Wrenn, Charles L., see *Beowulf.*

Wynne, Nancy Blue. *An Agatha Christie Chronology.* New York: Ace Books, 1976.

Yates, Donald A., see Borges *(Labyrinths).*

Index

THE JOHNS HOPKINS UNIVERSITY PRESS

This book was composed in Linotype Palatino text and foundry Palatino Semibold display type by the Maryland Linotype Composition Co., Inc., from a design by Susan Bishop. It was printed and bound by Universal Lithographers, Inc.